MOORLAND MATTERS

This is an extremely honest and informative book. It educates the reader about the much wider beneficial effects of grouse moor management and the unique environment this creates, rather than concentrating on the narrower argument for grouse shooting itself. Yet it shows clearly just what a disaster for conservation it would be if the zealots who wish to end grouse shooting got their way. A must read by all who genuinely care about our wildlife .

Kate Hoey (Baroness Hoey of Lylehill and Rathlin)

When the battle for our moorlands is won they will be teeming with endangered curlew, our upland villages thriving and the pubs full of gamekeepers. At that time we should raise a glass to Ian Coghill – the champion of pragmatism and science who wrote this book. In running the Game & Wildlife Conservation Trust he did more than anyone else to win against the shrill ideologues – the bitter people who use the banner of biodiversity to camouflage their hatred of what they regard as the toffs shooting grouse.

Ian is certainly no toff – his first home was a council house and he jokes that the only estate he owned was a Peugeot 207. Yet his balanced approach – of the need to protect the homes of birds as well as their lives from predators – is spot on. He conveys his fantastic knowledge with a wonderfully easy style. Everyone who reads this book will learn a great deal. For the RSPB this will be painful because page-by-page Ian is forensic at unravelling how that moneymaking machine has repeatedly failed the birds they profess to love.

Ian Botham (Lord Botham of Ravenscroft)

This is a beautiful book, giving the unique moorlands of Britain the credit they deserve as a conservation success story. It is also a devastating book, using deep and careful knowledge of the facts to expose the shocking distortions of the truth being told to the public by many activists.

Matt Ridley (5th Viscount Ridley, Author and Businessman)

MOORLAND MATTERS

The Battle for the Uplands against Authoritarian Conservation

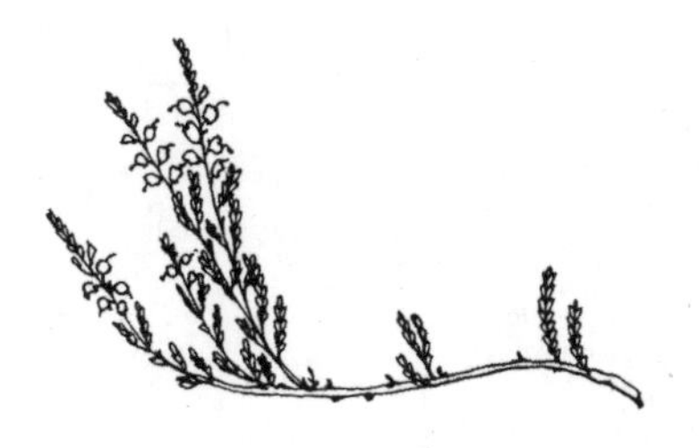

IAN COGHILL

Quiller

First published in the UK in 2021
by Quiller, an imprint of Amberley Publishing Ltd.

British Library Cataloguing-in-Publication Data
A catalogue record for this book is available from
the British Library.

ISBN 978-1-84689-347-6

Design by Guy Callaby

Printed in Great Britain by TJ Books Limited, Padstow

Quiller
An imprint of Amberley Publishing Ltd

The Hill, Merrywalks,
Stroud GL5 4EP
Tel: 01453 847800
Email: info@quillerbooks.com
Website: www.quillerpublishing.com

Contents

Foreword

IAN COGHILL FELL in love with moorland as a boy, on day trips to the Lammermuir Hills from his grandparents' council house in Edinburgh. At the age of 63, after a long career in local government, he shot his first grouse. By then, as chairman of the Game and Wildlife Conservation Trust, he had become a passionate conservationist, devoted to understanding and analysing the science behind the management of natural habitats. His command of the science behind conservation is unparalleled. Reason and passion join to great effect in this eloquent, funny and fascinating book.

Moorland Matters is full of common sense, spiced with not a little annoyance at the way that moorlands have been misrepresented and misunderstood while the public has been deliberately misled about them. This is a habitat virtually unique to the British Isles, with species that thrive at high densities nowhere else, including the curlew and the red grouse, and with a system of management in the service of nature that has evolved over the centuries into a sophisticated and effective whole. None of it happened because of command and control by government or because of campaigns by the big environmental pressure groups. Moorland is a fine example of private individuals risking their own money to do something for conservation and working out the hard way what works and what does not.

The result is rare birds breeding in abundance, rich mixtures of mosses and flowers and insects on deep peat that is steadily accumulating and acting as a sponge for rainfall. This brings jobs and income for young people in remote Pennine dales, in a landscape loved by and shared with walkers and picnickers. Where there are no grouse moors, the hills of northern England and southern Scotland have vanished beneath silent monocultures of alien Sitka spruce trees, grown at a taxpayer-subsidised loss, or turned to low-diversity acid grassland by overgrazing with subsidised sheep, or disfigured by vast steel towers to support huge wind turbines that kill rare birds with their fast-turning tips.

Yet far from thanking the grouse moor owners for this unique example of privately-funded environmental protection and enhancement, the big environmental pressure groups constantly assault them with criticism, most of it ill-founded as Ian Coghill demonstrates. The most vocal of these critics, the Royal Society for the Protection of Birds, has received many millions of pounds from taxpayers via the European Union and the British Government to save the curlew and to look after the uplands, yet has failed dismally. Its reserve at Lake Vyrnwy in North Wales, not far from where I live, has seen steep declines in its iconic moorland birds under the RSPB's stewardship, including curlews, merlins, black grouse, red grouse and golden plover. All were abundant breeders when the RSPB acquired the land and are all now teetering on the brink of local extinction. Yet that failure has been richly rewarded, with a £3.3 million grant to the RSPB to help prevent the disappearance of the curlew from Lake Vyrnwy. Meanwhile, on grouse moors in the North Pennines, curlews are so numerous and so successful at breeding, that in the springtime, at dawn, you literally cannot find a moment when they cannot be heard singing.

When I was Secretary of State for the Environment, one of my chief priorities was to manage the environment and, most of all, not to protect it but to improve it. I wanted to shift the mindset of conservationists from preserving nature to working actively to enhance it. We could do far more good by creating new habitats or transforming badly degraded habitats than by putting yet more bureaucratic regulation and protection around the bits of the countryside that had survived and were rich in rare plants and animals. The lack of ambition sometimes astounded me. A fine example is given in this book. In 2020 the EU's Life Fund gave the RSPB a large chunk of a £4 million grant specifically for protecting curlews in five locations. The ambition of the RSPB, with this money, was "that the number of pairs at these sites will be at least as high at the end of the project as at the start."

While at DEFRA I was acutely aware that the issue of conservation was to a large extent "owned" by the wealthy environmental pressure groups, who thought they knew best; they worked hand in glove with – and often frankly instructed – many of the officials who worked in the quangos that regulated the countryside. I tried to challenge this alliance between activists and civil servants, and to bring science, scepticism and not a little economic reality to their thinking. It was uphill work. Reading Ian Coghill's magnificent book has left me realising that I never knew the half of it. The story of Britain's moorlands is one of a spectacular conservation success story that the agencies and pressure groups are doing their utmost to destroy for no good reason than that it makes them jealous. The scientific evidence is overwhelming that it is the grouse shooting industry that has got this issue right, and their critics who have got it wrong.

Rt Hon Owen Paterson MP

Glossary of abbreviations and acronyms

THIS TEXT MAKES reference to a large number of organisations, official site designations, significant study reports, assessment notices, etc. that are often, or usually, best known by abbreviations or acronyms of their official titles. To spell out their names in full, at each reference, would make the text appear cumbersome, especially since, at times, several may be mentioned in the same sentence.

Usually, when a text contains a significant number of such references, the practice is to spell each out in full at first use, adding the abbreviated form in parentheses, and subsequently use just the latter, and that practice has been followed in this text.* However, since there are so many, it was felt that listing both the abbreviated and full titles here in alphabetical order (not the order in which they appear through the text) might serve as a useful *aide memoire* for readers. Please note that the list does not include those cases where a particular name (and its abbreviated form) appears only once, since in such cases the two elements will be self-explanatory.

* *Since quoted extracts from other sources (as in that from chapter openings and elsewhere) are verbatim, there are a few instances where the abbreviated form only of an organisation may appear within the quote.*

AIHTS	Agreement In Humane Trapping Standards
AONB	Area of Outstanding Natural Beauty
BBS	Breeding Bird Survey
BTO	British Trust for Ornithology
Defra	Department for Environment, Food and Rural Affairs
DOC	Dissolved Organic Carbon
EA	Environment Agency
EU	European Union
FoE	Friends of the Earth
FRS	Fire and Rescue Services
GBS	Game Bag Survey
GWCT	Game and Wildlife Conservation Trust

HHAP Hen Harrier Action Plan
HLF Heritage Lottery Fund
HRA Habitat Risk Assessment
IUCN International Union for the Conservation of Nature
LACS League Against Cruel Sports
SAC Special Area of Conservation
SEO Spanish Birdlife Partners (translation)
SGA Scottish Gamekeepers Association
SNH Scottish National Heritage
SPA Special Protection Area
SSSI Site of Special Scientific Interest
MA Moorland Association
MFF Moors For the Future
NE Natural England
NGO Non-governmental Organisations: a generic term for organisations that are not part of local or national government departments, but which might derive some of their income through grants from such bodies.

NB: rather ironically, the National Gamekeepers Organisation has the same initial letters as a Non-governmental Organisation but it is mentioned just once in quoted material in the main text and there was no need to add an abbreviated form for further reference. *All mentions of NGO within the text stand for Non-governmental Organisation.*

NRW Natural Resources Wales
NT National Trust

In addition to the National Trust, there are a number of local Nature Trusts, a term with the same initial letters as the national organisation. Within the text, the full name of these latter trusts may be preceded by, for instance, the name of a county. *Where this is not the case, Nature Trust is spelt out in full to avoid confusion.*

PDNPA Peak District National Parks Authority
RSPB Royal Society for the Protection of Birds
SNH Scottish Natural Heritage

Prologue

I WAS CONCEIVED when my mother decided that the risk of Father meeting a German with a gun had finally disappeared. I was born in my grandparent's bedroom on 5 September 1945 on our estate. That sounds a good deal grander than it was, as the estate belonged not to my family but to Smethwick County Borough Council. That said, it was a perfectly good one, with sturdy semis and healthy outside toilets, gas stoves and gas-fired coppers as standard. As a mark of distinction, we also possessed our own non-standard mangle, something which remains to this day my favourite household appliance.

The establishment into which I was born was fairly densely populated. The three up, two down semi held three families. The tenants were my grandparents, Walter and Hilda Sprigg; my parents, Sinclair and Lorna, had the use of the second bedroom and my Uncle Trevor and Auntie Vera had the back room downstairs. On that bright morning I was the only child in the establishment.

My father was a Scot from Haddington, a lovely old East Lothian town a few miles east of Edinburgh. Lying, as it does, on the main road from England to Edinburgh, it suffered grievously in the Anglo-Scottish wars and had been burnt down, according to my aunt, thirteen times. Eight of these were down to the Scots, something that I found out later gave her much satisfaction. At the outbreak of war, Father was a fishmonger, tasked with buying the fish fresh from the docks at Leith. He was called up into the infantry but, following his refusal to accept the rank of acting lance corporal unless he was paid to be one, he was sent to the pioneer corps where he thrived considerably. He rose to the exalted and extremely comfortable rank of regimental quarter master sergeant and it is to this fact that I owe my existence.

My mother was, by general consent and the evidence of photographs, a good-looking young woman, if somewhat inexperienced in the ways of the world. She was not without suitors when she encountered a smallish bespectacled Scotsman with wavy hair and a considerable amount of self-belief at a dance at the Ward Arms in Dudley. She was, she later admitted, somewhat surprised that someone as vertically challenged as Father should have been selected as a commando, and that someone as short-sighted would be one of the fortunate few to get back intact from the débâcle at Dieppe – but, as I said, she was a trusting soul.

Although Father's unit moved to Warwick, he was the only one of her potential suitors who showed the commitment to return, with monotonous but winning regularity. What she remained crucially ignorant of was that, as he not only controlled the unit's fuel but also access to its only motorbike, he had been able to completely neutralise the competition. He need not have worried. He made Mother laugh, one of the most winning things a man can do. He also provided enough bravado to compensate for her diffidence and they shortly became Mr and Mrs Coghill.

The months following my arrival passed and, as my awareness of the world grew, it all seemed very convivial. The house was always busy, the air reassuringly filled with fumes from smouldering nutty slack – an apparently essential ingredient of post-war home heating – and, of course, swirling clouds of cigarette and pipe smoke generated by everyone in the house except for me and the dog.

The other thing which developed into my particular delight was the livestock. Ours may have been an urban semi with a back garden only slightly longer than a cricket pitch, but it was stuffed full of livestock. During daylight hours, the garden was my playground, but it was one that I happily shared with hens, pullets, cockerels, ducks, geese and rabbits. As a treat I was taken over the back fence into the allotment, where Granddad grew fruit and vegetables, then two doors down, to where I was dangled over the fence to drop boiled potato peelings to the neighbour's pig.

The war had forced everyone to attempt a degree of self-sufficiency. Granddad was an old soldier who had survived Gallipoli and quite a bit of foreign unpleasantness, but he was essentially a countryman in a council house, and he was a dab hand at it. I just loved the chickens. When feeling in need of a nap I would invariably make a beeline for their sleeping quarters. If in the rough and tumble of that crowded house I went missing, as children are apt to do, the first place to look was the hen house. There I would be found, happily oblivious, slumped among the fowl. I still find the lovely soothing cluck of a contented hen one of the most relaxing and soporific of sounds, although these days I try not to soil myself quite as much as I did in those distant happy, nappy days.

To children everything is normal. Having no prior knowledge, things are what they are. The conditions we lived in were spartan even by the standards of the 1940s. By any modern measure we lived in poverty, but that is not to say we were particularly poor. When Father was demobbed he walked into a job as transport manager for a local haulage firm and earned a reasonable wage, as did my grandfather and uncle. With three wage earners in the house we were not short of money: there was simply nothing to buy. The country was broke. There were virtually no televisions, very few cars or refrigerators, no microwaves and we had no refrigerator, no central heating, no immersion heaters, no fitted carpets, no indoor toilet, no soft toilet paper. The sum total of our kit, apart from pots and pans, was a gas cooker and copper, a radio, a perforated zinc meat safe, a wash board and my beloved mangle. Hot water was courtesy of a back boiler or the gas copper. Heating was by coal fires that seemed to exist simply to draw freezing draughts under every door. If a way was found to prevent the cold air rushing in, the fire went out and the room filled with smoke.

Whilst it must have been utter misery for my parents, to me it all seemed great. I had a loving mother, whose side I never had to leave. I had grandparents as on-site back-up. Also, a personal menagerie and cousins in increasing numbers to play with (or be affronted by, as need arose) and my own mangle.

The twin facts that our resources were limited and that Father lived three hundred miles from his parental home made a happy conjunction when it came to annual holidays. We simply left my mother's parents and drove for thirteen hours behind a succession of lorries to stay with my father's for the 'industrial fortnight' every summer. My grandparents lived in the Scottish version of my home, a council house of the same vintage, but there the similarity ended. The estate was very spacious. The houses were divided horizontally, not vertically; one dwelling on the ground floor, the other on the first floor, reached by an external flight of steps. The ground floor had the front garden, the upstairs the back. The differences in location were far more striking. The industry and cities had gone, replaced by a small market town, a trout stream, a golf course and farmland, and everyone we met seemed to know my father.

There were other differences. There was no electricity and everything was cooked and illuminated by gas. However, there was an inside toilet, the first I was aware of. Best of all, there were my Scottish grandmother and my two maiden aunts, Chrissie and Kay, who treated me in a manner to which I felt I was both entitled and prepared to become accustomed. At home there were other children to distract adults; here there were none. At home any novelty value I had had long since dissipated; here, for two glorious weeks, I was the biggest show in town – which is exactly what a little boy wants, whether they admit it in later life or not.

The other difference was outside. At home the garden was unusually akin to a smallholding. In Haddington, on the Amisfield Estate, the gardens, all of them, except my granddad's, constituted a potato farm. Every garden on the estate, front and back, was entirely dedicated to the cultivation of potatoes. My grandfather and Aunt Chrissie were viewed as extremely Bohemian for their weird determination to grow dahlias and not, for reasons their neighbours could ever fathom, the trusty potato.

Memory is an odd thing, but I can't be sure if my love of the natural world was triggered by my holidays or whether it was always there. Either way, that was where it was nurtured. Both Chrissie and Kay were great walkers and, whilst Kay was quiet and unassuming, Chrissie was daunted by nothing and nobody. Walks with Kay were extremely well informed, but limited to the lawful bits. God knows, they were exciting enough, with stoats chasing rabbits, water voles, trout and house martins. However, Chrissie's walks were something else. She was like a small, dynamic combination of two people named Marx: Groucho from the famous brothers and Karl, adhering strongly to the view that all property is theft. A great deal of the countryside in the Borders is not just privately owned but part of large estates. Whilst this deterred Kay, it simply incentivised Chrissie. She was happiest when we were climbing over some locked gate, with the familiar 'Och, dinnae give it any heed. He's got mair land than he kens what to do with.' That said, it may not always have been as daring as it seemed at the time. She had a large circle of friends and friendly contacts, including a remarkable number of gamekeepers.

One happy day it was decided we would go en masse for a picnic in the Lammermuirs, somewhere I had heard spoken of, but which we never seemed to get to, and which had consequently grown into a place of myth. As a result I may have been particularly impressionable when we finally parked in the entrance to an old sand quarry. My parents began the stultifying process of preparing a picnic and I legged it with my aunt.

We set off up a sandy track and walked out onto my first ever grouse moor. I found its wildness and beauty stupefying. It was a perfect August day. The heather was in bloom, rolling away in a carpet of purple, patterned with greens and browns. The air was filled with the sound of bees and grasshoppers. Sand martins flew in clouds, chasing insects over the heather. As we walked, a covey of grouse rose from beside the track with that lovely whirr and their glorious rattle of abuse. I had never seen anything like it. It was like someone who had only drunk flat, warm beer being given their first glass of champagne. After that, every holiday was a plot to get onto a moor. Whenever the question was posed as to where we should go, my answer was always the Lammermuirs.

That was a long time ago, but I can go there still. Big and old and cynical, as I now am, I can still walk there and still feel as I felt then, and stand in awe and wonder of that beautiful place. Of course I know far more than I did then. How it came to be, and what has to happen to keep it as it is. But that in no way alters what it feels like to be there, and to see now what I saw then.

I fell in love with the heather moors that day: with the sight and sound and smell of them; their strange combination of vast landscape and intimate detail. It is a love that has never let me down, and never will. I have had to live much of my life, and earn my living, in cities and towns, far away from these beautiful places, but my heart has never left them.

Introduction

I SHOULD MAKE it clear that I do not own a grouse moor, nor have I ever done so. My life has been as far removed from the archetypal lord of the manor as one can get. Where I grew up, the best bits of wilderness I knew had been created by explosives. Someone had told the chap in charge of Luftwaffe operations that my home town made a lot of machine tools, nuts, bolts and ball bearings and they obviously thought it was their duty to the Fatherland to put a stop to it. We lived a fair way from the main industrial parts but the Germans were no better at hitting what they aimed at from way up in the clouds than we were and the destruction was fairly general. This resulted in my early years being lived in and around large areas of domestic and industrial destruction. This may sound bad, and it was indeed dangerous, but it was also really good fun. Nature reclaims its own with amazing speed and the variety of vegetation and wildlife that found these places congenial was remarkable. No one has ever invented a children's playground that is half as exciting as those I enjoyed courtesy of Reichsmarschall Goering. I still miss bomb sites but they were hardly the same as the Lammermuirs.

After university, I joined the local council as a trainee public health inspector, and remained a public servant in local government for the rest of my working life. I was not, I should make clear, a civil servant – there is a difference. Civil servants do policy and its implementation; public servants do *things*, which is far more satisfying.

In my case, working as I did for Birmingham, one of the largest urban local authorities in the kingdom, at the mucky end of their business, I had a great time doing all the things no one else wanted to do. Having no particular talent, other than a knack for solving complex problems by doing simple things, I was, in time, put to sort out almost everything the high-flyers weren't interested in. Food safety, cemeteries, licensing, fly-tipping, street cleaning, sickness absence, waste collection, recycling, pest control, community safety and a lot more. To succeed in these things, in the complex and thin-skinned world of modern local government, I had to work with the widest range of communities and tackle some of the most intractable of problems. I found that there is no insurmountable difficulty in getting very combative and antipathetic groups to work together for their common good. I ended my working life as Director of Environment and Community Safety, in charge of rubbish and crime. I thus come to the issue of conservation from a position which is informed by what it is like to work with communities of interest and place, what is expected of a statutory regulator (I was one myself for forty years), and how crime can be successfully reduced.

In my teens I discovered I possessed a hunting gene. Where it came from is unknown. No one in my family was in the least interested in pursuing anything beyond a quiet life, but I very definitely was. Unfortunately, having no money and no connections, my early hunting was limited to chasing rats around some local pigsties with my ever-present canine companion, Buster. Occasionally we would catch a bus to go upmarket bothering rabbits. Eventually, when I acquired a car and a shotgun certificate, my sporting endeavours reached the exotic heights, or rather depths, of lying for hours in the dark in a salt marsh creek hoping to get a duck, or even a goose.

From my earliest days, I have also been a passionate conservationist. I am aware that people find this combination surprising. 'How can you claim to be a conservationist when you shoot ducks?' is, to me, no more sensible than, 'How can you be a conservationist when you eat prawn cocktail?' The fact that I shoot my own dinner is no more relevant to my attitude to conservation than if I ate halibut or kept a cat. But I understand that many people see things differently, and carelessly cross people like me off the list of those who can be seen as trying to make the world a better place. I have experienced it all my adult life. Like all forms of discrimination, it is a costly mistake. Not because it hurts my feelings or offends me, but because it is counterproductive. The environmental crisis is something we all face and thus something we should all contribute to solving. The idea that those pretending to solve these huge problems can say, 'We don't need help from those people because they shoot or fish', seems extraordinary. But it happens.

In part, this is because it is far easier to find someone to dislike than actually to confront the vast complex reality of the problems to which you almost certainly contribute. As will become clear later, the issue of carbon sequestration by heather moorland is assuredly an important one. However, in the totality of the carbon generation it is dwarfed by an issue as mundane and commonplace as refrigeration. But shouting about heather burning is far easier than doing without a fridge or air conditioning.

I am also an inveterate joiner and the list of conservation bodies of which I am a member is long. The one that became my passion was the Game and Wildlife Conservation Trust (GWCT). Many years ago, I was invited, almost by chance, to sit on one of their research steering committees. Since I was a bureaucrat, meetings were my natural habitat; I would even claim to be a meeting connoisseur. My first GWCT committee was the best meeting I had ever attended. Scientists, farmers, gamekeepers, landowners and a bureaucrat from Birmingham, sat around for nearly a day, deciding how best to conduct research into what was adversely impacting the brown hare population, and how we might design ways to show people how to conserve them. I could not wait for the next meeting. When it came it did not disappoint, and they never have. The results of that first piece of work have enabled landowners or farmers to adjust their land management to ensure that brown hares do as well as the weather will permit. It is as valid today as it was then.

In the context of any rural organisation, I long ago accepted that a local government officer from Birmingham is not the norm, but nevertheless I was invited to become a trustee and, eventually, chairman. In this role I was able to see how the conservation industry works and some of the pressures the major players are under, and which they create for others. Furthermore, I had the privilege of meeting and getting to know people from across the debate about our uplands and have found good, honest people on all sides. I have also watched a broad consensus turn, with remarkable speed, into one of the worst conflicts in modern conservation, and I am deeply saddened by it. This sadness comes, not just because of what has already gone, and what may yet be lost, but because so much could be gained if everyone, or at least the reasonable majority, could find a way to work together for the common good.

I accept that I come to this issue from an unusual direction, but I believe that provides the opportunity of a different perspective. Having spent my life solving urban problems, working with all manner of minority groups and dealing with all sorts of regulatory and criminal challenges, I find what happens in the uplands extraordinary. Hardly any of it would be tolerated in inner city Birmingham or Manchester. What is clear is that a distinct narrative has been developed by those who want to end grouse moor management. That narrative is beginning to be accepted as unalloyed truth and it is being used to drive policy, regulation and legislation in a manner designed to bring about permanent change. At the moment the case for the defence is largely unheard.

However, this is more than simply an interesting argument. If we, as a nation, get this wrong we stand to lose something that will never be re-created on anything like the scale that now exists. As I write, it is still possible for me to park where my father parked by the old sand quarry and walk out into that immense landscape and see it apparently unchanged. There are very few landscapes for which I can make that claim. So many other places have changed and deteriorated. Only the moors are always 'changing to remain the same'. If this landscape is going to be destroyed, along with the way of life that goes with it, it is important that those responsible know that what they did was not the result of a universally accepted truth and that they will be held accountable for the consequences. At the very least, those driving this agenda should consider what those consequences are and be honest about them. The minimum requirement must surely be the stricture in the marriage service, 'That this should not by any to be enterprised, nor taken in hand, lightly, ill advisedly or wantonly.' This must surely be the minimum a landscape and a way of life can expect.

This book is not about grouse shooting (if you want to read about how to shoot grouse, get another book), nor is it intended to persuade people that grouse shooting is a wonderful thing. It is about the real danger that grouse moor management may cease to be possible, and what the consequences for the landscape, biodiversity and the common wealth might be. It is about considering the consequences of the extraordinary idea that the best way to conserve our landscape and the wildlife it supports, is to ignore and marginalise the people who own and manage most of the countryside, and give control over its destiny to the huge, wealthy and power-hungry organisations who make up what can now only be described as the 'conservation industry', working in concert with their authoritarian and bureaucratic allies in the environmental regulators such as Natural England (NE) and Natural Resources Wales (NRW).

There is a different view, which is that the best way to achieve the outcomes everyone says they want is through partnership based on mutual respect and a sensible and sensitive application of the principles of adaptive management. What follows in these pages is not intended to prove that case. Rather, it is intended to prove that *such a case exists*, and that holding a view that runs counter to the current narrative is both rational and honourable, and that not everything is as it is said to be. It is also intended to give a voice to the voiceless: the people, and there are many of them, who feel that it doesn't matter what they say, because no one will listen, and it doesn't matter what they do, because they will still get the blame. Their voices, mostly those of upland gamekeepers, have been included in the quoted matter at the beginning of the chapters. It is a sadness that, to protect their personal security, they have to remain anonymous.

1. Moorlands matter

I've lived and worked here all my life. I raised my family here and I love this place. They joke that the moor is my girlfriend, although if she is, she's getting on a bit. My granddad was the first of us to get here, when he came as a beat keeper. Just before he passed on, we were out checking my traps, and we were in the big ghyll on the boundary, when he said, 'Do you know, this place is exactly the same as when I came here sixty years ago?' He was right. It's odd really; you work away, you cut this, burn that, mend this, pick up that, and nothing changes. His life, Dad's life and now mine, all working away to keep a changing world the same.

I doubt if I'll say the same to my grandchildren. I'm drowning in paper. People who've never been on a moor are making up one crazy rule after another, and if I never see another ecology graduate with a clipboard and an attitude to go with it, it will be too soon. The things my dad and my poor old granddad did, were why this place got all its bloody designations in the first place, and now they hang around my neck like an albatross. God knows how the boss puts up with it. It must be costing him a fortune for less and less return. He's a good man to work for and I'm safe whatever happens but the moor, that's anybody's guess. By the time I follow Granddad it could be anything, a sea of sitka spruce, miles of molinia and bracken or burnt to a crisp. It's funny after what Granddad said, to think that I might last longer than the moor.

R.B., Yorkshire

THERE IS A battle raging for the future of our uplands. On the one hand you have the people who own large parts of them, who live and work in them and who have created what seems to them, and to the millions who visit the moors every year, to be rare and wonderful landscapes. On the other, there is an alliance of non-governmental organisations (NGOs), activists, civil servants and politicians who have theories about everything and experience of little, but who are united in the view that they can change these benighted wastelands into a new Eden if only the stupid locals would get out of the way.

The common ground which existed a few years ago has almost gone. Where grouse moors are concerned, it has more or less disappeared completely. This is an unmitigated tragedy. We sit on the brink of a catastrophe and the end of a way of life and a system of land management which has benefited the common good for centuries. Yet those who seek to drive change seem prepared to go to any lengths either to ignore or demonise the people who own and work this land.

The uplands have always been a special case for some reason: perhaps because they look wild and uncultivated they are treated differently from the rest of rural Britain. Perhaps because they are sparsely populated with people – who are, by and large, more given to thinking than shouting – they are treated as though they have no communities. Whatever the reason, the effects are clear. Governments, and to an even greater extent government agencies, encouraged by NGOs and special interest groups, are intent on taking charge and sweeping away the old ways to force the recalcitrant inhabitants to conform to a new dogma. Or, if they can't conform, to get them out.

What makes this all the stranger is that the heather moorlands of the UK are seen internationally as a jewel in our nation's environmental crown. Globally, heather moorland is much rarer than tropical rainforest. At the Rio Convention on Biodiversity in 1992, the delegates unanimously recognised the global significance of the UK's heather moorlands.[1] What still survives, after decades of disgraceful and tragic loss, makes up 75% of the entire earth's stock of this incredibly rare habitat.[2]

These heather-dominated moors are important, not just because they are achingly beautiful, but also because they support many biological communities that are either found only in the UK or are better developed here than anywhere else on earth. An EC Directive on the Conservation of Natural Habitats and of Wild Flora and Fauna lists thirteen such communities. These moorlands are also home to unique assemblages of bird species, eighteen of which are listed as being of European or wider international importance.

As a consequence of the increasing rarity of our heather moorlands, they are subject to a host of protective designations. They may be Sites of Special Scientific Interest (SSSI); Special Areas of Conservation (SAC); or a Special Protection Area (SPA), the last being an EU designation, but still extant at the time of writing. Some of them are all three simultaneously.

These rare landscapes also have practical value. They are the primary sources of 70% of our drinking water, store millions of tonnes of carbon and continue to absorb CO_2, and provide meat, game, energy and recreation for millions.

It is this last-mentioned contribution that is, perhaps, the most significant of all. The moors most important characteristic is their beauty and the place they occupy in the hearts of the people of Britain. Their wonder is recognised, not only by Areas of Outstanding Natural Beauty (AONB) accreditation but also by the fact that they are key features of several National Parks. These moorlands are visited by a staggering number of people. The Peak District moors, for example, see upwards of twelve million visitors in a typical year, and rising. Such a level of popularity with the public is an accolade beyond any official designation.

With this in mind, any unbiased observer might assume that Britain's heather moorlands and their management would be as universally celebrated and admired by the UK's conservation industry as they are by the general public and international observers. However, anyone making this entirely rational assumption would be wrong. Profoundly so. The people who are largely responsible for the survival of this rare and wonderful habitat are reviled and those whose skill and knowledge maintains it are at best ignored, and at worst demonised.

The main reason for this is that, while a succession of governments, acting on the advice of their experts, did everything they could to convert these beautiful places into forestry or farmland, almost the only people who refused the huge cash incentives to drain, fence and forest the heather moors were the landowners, who valued them as they had been for generations. This was, in large part, because in their ancient state the moors provided an annual opportunity to shoot red grouse, widely considered to be the finest of all game birds. The idea that something, which can be easily characterised as the exclusive pastime of the rich, benefited the uplands more than the conservation industry, government policy and a raft of quangos, is obviously anathema to all concerned.

Unsurprisingly, in these circumstances, everything possible is being done to ensure that credit is definitely not being given where it is due. The issue is made even more pressing by our nation's response to climate change, which is likely to see huge sums of public money directed into the peatlands, much of which is still functioning as grouse moors. Some of the larger players amongst the conservation NGOs predictably want to get what they see as their rightful share of this bonanza, and have no intention of being upstaged by people who shoot grouse.

As a consequence of these and other factors, we are now in an extraordinary situation. Imagine if you were fortunate enough to own a grouse moor. You would employ people to manage it and maintain it in its traditional state. Your family and theirs may have owned and managed the land for generations, as is often the case. But even if it's not, there will have been continuity of management technique. The land you own and manage is so valued by the public (who have free access to it), and so beautiful, that it is in an AONB and a National Park. The ecosystems and wildlife your land supports are so rich and rare that the moor is a SSSI, SCA or SPA, or any combination of all three of them.

This 'demi-paradise' only exists in this state because you, and the people who came before you, kept it as they found it – a functioning grouse moor. Your predecessors will have been offered huge sums of public money to drain it, more money to plant it with larch and sitka spruce, yet more money to fence it and to put in more tracks and hill roads and will have, at one time, been encouraged by way of the thankfully defunct headage payments scheme, to let sheep eat it to destruction. The fact that the moor still exists means that much, if not all, of this public largesse must have been refused. This will have been because everyone in the chain of ownership wanted to keep it as a grouse moor and doing what these governments wanted would have destroyed this wonderful place and with it any chance of shooting grouse. As a consequence of your interest in shooting grouse and the money you, and those before you, were prepared to spend on maintaining rare habitats and controlling predation, these precious places have survived and with them their extraordinary assemblages of ground-nesting birds, many of which have more or less disappeared elsewhere.

In the twenty-first century you will be used to the fly-tipping, the little presents of plastic bags full of dog excrement, the in-lamb ewes being chased by dogs, and the wildfires caused by discarded cigarettes, sky lanterns and disposable barbecues. You will have become accustomed to being increasingly excluded from most of the discussions surrounding the wider landscape of which you are a vital part. You will not have been surprised to discover that the Royal Society for the Protection of Birds (RSPB) blames you, and people like you, for, of all kind of things, the decline of salmon, pearl mussels and wood warblers in the rivers and woods you don't own.

But the real shock, for which no one is ever prepared, is when someone who has never managed a moor, put out a fire, caught a stoat, shot a fox or has any apparent interest in, or knowledge of, how this wonderful place came to be or how it has been maintained in its biodiverse beauty for generations, turns up and tells you to stop doing what you have always done and do something else.

Huge swathes of the UK have been changed beyond recognition. Not because landowners and farmers wanted them to change or didn't like the way they were. They changed because national and European governance, coupled with the demands of the marketplace, insisted on it. They were faced with economic suicide if they refused. One of the few places where these twin forces were successfully resisted was on the grouse moors, where the incentives for change were set against one of the rarest and most valuable sporting experiences in the world.

What is happening now is tragic. Grouse moor management is not perfect; nothing is. Grouse moor management can be improved; everything can. But what cannot be denied is that these wonderful places have survived because of grouse shooting, not in spite of it. Now those who are responsible for the very existence of these places, which are, never forget, SSSI, SAC, SPA and AONB, are being told to stop doing the things that resulted in these designations in the first place, by representatives of the organisations who have previously done their level best to destroy them.

Heather moorland is a dynamic habitat. Apparently unchanging, but in reality in a constant state of flux. The plant, invertebrate and bird species that thrive in this rare landscape, do so because they are adapted to this ebb and flow. Neither they nor the landscape take kindly to the dead hand of a risk-averse regulatory bureaucracy. This stultifying rigidity is compounded by the swarm of activists dogging the footsteps of the regulators, eager to fall on any perceived weakness or latitude shown to those who have the audacity to think they should have a say in how the landscape they own is managed.

The people who own grouse moors and the people who live on them and manage them are not mindless brutes intent on environmental vandalism. They are as intelligent and responsible as any other cultural minority. They have, at their own expense and with their own skill, wisdom and resources, maintained a wonderful landscape and its wildlife for generations. They are happy – indeed eager – to learn from new science how they might improve the ecological, economic and cultural performance of these wonderful places. Perhaps surprisingly, in light of the appalling history of external interference in the management of the uplands, they are not averse to change, where it can be shown to be of benefit. They deserve the same respect as anyone else and they deserve to be listened to and properly involved in managing the land they have preserved for so long.

Sadly, respect and a willingness to listen seem to be off the agenda as far as the environmental activists are concerned. Strategy papers are produced on the future of the uplands without anything more than token involvement from the people who own the land. Huge grants are given to NGOs to do things to, rather than with, estates and landowners. Many partnerships intended to effect change in the uplands are formed entirely of NGOs, without any representation from private landowners.

Almost everything that is done on these moors to keep them in the state that resulted in their designation in the first place, is attacked and traduced. Every natural disaster is examined minutely to see if there is any way it can be laid at the door of grouse moor management. Gamekeepers are one of the last cultural minorities about whom it is acceptable to be gratuitously offensive. Estates are subject to repeated criminal damage; the people who work on them are threatened, intimidated and sometimes attacked. All of this is done by a tiny minority of extremists, almost always from a militant animal rights background. But the big players in the conservation industry are never critical of what is going on and are happy to send little signals of approval, by being on the same platform or in the same photograph.

Something clearly has to change. The people who own and manage these grouse moors are happy to change what they do, *if it can be shown that there is a better way to do things*. They are not happy, however, to see the public misled or their communities attacked.

If progress is to be made and our uplands are to thrive, it is important that there is as much clarity and agreement about the reality of grouse moor management and its consequences as is possible between reasonable people. No one will ever convince a militant animal rights supporter that grouse moor management is acceptable. But the bulk of the population, who have open minds, are surely entitled to form their opinions on the basis of facts rather than fantasy.

It is not difficult to make an exhaustive list of the high crimes and misdemeanours that are regularly laid at the door of those who manage grouse moors. They have been rehearsed in the media with great regularity. What is harder to do is to get people to examine the alternative view. Moorland management does not have access to celebrities adept at sound-bites, nor does it have automatic access to prime-time media. The people involved have to rely on more traditional systems, which require a much longer attention span. If you have got this far, there is hope that you may be prepared to continue through what follows.

In summary

- *Our heather moors are one of the rarest and most celebrated habitats on earth. The vast majority have only survived because they are used for grouse shooting.*

- *These moors are internationally recognised as beautiful and biodiverse habitats* because *they are grouse moors, not* in spite of *being grouse moors.*

- *The people who own and manage them simply want to be allowed to keep them safe, with their biodiversity and culture intact.*

- *External interference in the moorlands has a disastrous history. Despite this, the upland communities are still happy to work with those who have practical contributions to make.*

- *The communities whose way of life depends on these moors deserve respect, and their long history of successful stewardship gives them a right to be involved in the decisions which will determine their future.*

2. A burning issue

The first I knew was a call on my mobile to say the woods above the lake were on fire. You can't fight a wildfire in forestry, not with any hope of doing any good, so I knew I had time to get organised. I got all our kit together, rallied the troops and got there in good order.

By the time I arrived it had got a good hold. There were the keepers who had come to the call, the fire engines parked as far up as the track would allow them to reach, and some odds and sods from the National Trust and the National Park milling about.

We lay in wait for the fire as it came out of the forestry. By the time it arrived it was already quite big. We threw everything we had at it and we had started to make a bit of progress when the National Parks mobile water bowser turned up and tipped over, which caused a bit of a distraction. Some people from the RSPB came and took some photographs, I think. They may have helped the hero with the bowser, but when you are fighting a fire you tend to focus on what you are doing and what is coming at you, so I can't be sure.

The fire boys are very good, but their big problem is access and local knowledge and that's where we can usually help. Because we have to be up on the moors all the time to set and put out so many 'cool burns', we know where the best places are to stop a fire. That said, these big wildfires are a different animal altogether and they take a lot of work to put out. We also have the quads and mules to ferry the FRS [Fire Rescue Service] folk to the places they can't easily get to, so we can help a fair bit.

Fighting a wildfire is a dirty, exhausting business, but after a very long day it was stopped, just short of the ridge line. If it had got over the ridge, there were miles of moor that hadn't been burnt for years, hundreds of thousands of tonnes of fuel, and no obvious place to stop it. With the wind as it was, it could have been enormous. We were still not sure it was totally safe when it got dark and the Fire Brigade had to withdraw its men until first light. The keepers stayed all night, putting out the embers and all the little fires the wind keeps making. In the dark you can see them better but you also see how quickly they can run away. By dawn all that was left was black burnt peat and wisps of smoke and we could go home to bed.

You don't do it for praise or money, which is just as well, because you don't get either. You do it because you can't help yourself. You do it because it's what your father, and his father did, and because it's the right thing to do.

But what did really upset everybody was when a National Trust spokesman, who had never been near the place and had done absolutely nothing on that long, hot, smoke-filled, back-breaking day, appeared on the local news and announced that they were not concerned in the least as they knew the sphagnum moss was going to stop it anyway. It makes you think, 'All right, next time we'll stay at home and you and sphagnum can get on with it.' How the poor beggars in the Fire Brigade feel about such rubbish, God only knows. It keeps happening, and people like us keep going to help, and people like that hero keep coming out with the same nonsense. Stalybridge, Marsden, Saddleworth, Crowden and every time it's been stopped by the magical sphagnum moss.

N.E., Derbyshire

IT IS IMPORTANT to bear in mind that the wide open heather-clad landscape of our grouse moors is not entirely natural. That is to say that these habitats are not exactly as nature left them when the ice sheets rolled back. Rather, they have been kept in a state similar to the present by a combination of rotational burning, grazing and the various activities of commoners, which have persisted for centuries. Thus we are not talking of a primeval landscape, but it is an ancient one and, in the profoundest sense, a cultural one. Whilst it will have seen changes over the centuries, it is nevertheless *largely* unchanged and those changes that have occurred do not render the moors artificial and worthless, any more than the changes that have been wrought on hay meadows, reed beds or coppiced woodland have that effect on these habitats.

The Ancient Britons or the Celtic tribes may have tried to farm the moors before the Romans came. The Saxons will have hunted on them and grazed their stock there. The great monastic houses, who moved in after the Norman Conquest, sent lay brothers from the abbey up onto the moors to tend the sheep whose fleeces enriched the Church. All of the graziers – Saxon, Norman, Plantagenet, Tudor, up to the present – refreshed the pasture, and rejuvenated the moor, by periodically burning the old vegetation. Ever since the land proved impossible to farm over two thousand years ago, these moors have been managed with fire.

It is, in part, the consequences of their history that makes these moors so beautiful and timeless. These centuries of management, coupled with the climate and soil making them impossible to cultivate, are the reasons they exist at all. The tradition of burning has continued, but its nature has changed. Gone are the old shepherds' big hot fires that cleared out half a parish. They have been replaced by lots of little 'cool burns' (see explanation below), scattered seemingly haphazardly across the moor. These are set by keepers to renew the life of the moor, just as the shepherds before them intended, but also to create a mosaic of different-aged plant communities, ideal for the reproductive needs of red grouse and many other species that thrive on the moor.

Let us begin with trying to understand what people are talking about when they address the issue of rotational burning. Language should be used to enlighten, but the people who want to stop all rotational burning prefer to confuse. Grouse moor managers are, according to statements made by, for example, the RSPB, burning peat, burning peatlands, and burning blanket bog, and, if given the chance, probably Joan of Arc into the bargain.

In fact they are doing none of these things. They are not burning them, but they are burning *on* them. Rotational cool burning burns some of the vegetation growing above the ground but not the ground itself. As the intention is to reinvigorate the vegetation, it would make no sense to kill the plants you hope will re-grow, which would be an inevitable result of burning the soil, peat or not.

The enthusiasm shown by the RSPB and others for using language that conceals this crucial fact cannot be based on them not understanding: the difference is both simple and clear and has been repeatedly explained to them. They know the difference; it's just that they prefer to pretend it doesn't exist. It is as though they could not grasp the difference between a haircut and decapitation.

So what is happening is correctly referred to as heather burning, because it is the heather that burns. It can also be correctly called rotational burning, cool burning and prescribed burning. This is because the burning rotates across the landscape on a cycle of ten to thirty years, because it is done in winter and early spring in a manner that ensures that the underlying substrate remains cool and wet, and because it is conducted in a manner prescribed by statute and the statutory agencies. The term cool burning requires a little more explanation as it might seem an oxymoron. It refers not to the fire itself – fire is always hot – but to the substrate over which the fire passes. The intention is that the vegetation burns rapidly but the ground beneath stays relatively cool. This is so that the mosses survive intact and the heather plants can start to re-grow almost immediately. Cool burning takes place when the ground is wet and cold, sometimes even when snow is lying, and that, coupled with the fact that heat rises, means that cool burns have minimal impact on the underlying moss and detritus layer and even less on the peat beneath it. Keepers have a party trick to demonstrate the point. They will put a chocolate bar in the moss and burn over it. When picked up after the fire, the chocolate can be seen un-melted. An even more impressive demonstration was witnessed by Glossop Fire and Rescue Service personnel on a training day on a Peak District moor in 2020. The moor owner put five £50 notes under the heather before it was burnt, and retrieved them undamaged when the fire had passed. So, on the evidence, cool burning would seem to be a fair description. It is telling that these terms, which reflect accurately the nature of the process, are never used by the people who want to ban it.

How is a burn conducted? On a well-managed moor the vegetation will already be a mosaic of different ages and heights. It will often have a range of peat depth, have areas that are dominated by plants other than heather, and be intersected by walls, tracks and streams. The keeper will decide on the area to be burnt on the basis of the age and condition of the vegetation, the wind direction and the places where the fire can be conveniently stopped. This may be an existing feature such as a wall or stream, or the keeper may create one by cutting or burning a fire-break. If a cutter can reach the area, they may also cut all round the patch to be burnt, otherwise they will physically control unwanted lateral spreading as the fire progresses.

The fire is ignited along an extended front, usually about thirty metres wide, and will run down the wind until half to one hectare has been burnt. By then it will have reached the pre-selected stopping point and the keepers will put the fire out either by the traditional beating or, more likely in these well-equipped modern times, using fogging equipment to dampen any embers after blowing the fire mechanically back on itself and thus exhausting its fuel.

This activity can be seen only during the legal burning season, which in England runs from 1 October to 15 April. Furthermore, on many sites, the whole process is already subject to approval by the statutory environmental regulator, in England, NE. Sadly this careful, controlled and lawful process is in no way reflected in the statements made by those who would stop all burning, who simply portray it as a form of uncontrolled environmental vandalism.

This is particularly unfair, as until recently the RSPB, the most strident critic of heather burning, took a very different view. A few years ago I picked up an RSPB leaflet on heather burning from their stand at the Royal Welsh Show (Leaflet 223-1194-06-07), entitled *Heather Moorland Management*. In this can be found numerous positive references to heather burning, along with a splendid photograph of burning progress, with the caption, 'Well-managed heather burning and cutting, in association with appropriate grazing, can have a positive effect on moorland diversity.' Nowhere does it refer to burning peat, or peatland, or blanket bog. It is also full of helpful tips. We read: 'Burns of up to one hectare, carried out during the building stage of heather growth, benefit a number of birds', or 'Smaller burns – between 0.5 and 1 ha, made up of long strips about 30 metres wide – provide a greater mix of heather structures than large, extensive burns.'

Next, we should consider the terms used to describe the places that may be subject to rotational cool burning. In the context of grouse they will all be moorland, and largely heather- dominated moorland, but even that does not mean it can be assumed to be peatland, deep peat, or blanket bog, although it can be all or any of them. Moorland may also include dry heath, upland grassland, exposed rock, scrub and much more. Moorland is a landscape, not a soil.

That said, much heather moorland used for grouse shooting sits on peat of varying depth and it is good news for all of us that it does. It is in large part thanks to the economic and cultural value attached to grouse shooting through the last two centuries that much, although sadly not all, of this precious and beautiful landscape has survived with its wildlife and its vast carbon stores intact.

The RSPB frequently talks about burning peatland. This is nearly as meaningless as saying we are burning Yorkshire. Peatlands are lands that contains peat. Peat is any soil that contains 35% or more organic matter. Such soils occur widely, so lots of places are peatlands – so many in fact as to make the use of the term little more than a device, intended to make what is going on sound worse than it is. This is because the RSPB's other claim that grouse moor managers are burning peat is so easily discredited as fiction. That said, even now, when they get overwrought, they sometimes still say that gamekeepers are burning peat. This is well beyond a mistake. The people who say this, including, regrettably, representatives of supposedly respectable organisations, know perfectly well that the keepers are burning vegetation, not peat. They know that what they are saying is not true. It is true that peat can catch fire, but for it to do so as part of a cool rotational burn is something that is extremely rare. The legal burning season only allows rotational burning to take place when the risk of such an event is remote because at that time of the year the soil is cold and wet. Peat does burn, a lot, but this is in the fierce hot wildfires of summer droughts and heatwaves, outside the legal season for rotational burning. Be in no doubt, the people who are campaigning to get burning banned, and who tell you that gamekeepers are burning peat, are not telling you the truth.

Then, and most importantly, there is blanket bog. This is where the trouble really starts because blanket bog isn't a 'thing' (it need not even be a bog, although it sounds like one), it is an administrative artefact. It is, in England, anywhere with a depth of peat of 40cm or more – roughly the thickness of a bale of peat-based compost in a garden centre. Just to show how arbitrary this is, in England it used to be 100cm, after that it was 60cm, before being horse-traded down to 40cm and, just to prove the arbitrary nature of the definition, in Scotland it is 50cm. Added to which it does not have to be a bog at all. It may even seem to be dry to the casual observer, especially in a long hot summer drought.

Why does this matter and why all the fuss? There are three causes of the conflict around burning. The first is that the EU Habitats Directive identified blanket bog as a habitat that member states had to protect, particularly on designated sites. The second is that the impending climate catastrophe brought on by our profligate use of fossil fuels has generated a desperate search for solutions, especially ones that don't inconvenience urban voters, and improving carbon sequestration in upland peat is an easy sell to a worried politician. This has meant that huge sums of public money are being spent on improving the carbon balance of upland landscapes and the conservation industry intends to get their share. The last cause of conflict is that the conservation industry led by the RSPB has decided that it will use any convenient stick to beat the grouse moor community with and this looked a good candidate. In this they found enthusiastic support, at least in the English context, amongst some elements within NE.

As a result of all this, moor owners found that their world had suddenly changed. Having been congratulated on preserving these wonderful landscapes and their wildlife at their own expense, having been praised for their careful management, including rotational burning, they found that anywhere with peat deeper than 40cm was defined as blanket bog and any sign of burning was defined as evidence of damage. Having been told that nothing would change, because everything was just wonderful, they woke up one morning to find a man with a clipboard telling them to stop and stop now.

They can hardly be blamed for being less than happy or feeling a trifle double-crossed, and eventually one of them refused to ask 'How high?' when told to jump, and ended up in court.

The outcome was that NE, who cut a sadly unimpressive figure in the witness box, partly as a result of a serious lack of evidence to prove that they were in the right, decided to cut their losses and negotiate a settlement. This, in turn, resulted in a management plan, which they could have had in the first place. All parties seemed roughly content and, more importantly, there would be positive outcomes for the moor and its wildlife. So a sort of happy ending.

Well, no. There was one organisation that was very, very upset. That was the RSPB. So upset were they that they took the matter, and NE, to the European Commission, and in 2016, in response to the RSPB's complaint, the EC threatened legal action (infraction proceedings) if the British government failed to stop rotational burning on blanket bog within English Special Areas of Conservation. The consequences were potentially severe, infraction proceedings that could result in a penalty of a million pounds a day. NE was caught in a net of its own making. It had defined blanket bog as 40cm and evidence of burning as damage, so it was always going to lose.

It is fair to ask, at this point, why all the fuss? Doesn't the RSPB do birds? Is heather burning bad for birds? Well, no, it isn't: as the RSPB was happy to admit until recently, it is actually good for many, and borderline essential for some. It is not the birds who are at the root of all this, it is climate change and money.

The urgent need to deal with the worsening climate crisis has led to a search for solutions, other than the obvious one of reducing our own species' dependency on, and profligate use of, fossil fuels. It was noticed that the uplands contained huge stores of carbon in the form of peat. From this it was a short step to the idea that these places could absorb more CO_2 and thus save the day. Imagine being a hard-pressed politician looking for something that might help but would not enrage the voters by putting up the price of refrigerators, or petrol. Then, one morning, you have a bunch of apparently altruistic conservationists turn up with solutions that only cost millions, that will look good on *Countryfile* and that don't upset your constituents. Anyone could be forgiven for saying 'Yes, please'.

So, peat has gone from boring to a goldmine in the space of a few years and the conservation industry has noticed and intends to make the best of it. The grouse moor owners, who were responsible for keeping many of these vast carbon stores safe until their value dawned on the rest of humanity, were now an inconvenience, and their meddling risked the smooth acquisition of huge funds, so they, and their management practices, went from good to evil in the space between meetings.

There are three things the conservation industry says are essential to facilitate the upland's capacity to save the planet. They are that drained areas of deep peat should be re-wetted, bare areas of exposed peat must be re-vegetated and all rotational burning should stop. To this should be added the other part of the strategy, that this can be best, or only, achieved if they are given control and huge amounts of public money.

Just to be absolutely clear, I have yet to meet someone in the grouse moor community who is not happy to adjust their management to assist in the fight against climate change. The argument that re-wetting moorland by blocking surface drains or grips is a good thing meets no resistance. In fact, they thought of it first. The GWCT was saying that moorland drainage was a bad thing forty years ago, and some grouse moor owners were among the few who refused drainage grants in the first place. Many of those whose land had been drained or gripped (surface drainage ditches are known as grips on the uplands) have already happily re-wetted huge swathes of it. Similarly, the same people are more concerned about bare peat exposed to the atmosphere than anyone else. Not only is it leaching carbon, without vegetation it is not producing grouse or anything else, so they are equally keen on re-vegetating bare peat. Figures released by the Moorland Association (MA) in 2021 showed that their members, who make up the bulk of English grouse moor owners, had, in the preceding decade, already completed 60% of the work needed to restore their moors. They had re-vegetated over 3,000 hectares of bare peat and re-wet over 6,000 hectares of moorland, by blocking 2,945 kilometres of grips.

Surely this enthusiasm for implementing the two proven methods of restoring peatland would please the conservation industry? Not entirely; the self-reliant grouse moor managers often simply did it with their own staff and equipment, or hired a competent local contractor. When you are promoting a huge prospectus costing millions of pounds over decades, having a bloke down the road with his own digger do something that looks the same in a few weeks for a few thousand pounds, is not entirely welcome news.

The other problem was that to make the case for the conservation industry to essentially take over the management of the uplands they needed to demonstrate that the people currently in charge could not be trusted. This brings us back to the burning issue. Here, the grouse moor community was unconvinced. Without the ability to manage vegetation, the landscape and its eco-system would be compromised. Within a few decades the place would revert to an uninterrupted sea of rank vegetation. By that time all the species that used to thrive on the existing mosaic would have gone. At some point there would be a hot dry time and there would be a wildfire and you would lose everything, including huge amounts of the underlying peat, the very material you had set out to protect and enhance.

The response was simply to attack. Grouse moor managers burn. Burning generates CO_2. Grouse moors are causing climate change. Give us the money and the control over these people and we can stop all this and save the world.

This has led to attacks on the use of cool burning, reaching levels of hyperbole rarely seen elsewhere. One of the silliest claims by an RSPB spokesman was that cool burning small patches of heather on a grouse moor is like burning the rainforest. In fact, it is the opposite. The carbon in the rainforest is almost all above ground in the trees and there is relatively little stored in the soil. These tropical systems are able to produce oxygen at the rate they do because the elevated levels of heat and moisture drive the system along at breakneck speed. It is the botanical equivalent of a Formula One racing car. A Pennine moor is the complete opposite. Virtually all the carbon is underground; it has been accumulated over millennia by tiny annual increments, in the cold and wet, by a system that could hardly work more slowly. It is the botanical equivalent of a broken-down van.

The normal way to deal with a problem of this kind is to have recourse to science to decide where the truth lies. Unfortunately, this is not entirely straightforward. The first problem is that the science is still developing and is yet to reach a settled state. Before people started worrying about climate change there was little interest in, or money for, researching bogs or peat. Until recently bogs were seen by most policymakers as expendable at best, and a nuisance at worst. Huge areas of bog were drained to grow trees or just to sit there, amusing an odd sheep. Vast sums of public money went into draining anywhere and everywhere. The second problem is that these systems work very slowly and over millennia. Think of the 40cm of peat needed to qualify as blanket bog. It may have been accumulating for eight or nine thousand years. Third, the moorlands are also very extensive and varied systems. If people mislead when they talk about heather monocultures, the same applies to the substrate on which the moor grows. The most complete inventory on the subject to date[1] identified no fewer than twenty-five peatland condition categories. Not only is there variation between moors, but there are huge variations within each one.

The result of these factors is that the science needs to be employed for years, or even decades, to capture the full impact, for good or for ill, of any system of management and to combine this long-term approach with a difficult combination of both extensive and intensive research. There is only one piece of research that has any resemblance to this. Almost everything else has, of necessity, been of small scale and short duration. Obviously CO_2 is released by cool burning, but more is then sequestered in the re-growing vegetation, and the ash, charcoal and charred stalks can also be incorporated into the peat, so it is obviously questionable to draw conclusions from only the first few years of the cycle. According to the RSPB's leaflet, heather should be burnt towards the end of its building or mature phase. They say that, 'On average, this means leaving about 15 years between burns, although re-growth time varies across the country, depending on climate, altitude and soil fertility.' So what sort of conclusions can be reached in five years and how applicable will that timescale be elsewhere?

The search for better science continues and the evidence changes, but nothing arising from these factors is yet certain. There have been two major reviews of the emerging science, which are known colloquially as 'Glaves' and 'Post Glaves' [2, 3], although the latter was written by a scientist named Ashby. They are well worth careful study and are capable of a variety of detailed interpretations, but what is noticeable is that both lead one to the conclusion that more research needs to be done, that there is doubt and uncertainty about almost everything and that the scientists are careful to avoid creating any impression of certainty.

What *is* certain is that huge decisions are being made and they may have huge consequences. The pressure to make the decisions now has been created by, and arguably for, the conservation industry, who are positioned to be the main beneficiaries of the vast sums that they intend government will spend restoring the peatlands, and to acquire the ownership or control of huge swathes of land currently managed as grouse moors. They have succeeded in creating a narrative that says these moors contain vast stores of carbon in their peat, and the people who currently manage them are recklessly burning the peat just to get a few more grouse. If you give us control and enough money we will stop that nonsense and sequester vast amounts of carbon.

For their part, many moorland managers take a different view. They say that these places have survived with their huge carbon stores intact under their stewardship and using their management systems. They are happy, indeed eager, to do those things that will prevent carbon loss and increase sequestration but the cessation of vegetation management at this state of knowledge, and at a time of increasing climate extremes, is reckless and can be predicted to have profoundly damaging impacts on biodiversity and the landscape, and, most importantly, potentially catastrophic consequences for the carbon already being safely stored in these places. Nor can rotational burning be replaced by cutting, as many, with no experience of either, suggest. Moorland managers already cut heather but there are huge areas where cutting machines cannot operate and so little research has so far taken place into any adverse effects that cutting may have, and also that it does not yet provide anything approaching a sufficiently safe and proven alternative to allow the immediate abandonment of cool burning.

The catastrophes to which the moorland managers refer are wildfires. Whilst the primary purpose of rotational burning has been to create the mosaic of vegetation of various ages, it has had the extremely important secondary purpose of reducing the risk and severity of wildfires. The moorland community is very clear that the abandonment of rotational burning is taking an enormous risk. It will create a huge, annually increasing, fuel load which, with hotter, drier summers and ever more people visiting the moors, will eventually burn.

Does it matter? A fire is a fire. Why is a wildfire worse than the fire that a keeper starts? There are four important differences between them.

1. Extent. Small cool burns that take place in the winter and early spring enrich the habitat by creating a mosaic of plants of different ages. Big wildfires, in hot dry springs and summers, impoverish the landscape by creating, when the vegetation eventually recovers, huge single-aged stands of vegetation. This is of far less value in terms of biodiversity. Two fires at Saddleworth in the Peak District burnt out blocks of moorland of some 1810 and 390 hectares respectively which, when they eventually recover, will be huge blocks of single-aged vegetation.

2. Cost. Rotational burning costs the state nothing: the keeper is simply doing the job he is paid to do. Wildfires make huge demands on the public purse, costing millions of pounds when they burn – as they often do – for days or weeks. The wildfires on Winter Hill in 2018 lasted for 41 days and burnt 1810 hectares of heather and underlying peat. The FRS report to the Upland Management Group said that it involved '950 appliance mobilisations. These resources came from as far afield as Newcastle and London. Air resources dropped over 400 tonnes of water, there were 77 reconnaissance flights by FRS drones, 35 km of hose was run out.' This is in stark contrast to the cost to the public purse of rotational burning on a grouse moor, which is zero.

3. Health. The health impacts of small burns are almost non-existent: the relatively small amount of smoke generated by the rapid, oxygen-rich burning of twigs above the ground is usually rapidly dispersed. Big wildfires, by contrast, can constitute huge air pollution events, especially when they get into the underlying peat. In 2018 the huge Saddleworth wildfire is estimated to have resulted in 4.5 million people inhaling micro-particulates.

4. Carbon. While the gamekeepers' cool burns hardly even warm the underlying soils, summer wildfires, burning big tinder-dry fuel loads on drought-affected peat, routinely ignite the immense stores of carbon already locked up in the moors. The Sutherland fire at the RSPB's Forsinard Estate in May 2019 released the equivalent of 290,000 tonnes of CO_2 into the atmosphere, almost 3% of Scotland's total emissions that year.

This last point is crucial. One of the reasons why people have accepted the idea that rotational burning should be banned is that there is an understandable wish to increase the rate at which moorland continues to add to the carbon it already stores. As it happens, the science is unclear as to whether or not this assumed outcome would be realised if rotational burning were banned, and, if it were, whether the difference would be significant, but there can be no doubt about the intention. The intention is that the moors will sequester carbon, as they already do, but a little bit quicker. Those in the conservation industry are very clear on this and, despite the paucity of evidence to support them, they have made many impressive claims about how much carbon can be captured if they are given control (and, of course, enough money). What is less clear is why anyone would believe that they could do this: some of the moors where their theories have already been applied are now vistas of black ash. The problem is that what appear to be laudable attempts to increase the rate of carbon sequestration slightly, may put at risk the huge stores we already have.

In June 2018 Saddleworth Moor, managed under direction from NE on the non-burn model promoted by the RSPB, caught fire. When the fire was finally extinguished three weeks later, eighteen square kilometres had burnt out. Researchers from Liverpool University estimated that a depth of seven centimetres of peat had been lost across the site, releasing an estimated half a million tonnes of CO_2 into the atmosphere. They calculated that it would take at least two hundred years to replace this loss. But if NE continues to enforce its no burning policy, the fuel load will build up again and there is every chance that it will burn again in twenty or thirty years, and the time needed to replace the lost carbon will increase again, to three or four hundred years.

After the fire had eventually been extinguished there were two noteworthy public statements made. One was from the RSPB, whose spokesman said that the wildfire was a result of grouse moors being drained wetland. The other was from a globally recognised expert on blanket bogs, peat and carbon sequestration, Professor Marrs of Liverpool University. He took a different view, saying that: 'Leaving the land alone causes much more damage than controlled burning because there is more heather to burn so it gets hotter and spreads to the peat, which in turn spreads the fire', and 'It wasn't a matter of if, but when.'

The abolitionists' answer to all this is that it is simply nonsense; a fairy story dreamt up by grouse shooters to let them carry on their selfish ways. If they can re-wet these places, they will not burn. The issue of fuel load and fire-breaks is a red herring and anyway it's the gamekeepers who start the wildfires with their rotational cool burns.

This latter point is an outrageous example of victim blaming. If any of the appalling wildfires at Marsden, Saddleworth, Stalybridge, Winter Hill, Forsinard and elsewhere had been caused by a gamekeeper, you can guarantee that it would have been front-page news, but none of them were. But this simple fact did not stop the RSPB from using people's awareness of these incidents as a tool to attack grouse moor management. In July 2019 they organised a meeting in the Houses of Parliament to promote their views on grouse shooting. The invitation to parliamentarians said that, 'In the last twelve months several wildfires have broken out on land managed for grouse shooting.' It was true that grouse shooting took place where these fires had occurred but the RSPB knew perfectly well that the owners and tenants were prevented from carrying out rotational burning, either by NE or their landlords.

In 2020 the Mayor of Manchester, Andy Burnham, speaking out against the supposed iniquity of rotational burning as part of an RSPB campaign, actually cited a huge wildfire on Winter Hill as an example of what needed to stop. He was apparently oblivious of the fact that what he was talking about was the antithesis of rotational burning and his handlers in the RSPB didn't even bother to tell him that his statement was nonsense. Had he asked the FRS or any moorland manager, he would have found that the rotational burning he was attacking could have stopped the fire he was complaining about from happening in the first place ...

The continued denial that a problem exists, or worse, is caused by the very people who are trying to stop it happening, is a disgrace.

The reason why the conservation industry believes that the moors will not be at an increased risk of wildfire if rotational burning is stopped, is that they will have been re-wetted. The grips that were installed using government grants intended to increase the capacity of a moor to carry sheep or cattle, are to be blocked. In that event, they will fill with water and the water table will rise. The now wet blanket bog will not burn. As a result, the need to reduce fuel loads, create fire-breaks or even facilitate access for fire-fighting equipment would now be redundant because wildfires can no longer happen. According to their narrative, a fire is supposed to be impossible on re-wetted blanket bog. The wet peat and sphagnum moss will stop it.

Leaving aside the obvious point that, if this were true, there would be no need to ban burning on blanket bog as it would be impossible anyway, the sad truth is that it is nonsense. As ever with grouse moor management there is no need to speculate. There are lots of places where this theory has been put to the test, either because the moors are managed by the RSPB, or owned by the National Trust (NT) or because burning has been curtailed by NE.

The truth is that re-wetted 'no-burn' moors can burn furiously in the right conditions. The hot, dry late springs, which have now become such a feature of our lives, are perfect wildfire weather. Not only is the vegetation tinder dry, but the supposedly wet peat dries out. The final factor is the sad fact that the hotter it gets the more likely it is that idiots will go to the moors, smoking cigarettes, wild camping and having barbecues. This is not a theory. Huge wildfires in 2018–2020, burnt vast swathes of land at Saddleworth, Stalybridge, Marsden, Crowden, Dovestones, Winter Hill,

Darwen, Moray, Forsinard and more. All are managed as the RSPB recommend: re-wet and leave alone. The amounts of CO_2 equivalent released in these events is stunning. The first, Saddleworth, was 500,000 tonnes; Forsinard was nearly 300,000 tonnes; Moray was 700,000 tonnes. That is 1.5 million tonnes in just three wildfires on ground where decreasing the fuel load and reducing the risk of wildfire by rotational burning had been stopped to increase carbon sequestration.

Such mayhem must have given the people who manage these places pause for thought. Not a bit. Their response to the fire on Saddleworth was to say that the problem occurred because grouse moors were drained wetland. This was said in the full knowledge that if you wanted to find a drain on that moor you would be well advised to bring a spade and dig one. It had never been drained in the first place.

The fact that the ground they own and manage, and the ground where the regulators can prevent sensible risk management by 'cool burning' or even, in extreme cases, by prohibiting cutting, keeps going up in flames in direct contradiction to their theory bothers them not a jot.

What is more, this is a really bad time to force the ending of rotational burning. In the UK, because of what used to be our climate, the tradition of rotational burning and, partly, because there were relatively few people in the uplands, wildfire was formerly an occasional issue, rather than a serious problem. However, the scientific consensus amongst those who study wildfires is that, as the climate changes, the risk is increasing and moving north. Historically, wildfires in Europe were a problem in Spain, Portugal and the South of France but now there are even fires in thawed permafrost in Arctic Norway.

The scientists who study wildfire, as opposed to those who study blanket bog, are clear that using controlled burns to reduce fuel load and create fire-breaks is a good idea. One of the biggest wildfires in 2019, on what had been grouse moor but was now full of trees and wind turbines, and had not been rotationally burnt for years, was at Moray in Scotland. It burnt for two weeks, and was fought by nineteen fire engines, two helicopters, eighty firefighters plus volunteers. It destroyed nearly 6,500 hectares of moorland, trees and peat. The chairman of the Scottish Wildfire Forum said, 'Seasonal burning following the guidance in the Muirburn Code is one of the key means of significantly reducing the risk of damage from wildfires in the rural environment.' The drier springs and hotter summers, and the millions of people who use these moors, make the risk far greater, at precisely the time that the conservation industry wants a key mitigation technique – possibly the best – taken away.

The FRS is in no doubt about what needs to be done. In 2018, following the Winter Hill catastrophe, the FRS advice given to the Upland Partnership, a body that includes amongst its members the people who own or manage the moors that burnt in 2019 and 2020, was clear. As a consequence of the practice of rotational burning having been stopped, there had been no fuel load reduction, no functional fire-breaks and no mosaic of shorter vegetation, or anything else to impede the fire. The FRS report states with chilling simplicity that, 'The fire, supported by an easterly wind, spread rapidly through a continuous arrangement of surface fuels ... its rate of spread at the head part of the fire reaching approximately 1000 metres per hour.'

The FRS identified several major challenges that had contributed to the disaster and which, in the FRS expert's view, needed to be addressed. The first three on the list were telling:

1. Unbroken and continuous arrangement of vegetation across the landscape.

2. Combustible ground fuels.

3. High surface and ground fuels.

Further on the expert also lists 'Deep seated fires in the peat layer' and 'Limited access to and across the landscape'. He concluded his report with the clear statement that 'The combination of very supportive weather and the presence of high fuel loads on the landscape presented the FRS with the most difficult wildland fire-fighting operation ever encountered in NW England.'

Interestingly, the recipients of these clear and unequivocal views appear to have carried on as though nothing had happened. Perhaps they thought the FRS were in the pay of the grouse shooters and could be ignored with impunity. Events on the land these people own and manage have since proved that the FRS shared with Cassandra the gift of prophesy and the curse of disbelief.

The only thing that is certain is that, when it all goes wrong – and it keeps going wrong – the people responsible will be nowhere to be seen.

When a wildfire starts, it is in the DNA of farmers and gamekeepers to get there and help. Direct observation indicates that the same does not apply in the staff of NGOs. Their instinct seems to be to get to a keyboard as quickly as possible and start explaining why this latest conflagration proves they were right all along. To be fair, they can do little else, as they are so convinced that these wildfires won't happen that they have not bought the kit to fight them when they do. The gamekeepers have the modern equipment needed to manage fires. If they find a wildfire early enough they can put it out, often single-handedly, without recourse to the fire service.

Perhaps the strangest part of the debate, about the urgent and crucial need to save the planet by stopping heather burning, and giving millions of pounds to the conservation industry to watch the re-wetted, unmanaged moors guzzle carbon, is that the claims and the figures just don't add up.

The amount of CO_2 emitted or absorbed by a grouse moor is going to vary, because all moors vary, between one and another and within themselves. Some moors are almost certainly carbon neutral and many will have areas that are absorbing more carbon than they emit, but estimates range from as low as 0.65 to as high as 4.48 tonnes of CO_2 per hectare per year. But, again, this means nothing without context. Average estimates for other uses for peatland help. The same measure gives forestry averaging an emission rate of 9.91 tonnes, re-wetted fen 6.37 tonnes and cropland 38.98 tonnes (GWCT Peatland Report 2020).[4] So it is fair to ask why everyone is getting so excited about something that is well down the list in terms of emissions per hectare. The other interesting fact that does not feature prominently in the conservation industry's pitch for huge sums of money to save the planet is that when, as we all want, the blanket bog is re-vegetated and re-wetted, it will be approximately carbon neutral.

Where carbon and moorland are concerned we keep coming back to uncertainty. In view of the fantastic variation of the places we are talking about this may be frustrating, but it is inevitable. Altitude, rainfall, wind, vegetation, subsoil, peat depth, exposure to pollutants in industrial times, grazing and so on and so on, variable after variable. We can't even be sure of the area managed for grouse in England, let alone the whole of the UK, so how can we be sure about anything?

We can't be, but we can make an estimate and the current worst estimate for England, albeit a crude one – they all are – is just over 240,000 tonnes of CO_2 equivalent emitted every year by England's grouse moors (GWCT Peatland Report 2020).[4] This is roughly 2.3% of England's total peatland emissions, of which 94% come not from grouse moors or even the uplands, but from the lowlands. The grouse moor owners have been working to reduce emissions for some time and will continue to do so by the two methods that have a demonstrable record of success, re-vegetating bare peat and grip blocking. When the figures are examined it is obvious why they are resisting the RSPB's campaign to stop them using cool burning as a tool to keep their carbon safe. Several of the wildfires on land where the RSPB policy was in operation have individually released more CO_2 in a few weeks than the whole of England's grouse moors do in a year.

There is one other fact that it is worth extracting from the pool of developing science; that is, to date, 'Every carbon stock survey conducted thus far has recorded positive carbon and peat accumulation within flat wet areas of blanket bog whether subject to burning or not' (GWCT Peatland Report 2020).[4] For any reader who wishes to form their own view of the validity of focusing exclusively on upland carbon storage in general, and grouse moor management in particular, I would recommend reading the GWCT Peatland Report in its entirety. They will find a world of great complexity and uncertainty but where even these issues cannot conceal some striking facts.

1. Even in their present less-than-perfect but improving state, grouse moors are, hectare for hectare, performing better in terms of carbon emissions than almost any other modified peatland.

2. Even if they were perfect they would not save the world from disaster, as the best that can be hoped for is a few kilogrammes absorbed per hectare per year, and more likely carbon neutrality.

3. The principal problems – and the major gains – lie not in the uplands but in the lowlands. Grouse moors may produce just over 2% of peatland emissions, possibly even less. Cropland produces 66%; intensive grassland 20%; even the much-vaunted saviour, forestry, beats grouse moors at 6%.

4. There is no doubt that these moors and other parts of the uplands that

> store deep peat are essential to fighting climate change. But that is primarily because of what they already hold, rather than what they might gain.

None of this means that we should stop trying to improve the carbon performance of the uplands and their grouse moors. Of course we should do what we can cost-effectively to improve. But it calls into question why the conservation industry makes the claims it does, and why the RSPB is focused so myopically on what is, in terms of carbon loss, one of the least problematic forms of modified peatland use.

Millions of pounds are being spent in the uplands to save the planet and the major outcome of the expenditure so far is to whet the appetite of the conservation industry for more. If you want to maximise carbon performance as speedily as possible, re-vegetating moorland and blocking grips are well tried and tested and can be done quickly and cost-effectively by landowners using local or specialist contractors, often for a fraction of the cost per hectare charged by the conservation industry. But the team leading the Great Northern Bog project announced to the world in February 2021 that they would need £200 million over twenty years.

The conservation industry is not interested in explaining that grouse moors already outperform most other uses of peatland. They will not be telling anyone that, no matter how much money is given to them to re-wet peat, the best you can normally expect is tiny accumulations or tiny losses. They will certainly never agree that fifty years of tiny gains can go up in smoke in a day, for no better reason than they, as an article of faith, refused to reduce the fuel load or make fire-breaks.

None of this counts for anything. The organisations campaigning to ban rotational cool burning on grouse moors simply deny that any of this matters. The fact that some of the places they manage are a sea of blackened ash troubles them not at all. They simply plough on and double down on the rhetoric and hyperbole, desperate to persuade, threaten and bully government into banning rotational burning, first on deep peat and then on all peat soils. They do this despite the fact that governments around the world are increasingly looking for ways to reinstate the practice and regenerate the lost skills needed to do it successfully.

But I have no wish to mislead. Those who want to retain heather moorland in a safe and biodiverse state need to have access to rotational cool burning as an essential management tool, but that does not mean that it needs to be, or should be, used everywhere or all the time. Nor does it mean that it is never done badly, or that it never causes unwanted damage. All management techniques can be misused, misapplied or go wrong, and rotational burning is no exception. But these are facts of life, not reasons to ban the entire activity. They are grounds for ensuring everyone is trained to operate to best practice and that the best practice evolves as the science evolves. To have the maximum benefit it must also be recognised that these moorlands are complex, dynamic and enormously varied landscapes and that any government policy must encourage site-specific, adaptive management, designed to deliver the best outcomes both for the environment and for the owners and their wider community.

But none of this matters to the RSPB, who have consistently led the charge to get all burning banned, everywhere. There is no nuance, no need for debate or further research. Their attitude is we say it is bad; ban it.

Who is to be believed? In view of the RSPB's power and its willingness to use it, it is increasingly unlikely that their world view will be challenged by anyone other than those fighting for survival. It is therefore rare to find people who will break ranks to challenge the increasingly furious attacks on burning. A remarkable exception appeared, peer-reviewed, in the august pages of the *Philosophical Transactions of the Royal Society* in the form of a paper entitled 'The role of fire in UK peatland and moorland management: the need for informed unbiased debate.'[5] Anyone who wishes to understand more about some of the issues that have been touched on in this chapter is recommended to read the whole, splendidly informed and balanced document. But here are two short passages that deal with the issues we have been addressing.

> Fire is a valued and integral component of the eco-system manager's tool kit capable of being used as well as abused in a multiplicity of different ways. Throughout Europe, managers, ecologists and conservationists value prescribed burning as a tool to protect and restore globally rare heathland and moorland eco-systems and there is a growing body of scientific literature to inform best practice. Much of this knowledge comes from research in the UK and it is ironic that while the public debate here has shifted strongly against the use of fire, scientists in other countries are using this evidence to promote the re-introduction of burning.

> However, if we want to retain moorlands as one part of a diversity of upland landscape structures, fire will need to be part of their management. Although managers seem to mostly follow current recommended guidelines on burning, traditional approaches to managed burning have room for improvement but do deliver conservation benefits. Our objective should be to use fire as one tool in management that aims to produce structurally diverse upland landscapes that protect a range of ecosystem functions. The conversation needs to move away from unhelpful hyperbole about banning part of the ecosystem manager's toolkit and focus on learning how to use it well.

The grouse moor community has no problem with these wise and measured words, and has expressed a willingness, backed by action, to follow the path suggested in the Royal Society paper. The RSPB's reaction mirrors its response to wildfire after wildfire devastating landscapes managed to their prescription. They just ignore it and plough on.

As a result of the RSPB's campaign, bolstered by its friends in NE, NRW and other regulators, and an unquestioning media, who are happy to compare 40cm of cold, wet peat on the top of the Pennines with Brazilian rainforest, the people who love and manage the heather moorlands waited with dread for a statement about the future of controlled burning, which had been coming since the RSPB obtained their judgment from the EC. The pressure on Defra from the RSPB and others had been relentless. NE were supportive of a ban and had even blocked some ongoing research that seemed likely to undermine the party line, so the probability of a decision that would end rotational burning seemed high.

In the event, when the Heather and Grass etc Burning (England) Regulations 2021 appeared in February 2021, to many people's surprise, they did not do exactly as the campaigners had instructed. While the regulations did ban burning on peat deeper than 40cm, they allowed a number of exemptions. Burning would be allowed where the ground was too steep or too rocky to cut. On flatter areas, where cutting was deemed to be possible, burning would only be allowed under licence for reasons of conservation and wildfire mitigation, but at least it might be allowed. The secretary of state made it clear that he considered wildfire to be the greatest threat faced by the peat stored in our heather-dominated moors. The people who use fire as a tool were cautiously relieved. The regulations could have been worse.

The RSPB and its allies were predictably and entirely outraged, and will not be satisfied until the regulations are rendered null and void. But their campaign has not entirely failed; it has caught the imagination of some of the public, as it was presumably supposed to do. As a consequence it is now perfectly normal for gamekeepers and other estate workers who are carrying out legal controlled cool burns to be abused and threatened by outraged members of the public who have absorbed the anger that is inherent and intended in the RSPB's more extreme statements.

Why has this become such a totemic issue for the RSPB, in particular? We can only speculate but it can hardly be about birds. Before they decided that their best interests lay in attacking heather burning, they were clear, as has been demonstrated, that burning benefited upland birds. The ones they list as using 'pioneer' or 'building' heather after a fire, include merlin, hen harriers, short-eared owls, red grouse, golden plover, curlew and dunlin.

A more likely explanation might be that they want to make grouse moor management impossible so that they can acquire control of grouse moors. They have had to watch utility companies and other institutional landowners continue to lease land to grouse shooters that they would like to manage themselves. They have also had the embarrassment of seeing vast swathes of the land that is owned by these landowners, and managed to the RSPB prescription, go up in smoke with monotonous and increasing regularity. Stopping anyone burning, anywhere, would have the twin advantages of making it more likely that the shooting tenants would walk away, whilst sparing the RSPB from being subject to painful comparisons of relative managerial competence.

In summary

- *Moorland landscapes have been managed by burning for centuries and burning remains an essential tool for eco-system managers.*

- *Cutting cannot replace burning on large areas because the terrain is unsuitable.*

- *There is little evidence that the alternative proposal of re-wetting and abandoning management has any advantages in terms of carbon sequestration or biodiversity. The moorland community's belief that this alternative makes the landscape more vulnerable to wildfire has been borne out in practice.*

- *These landscapes are complex and not best served by 'one-size-fits-all' solutions.*

- *The claims of climate effects and the demand for public finance are exaggerated.*

- *Grouse moor managers have already done much to mitigate historic problems by re-wetting and re-vegetating, and remain happy to do what works.*

- *The campaign to ban all burning has been crude and resulted in unjustified demonisation of an essential management tool and the people who use it.*

3. Does grouse shooting cause floods?

If you can bear to hear the truth you've spoken
Twisted by knaves to make a trap for fools,
Or watch the things you gave your life to, broken,
And stoop and build 'em up with worn-out tools.

Rudyard Kipling, *If*

A FLOOD IS awful, in the literal sense of the word. Anyone who watches a big flood must be awestruck. We are used to nature in safe little packets, cleansed of any risk or unpleasantness. Even some of the *Countryfile* calendar photographs are taken in studio conditions. We rarely see what is really going on and, when we do, it can be a shock. Rivers are *supposed* to flood. It is what they do when there is more water than their normal channel can cope with. It is why we talk of a flood plain. Yet when it happens, as happen it must, someone must be to blame.

It has become standard practice in some quarters to blame grouse moor management for flooding. This is based on a series of assertions supported by wisps of science and reality – which is all a good myth needs to become an article of faith. First, comes the view that rainwater flows faster over the surface of the allegedly bare ground left by a burn. Second, that grouse moors are drained wetlands that should have a higher water table, which would itself halt flooding. Third, that heather burning destroys sphagnum moss, the twenty-first century wonder plant that will single-handedly both prevent flooding and stop global warming if the NGOs are given enough money and the excesses of grouse moor managers are curbed.

There are scraps of truth in these assertions, but they are not wholly true. The people who use them to fool the victims of flooding are perfectly well aware that no act or omission by those who manage grouse moors has ever caused a flood, and that there is nothing they can do to prevent one. Obviously if your aim is to damage grouse shooting, or even, as stated by many involved in this particular business, to get it banned, then anything goes. As has been shown repeatedly in history that if you repeat a lie often enough and loudly enough, people will believe it. You would expect no better from the extreme end of the animal rights movement, but what is far more reprehensible is the silence of the more respectable elements of the conservation industry. In spite of knowing that these claims are nonsense, they never utter a word of correction and, if forced to comment, trot out the usual quotes about grouse moors being drained wetlands.

Floods are caused by extreme weather events, not moorland management. They have become worse and more frequent because extreme weather events have become worse and more frequent, not because moorland management has suddenly changed, because it hasn't. The conservation industry's enthusiasm for removing management from the nation's uplands is based, if anything, on the assumption that the more natural the better. In the case of flooding this ignores the fact that flooding is entirely natural. The fundamental problem is people being led to believe that they can live near a river, at no height above its banks, and not expect to be flooded. This is, of course, now compounded by the fact that, thanks to climate change, the extreme weather events that cause flooding are increasing in frequency and severity. We are having to get used to what was 'a once in a hundred-year probability' now occurring three times in a decade, and the plaque on the wall, showing the record flood height, now a metre or so under water. That said, it is obviously desirable that everything should be done to relieve the situation and it is important to address the issues that the detractors of grouse moor management raise.

First, does water flow over burnt ground faster than elsewhere because it is smooth and non-absorbent? If it does, does it contribute to flooding downstream? If you look at a recently burnt moor, 'smooth' and 'non-absorbent' are not the first words that spring to mind. Compared to a well-grazed pasture in the adjacent fields, or the nearby road, it is clearly very rough and very absorbent. Of course, it isn't quite as rough and absorbent as the rest of the moor, which having been burnt rotationally is in stands of heather-dominated vegetation varying in age between three and thirty years. But very few ground surfaces can compete with heather moorland when it comes to slowing water flow, so that is hardly surprising. Such science as is available indicates that at very, very high levels of precipitation, run-off is faster on the burnt ground. But on a rotationally burnt moor even this is rendered largely academic, as within a few yards any run-off hits an adjacent stand of vegetation that has not been burnt for years and is slowed down again. Would cutting be better in this regard, leaving the chopped brash lying on the cut ground? It might, but the difference would be academic as neither surface is the cause of the problem. It is the quantity of rain falling in a short period of time that causes the problem, not the fact that it falls on a grouse moor. Burnt, cut or abandoned makes no significant practical difference.

Then we have the allegation that grouse moors are drained wetlands and the drains have lowered the water table and thus made flooding more likely. As has already been explained, many grouse moors were, and are, wet land, but this is different from being wetland. Furthermore, not only were a lot of grouse moor owners amongst the few who resisted government pressure to drain the hills in the first place, they have, almost without exception, been enthusiastic supporters of re-wetting. This is in contrast to all the other people who drained the hills, especially the draining done to facilitate forest planting, none of which has been re-wetted and none of which is, strangely in the circumstances, ever mentioned in the context of flooding.

Thus, the lowered water table is now increasingly an imagined problem. In the welter of generalisations used to attack grouse moor management, no one is interested in letting reality spoil their argument. Grouse moor owners have blocked the grips on vast areas and raised the water table as high as it can get, but that doesn't stop them being accused of the exact opposite in the wake of a flood. Unfortunately, whilst re-wetting can dampen flows by releasing water over longer periods, thus maintaining flow rates for a few days longer or buffering smaller downpours, it is doubtful that raising the water table makes much difference to really severe flooding events. A moor is like a sponge. It can hold so much water but no more. Raising the water table doesn't make the sponge bigger, it simply fills it up. The more water already in the sponge, or the moor, the sooner it is full and starts to overflow.

Of course, if you put a series of drainage ditches on a slope, the rain that falls will run off the hill more quickly; that is what the drains are there to do. But this pattern of intensive drainage is more a feature of forestry than grouse moors. Where moors have been drained at the behest of government, smaller spates may well be more intense and shorter lived, but the now standard practice of grip blocking undertaken by the vast majority of grouse moor managers has dealt with these problems as far as can be practicably achieved.

The big storms are beyond the capacity of the best grip blocking in the world to deal with. This is, in large part, down to the rest of the landscape, the non-grouse moor elements, but in the rush to blame grouse moors every other land use is ignored. In fact, old-growth deciduous woodland is probably the only land that sheds water more slowly than a grouse moor. Roads, car parks and urban hard landscaping have the water flow retardant capacity of a flagpole. Most farmland is deep drained and sheds water rapidly, while modern forestry is also criss-crossed with masses of drains, often even on steep slopes. But when the storm comes roaring along the jet stream it is the grouse moor managers draining the wetlands or cool burning who are held to blame.

Can you imagine how it feels to be told that you are to blame for some poor devil being flooded out because you have drained your moor, when the reality is that you have done the exact opposite, and when you turn to any conservation industry representative to confirm that what you are saying is demonstrably true, they make some vague statement about grouse moors being drained wetland?

The scientific base for the remorseless misleading of the victims of floods by those who want to attack moorland management is slight. The UK National Ecosystem Assessment (2011) found that the capacity of peatland restoration to modify water runoff was likely to be slight and uncertain. An NE report by Glaves et al. (2012) stated that 'no evidence was identified specifically related to the effect of burning on watercourse flow or the risk of downstream flood events'.[1] The study on which much of the 'grouse moors cause floods' sentiment appears to be based, and which has itself been called into doubt because of potential bias generated by study site selection, is hardly a ringing endorsement for the idea. What it actually says is, '... catchments where burning has taken place appear slightly more prone to higher flow peaks during heavy rain – however this is not a conclusive finding.'

Based on this, a bag full of prejudice, and a TV celebrity or two, the anti-grouse shooters have spent an enormous amount of resources getting the residents of towns like Hebden Bridge to believe that little strips of burnt heather and a few as yet unblocked grips are to blame for their repeated flooding. The cycle of misinformation was recently completed by none other than RSPB's Vice-President Chris Packham, CBE. When he was challenged on the absence of any science to support the view that heather burning causes floods, he unblushingly replied, 'I want you to explain that to the residents of Hebden Bridge downhill from Walshaw Moor.'[2] So the plan is you get people to believe something that isn't true by pretending that there is an unequivocal scientific base for what you are claiming, when there isn't. You then use their belief, something that you created on a false premise, to confirm what you asserted in the first place as true.

Rarely has a plant leapt from obscurity to centre stage with the speed of sphagnum moss. It has been useful to man since the Stone Age. It was found in a fire-lighting kit in the satchel of the 'Iceman', whose body emerged from an alpine glacier after thousands of years preserved in the ice. It has been used as a wound dressing for probably as long. These uses are as nothing compared to what is now expected of it. It is now claimed to be going to solve the climate crisis whilst simultaneously preventing flooding. The narrative says that the only thing that stands in its way is grouse shooting – but this is demonstrably false.

The argument is that rotational burning has destroyed sphagnum. This is, in itself, surprising as the same people also claim that sphagnum will stop a wildfire which, it must be said, seems a little contradictory. But does burning destroy sphagnum? It can, but mostly it doesn't. The science indicates that if other things are equal, there will probably be more sphagnum on rotationally burnt moors than on moors that are not burnt. This remained true even when comparing short burning rotation (ten or so years) with heather that had not been burnt for sixty years.[3] It may seem counter-intuitive but a lot of things are on moorland, because it is a dynamic environment full of species evolved to deal with fire and thus very different from most of the places we are accustomed to and where our ideas of what is 'normal' are developed.

Sphagnum, like all green plants, needs water, light and an absence of toxic atmospheric pollution. In our post-industrial world, most of the atmospheric pollution challenges are gone and if sphagnum gets plenty of sunlight and water it will thrive. These are precisely the conditions it encounters on many well-managed moors, which is why it is found there in abundance. If there is no burning or cutting, the sphagnum is eventually shaded out by the heather and other vegetation. Where there is rotational cool burning, whilst the plants may be charred and temporarily damaged, if the conditions are right they will recover very quickly and thrive whilst they have the moisture and sunlight they need, but eventually the taller plants will be dominant and the moss will need help to see the sunlight again.

This doesn't happen everywhere. In the midst of a true blanket bog it may be too wet for the taller shading plants to grow well or at all. Even where they can, the moss may dominate them. But much of the land defined by NE as blanket bog is nothing like that and never has been or will be. If it is considered desirable to increase the extent and success of sphagnum – and this seems an article of faith in the conservation industry – it is perfectly possible to do so without impacting adversely on grouse at all. Where rotational burning or cutting have been carried out in the proper manner there should be little problem. Where there have been the far more damaging impacts of wildfire, burning down into the peat and destroying the moss entirely, as long as action is taken immediately by a skilled contractor the moss can be regenerated relatively cheaply if the substrate is naturally wet. What cannot be done is to make a naturally dry place wet by using sphagnum.

This moss needs to be wet, so it grows in wet places. It tends to retain water, so it makes an already wet place wetter. From this simple observation, a view seems to have formed that sphagnum will make dry places wet and now large sums of money are being spent in the fond hope that what is dry will become wet. The problem is that this is happening long after the optimum time to regenerate sphagnum has passed, and in places where it is disinclined to grow. Plants often disappoint and show a reprehensible disinclination to do as they are told. Rice, for instance, would be even more useful if it grew in dry soils, but unfortunately it won't and neither will sphagnum.

But all this is of no matter as far as flooding and grouse moor management are concerned. The fact that there is more sphagnum on grouse moors than there is on adjacent land, which has been turned into forestry or pasture and where there is none, does not stop grouse moors being accused of destroying the stuff. Nor does it stop its fictional absence being used as another untruth to support the claim that grouse moors cause floods The reality is that sphagnum moss is no better at stopping flooding than it is at stopping wildfires. It is an important and valued plant, but it is not going to stop a flood for the simple reason that nothing can.

No one is against the idea of grip blocking. It is thought likely to slightly reduce carbon emissions and improve a moor for grouse and a host of ground-nesting birds. It is relatively cheap and a great deal has already been done. Grouse moor managers are happily engaged in re-vegetating peat, blocking grips and even natural erosion gullies, and supporting other measures on their land that might help flatten flow peaks, but their willingness to do anything that can be shown to help – and even things that are still speculative – is not evidence that they cause floods.

The painful reality is that none of these things is true. There is plenty of sphagnum moss on grouse moors. The amount of freshly burnt ground on a properly managed moor is far too small and too integrated into other states of regeneration to make any significant difference to flow rates. The sad truth is that these tragic incidents, which are getting far more frequent and more damaging, are the result, not of the mismanagement of heather moorland, but of extreme weather events, which are a result of a much wider mismanagement of the environment. And extreme they certainly are.

If 100mm of rain falls on 10,000 hectares of countryside, roughly the area of many smaller dales or straths, the total weight of water is a million tonnes. If that, or more, falls in a few hours onto already saturated ground you are in trouble, whatever the land use. All the sphagnum and all the little dams in the world are not going to prevent a million tonnes of water trying to get back to the sea. To pretend to the poor victims of such an event that there is someone they can blame is doubly dishonest: it misleads the victim and damns the innocent.

What is needed is greater honesty and clarity. If there are things that the people who manage the uplands can do that really will make a contribution to reducing flooding, let them be made clear and acted upon. If there are not, it would be honest and humane to cease tormenting both the victims of these awful events and the innocent land managers with nonsense and half-truths.

The focus on grouse moors as the imagined cause of flooding is a politically motivated distraction. Climate change is real and it is beyond our capacity to prevent the increase in frequency and severity of extreme weather events. If we are to reduce the damage these events cause, it can only be done by addressing the issue at a catchment scale, involving all land uses, considering at every point what will be the most affordable contribution that can be made. Much of what needs to be done is nowhere near a grouse moor, and will include some hard decisions about the built environment and some frankness about what is possible, but without such landscape-scale action the problem will simply get worse.

Grouse moor managers have already done much – remember that the MA, supported for once by elements of the conservation industry, are clear that their moors are being re-vegetated and re-wet as fast as is practicable. In the spring of 2021 the work had been completed over 60% of their land and this figure was increasing rapidly. They have blocked nearly 3000 kilometres of grips, enough to run a drain from London to Athens. They remained ready to do more, if it could be shown to work. It is ironic, but sadly typical, that grouse moor managers, who have been some of the most willing to do what they are told will help, are the group most likely to be blamed.

There is also the question of quality as well as quantity. The critics of grouse moor management claim that the water flowing from the moors contains more dissolved organic carbon (DOC) and is more discoloured than should be the case. As a consequence, the water companies have to spend large sums of money removing the brown tinge in the water, and carbon leaches from the vast amounts stored in the peat. The critics also claim that silt from the moors adversely impacts on aquatic invertebrate communities and through them the fish of these upland streams, primarily trout and salmon parr, whose numbers are consequently reduced.

Once again the science is equivocal. The issue is still being studied and the results are frustratingly variable with evidence from different studies suggesting different outcomes. Some have indicated that there was more loss of DOC on burnt sites than on sites that had never been burnt, or had not been burnt for many years. Since then, other studies have found it impossible to replicate these findings and it is suggested that the variation may be related to site selection.

It is now not possible to re-create the initial experiments as two of the sites that were chosen because they were supposed not to have been burnt were consumed in the wildfires. This brings us back to our old friend, small annual gains versus the risk of huge losses. Such differences as emerged from the initial study were relatively small, and if the pursuit of these small gains increases the risk of wildfire, as was apparently the case on these moors, decades of small gains can be lost in an afternoon.

There is no doubt that water flowing off peatland will have a brown tinge. This is universally the case, whether grouse moor management is taking place or not, and it is deemed necessary for water companies to remove the brown stain before it enters the domestic water supply. It is entirely understandable that, faced with the associated costs, the companies are keen to reduce the problem at source and they are currently content with the arrangements they have made. On grouse moors this may involve a decrease in burning and an increase in cutting. On areas managed by NGOs the heather may be cut or, more likely, left to grow without any rotational interventions. Very little research has taken place into the impact of cutting on water quality. Yet, it is being promoted, apparently on the basis that it isn't burning, which is a poor substitute for knowledge. The problem with the 'leave it alone' strategy is the ever-increasing fuel load and the consequent risk of wildfire, which in many areas impacted by centuries of industrial pollution may release not just ash, carbon and colour into the water supply system but also a range of unwelcome heavy metals and other pollutants. The 2018 Stalybridge fire is thought to have released an estimated thirty tonnes of industrial lead into the river system. So, as ever, it is a balance between necessity and risk, which needs local decisions to get the best local outcomes. It is not a binary choice between good and bad – and the best outcomes are not achieved by 'always' and 'never'.

The idea that grouse moor management damages aquatic invertebrate populations to the extent that it compromises the viability of local populations of salmon and trout is an interesting one. As is usual in the attacks on grouse shooting, it seeks to avoid comparisons with other potential forms of land management and instead seeks to compare it with some imagined perfect state. Furthermore, those making the assertions avoid looking at the outcomes on a landscape scale, whilst ignoring the fact that every site is so variable in itself and different from any other that the best outcomes will be site-specific and neither universal nor binary.

A simple comparison between the known impacts of forestry and grouse moor management in relation to fish populations and aquatic invertebrates is all that is needed to demonstrate the point. Whilst elements within the conservation industry are apparently outraged by an alleged adjustment in the mix of invertebrates found in streams flowing from grouse moors, they remain apparently uninterested and certainly silent on the well-established fact that many otherwise identical water courses which flow from forestry are completely devoid of invertebrate life. They also fail to notice that most of the great salmon rivers of Britain – the Spey, Tyne, Tweed and Dee to name a few – all rise in, and get most of their water from, grouse moors. In common with all salmon rivers, they are currently going through a lean time because of unprecedented losses of smolts in the marine environment. However, they were in their pomp when grouse moor management was more intensive, and grouse bags larger, than is the case today. Look at the alternative land use, which is rarely mentioned, and the upper reaches of rivers such as the Severn, the Wye and the Towy, draining vast conifer forests. These are in places literally devoid of any aquatic life – let alone salmon. That this is caused by acid flushes coming from the forests has been known for decades and has been confirmed by liming some of the affected streams, resulting in the return of aquatic life. Curiously, this widespread and well understood problem has been the subject of considerable comment by anglers but none from the RSPB and conservation industry. Conversely, the assertions about grouse moor management damaging fish populations are something that loom large with the RSPB and seem to be discounted by the people most interested in fish.

Every human activity creates an impact. Whatever you do in the uplands has an effect – but that's not the point. The real question is how significant is the effect, and does its seriousness justify destroying the form of land management which has created and maintained these wonderful places for so long? The various impacts on water quality are either capable of resolution by relatively minor adjustments to existing practice or are so minor as to require no action, as the alternatives would be no better or potentially worse.

Climate change is happening, and nothing we can do in the short term can alter the fact. The current focus on grouse moors is not just absurd, it is seriously damaging. What is needed are catchment-specific plans that combine the best practical solutions for the entire landscape, everything from heather moorland to the built environment, and town and country working together to deal with the new circumstances with which we have to live. How does focusing blame on a single land use help to create the spirit of partnership that is needed for such an endeavour to succeed?

In summary

- *Floods are caused by extreme weather events, not by grouse shooting or grouse moor management.*
- *Nothing can be done to stop a million tonnes of water falling in a small catchment in a short period of time from causing problems.*
- *The people who own and manage these catchments are prepared to do whatever they can to ameliorate problems but, to date, nothing has been suggested that would prevent an extreme weather event from causing flooding.*
- *The EA, the body with the statutory duty to deal with flooding, does not consider grouse moor management as the cause of flooding events.*
- *Grouse moor managers have no difficulty in accommodating the requirements of water companies and river trusts.*
- *The quality of water coming from grouse moors and the aquatic life it supports is excellent and superior to that which flows from many other land uses.*
- *Grouse moor managers are not draining the uplands.*
- *What is needed is the detailed examination of entire catchments and catchment scale planning and action that all landowners can engage in, and not the demonisation of grouse moor owners.*

4. Never mind the quality, feel the width

I force myself to watch Countryfile. *To be fair, it's not the worst programme on the television and at least it doesn't have Chris Packham patronising his female co-presenter and being smug. The presenters seem to try to be fair. But when Lake Vyrnwy and the RSPB appeared it was very nearly the straw that broke the camel's back. How they've got the barefaced cheek to promote it as a success story, I simply can't imagine. It was one of four locations selected for special funding because of black grouse, one of the others was Ruabon away to the north, where they still shoot and have gamekeepers. Millions were spent. When I last went to Ruabon it was wall-to-wall lekking blackcock. I've never seen anything like it. I doubt if there is anywhere in Europe that had more lekking birds than Ruabon did that day. I went to Vyrnwy the next day and it was like a tomb. The structure was there, it looked OK but not a single blackcock. They spend millions, they oversee the extinction of a bird they were paid a fortune to save, and they stand there going on about how marvellous they are. They have no shame.*

E.W., Shropshire

CENTRAL TO THE future of the survival of our nation's heather moorlands and their unique wildlife is the attitude of the major players in the conservation industry. The most influential of these by far is the RSPB, one of the richest and most powerful organisations of its type in the world. The RSPB tells anyone who will listen that the way in which grouse moors are run is a disaster. A paper published in the journal Ibis, written by a group of senior RSPB staff and vetted by trustees, could find nothing good to say about grouse moor management. Its only positive suggestion was that all grouse moors should turn to walked-up shooting and be run along the same lines as the Langholm Moor project, with which they had been involved for many years. This was not particularly sensible or helpful. They were perfectly well aware that this project was such a profound failure from a shooting point of view that, despite employing five gamekeepers at considerable expense, no sustainable shooting had ever been possible and the estate had become so disenchanted with the whole business that they had reluctantly had to make the keepers redundant and put the moor on the market.

The views of the RSPB are very important. They are a very rich organisation with a great deal of political influence and soft power as a result of their million-plus membership. At one time, not long ago, they were very supportive of grouse moor management. One of my favourite quotes from them is: '... management of land for grouse shooting has protected upland areas from the worst of over-grazing and blanket conifer plantation whilst generating income for upland communities and forming a uniquely British form of cultural landscape.'

Sadly, those days appear to have gone. It is said, by its detractors, that this is because grouse shooting has become more intensive. But while this might be the case in a few places, in most it just carries on as before. If anything, keepers and moor owners are more amenable to change than was historically the case. Their only condition is that before they make swingeing changes to processes that have stood the test of time they are given real evidence that they work and produce better outcomes.

Unfortunately there is a strange reluctance to provide this evidence. The debate on how our heather moorlands should be managed is bedevilled by theory, but not in the usual way. The critics of grouse moor management are strangely content that their plans have the appearance of being largely theoretical: 'Do this and we think this will happen'; 'Give us this money and we will do this and see what happens in twenty years' time.'

The reason for this is not hard to find. There is absolutely no need to theorise or speculate. The national decline of heather moorland in the last seventy years means that virtually every alternative use and management system already exists, hidden in plain sight. The current list of potential options can be experienced and evaluated. We can see what happens when grouse shooting ends and the keepers are made redundant.

We can, according to suggestions, start with using the moors to plant trees – once again a fashionable idea, especially with virtue-signalling politicians. The Southern Cheviots, the subject of a huge afforestation programme, provide a perfect example. The hills were drained, because trees won't grow in a bog, and millions of non-native conifers were planted. As they grew, the trees continued the process of drying the peat (as all trees do), sucking the precious moisture up with their roots. When the forest canopy closed, the sunlight that the peat-forming mosses need to function disappeared, and the process of carbon capture, which had operated for millennia, ended – probably forever.

This was not the only impact. For a few years there was a boost in numbers of some species: short-eared owls and hen harriers prospered briefly, thanks to a temporary increase in vole numbers, and black grouse often do well in young plantations. But these few good things came to an abrupt end when, after fifteen years or so, the forest canopy closed. This saw the extinction of an entire ecosystem which, having survived since time out of mind, was expunged in a decade and a half. The losses were almost too great to comprehend: 1,750 pairs of curlew, 1,200 pairs of golden plover, 200 pairs of dunlin, 25 pairs of merlin, 11,600 pairs of red grouse, all the larks, meadow pipits, ring ouzels, and on and on.[1] A similar calculation for the moorland habitat lost to forestry in Galloway put the lost curlew alone at 5,000 pairs[2]; that is twenty times the number currently surviving in England south of Birmingham. But these were only the obvious ones. Along with them went the rare and rich mix of vegetation and the invertebrate communities that relied on the heather-dominated moorland with its multiplicity of micro-habitats, interlinked, always subtly changing, but always essentially the same.

The final irony is that, having used vast amounts of taxpayers' money to grow trees for use as pit props in the now non-existent coal industry, and having trashed a rare and beautiful landscape and its wildlife, some landowners can now claim public funds to get rid of the trees and do whatever is necessary to return it to moorland. Faced with these circumstances it is probably safe to assume that trees are not the answer.

Next, the Peak District, singled out for criticism by the chairman of the

RSPB as an area where the continuation of grouse shooting was 'one of the main reasons for the decline of wildlife in the uplands'. This statement has, happily, been shown to be wrong by the independent Breeding Bird Survey (BBS). This makes it clear that many of the relevant species are doing better on the grouse moors of the Peak District than elsewhere.

The curlew is an interesting and important example; a species in steep and worrying decline. There are probably fewer than 250 pairs attempting to breed in the south of England; the last remnants of a population measured in thousands a few decades ago. The species became extinct as a breeding bird on Dartmoor, home of the RSPB chairman, in 2020.

The grouse moors of the Peak District have a different story to tell. In 1990 the count gave an estimated breeding population of 382 pairs. By 2018 the BBS showed that this had risen to an estimated 1,346, an increase of about 350%. Interestingly, the RSPB immediately challenged the figure as too high as a result of double-counting curlew. But even if you halve the 2018 figure the curlew population is nearly twice what it was, and stands in stark contrast to the extinction on the moorlands where the RSPB chairman lives, hundreds of miles from a grouse moor.

Other species increasing in the Peak District's grouse moors, according to the BBS, include lapwing, golden plover, snipe, ravens, buzzards, peregrines and kestrels. Add to this that the Peak District contains nationally important populations of short-eared owls and merlins, 1–2% of the nation's ring ouzels and breeding hen harriers, and you may see why some of those responsible for this success are concerned that the RSPB's chairman's remarks may be more to do with a personal animosity towards grouse shooting than a grasp of science or reality.

This is especially the case when you take into account the fact that not everywhere in the area has been as successful as the reviled grouse moors. The Peak District National Parks Authority (PDNPA) acquired the Warslow Estate in 1986. Until then the estate had included a successful grouse shoot and was renowned for its large populations of breeding waders as well as the only sustainable population of black grouse in the Peak District. In 1985, before it was acquired by the PDNPA, the Warslow Estate's pair counts were snipe 654, curlew 421, lapwing 306, golden plover 12. One of the PDNPA's first actions was, of course, to get rid of the gamekeeper. By 2005, with the keeper gone and grouse moor management finished, the pair counts for that area of the Peak District were: snipe 25, curlew 26, lapwing

24 and golden plover 2 and the black grouse were completely extinct. In 2017, faced with the risk of local extinction of the remaining species, predator control was restarted, albeit in a limited way. Thirty years too late – but let us hope it works.

Finally, Lake Vyrnwy, the RSPB flagship Welsh reserve. This has been under the management of the RSPB on behalf of its owners for decades. The estate is huge and was, prior to the RSPB taking control, one of the largest grouse moors in Wales. Not only have the RSPB had the time and opportunity to demonstrate how a former grouse moor should be run, they have had the resources to do so. During their tenure, in addition to their core funding of over £120 million a year, they have had millions of pounds from the Welsh Government and through grant regimes such as the plastic bag levy and the Heritage Lottery Fund (HLF).

In their public pronouncements the RSPB is strangely opaque when it comes to the evaluation of the success of its reserve management, but occasionally the veil will slip. In the important case of the success, or otherwise, of their stewardship of the Vyrnwy grouse moors, such a slip occurred with their application for £3,299,900 to the HLF. This contains the following clear and unequivocal statement: 'Without the serious interventions RSPB is proposing in this bid, in the next few years curlew, black grouse and merlin will cease to appear as a breeding species in this area of Wales. It is likely that the same fate would befall red grouse and hen harrier within the next decade.'

The application goes on to make clear that the £3,299,900 is not all that the RSPB deem necessary to stop all these species becoming extinct on their watch. During the life of this project, this vast sum of money is intended to receive, according to the application, matched funding from Welsh Government, Severn Trent Water, United Utilities, Powys County Council and Visit Wales.

Just to be clear, the RSPB has had complete control of this huge grouse moor for decades, during which time it has received millions of pounds from the Welsh Government and grant-giving bodies to facilitate its conservation work. At the end of that time the RSPB is perfectly clear that the land it controls is in a parlous state, and that the bird assemblages it set out to protect are on the verge of extinction and will disappear unless its palpable failure is reinforced by eye-watering amounts of public money. Even then they are giving no guarantees. After all, the money is for process not outcomes. Heaven forbid that they would have to ensure the survival of merlin and black grouse to get the money. The money is for a process. Nowhere in the application does it give any undertaking to actually achieve the recovery of even a single species. It says if we don't get this money, black grouse, merlin and curlew will disappear – nowhere does it say that if we do get this money they will survive.

To be fair, this is not surprising, as a lot of the money will be spent on renovating a derelict chapel and turning it into a RSPB shop, so obviously quite a bit less than the headline £3.3 million will actually be spent on preserving the birds. It is surely beyond parody that those responsible for this catastrophe presume to lecture others on how to manage their land. But they do.

When some of this shambles was discussed in the pages of the Farmers Guardian, the RSPB were stung into responding. We read:

> Lake Vyrnwy is a complex, landscape-scale estate, with an array of stake holders involved in its management. The charity said it was working to improve the condition of the area by restoring thousands of hectares of blanket bog and upland heath, removing non-native conifers, reinstating active heather management, creating wildflower meadows and restoring ffridd habitat [a type of woodland found in the Welsh hills].

'Lake Vrynwy is a complex, landscape-scale estate, with an array of stakeholders.' Goodness me, how utterly amazing. One of the reasons why the RSPB can't manage their moor of some 3,240 hectares is that it is large and complicated. In other words, it is just like a typical estate with a grouse moor. The fact that they can't manage it in a manner that has the outcomes they said they wanted is a result of their lack of competence, not an inevitable consequence of the estate being large and complex. Any competent head keeper could have outperformed them. In fact hundreds of them already do, on large complex estates all over the uplands.

The RSPB is 'reinstating active heather management'. That's good to hear. We should all be grateful that they have just taken control and can save the moorland from the previous manager's neglect. Well, no. The RSPB has been in charge for decades. It has to be asked who stopped the active heather management in the first place. I couldn't possibly guess. The only clue we can find is in a statement by the RSPB made in 1984 when they were definitely in charge: 'Because of the regime of burning and despite grazing the moorland, there is still a healthy population of red grouse and large numbers of breeding curlew and whinchats. Less common are golden plover, hen harrier, merlin and stonechat.'[3]

At the time of writing, that was thirty-seven years ago. Thirty-seven years during which, at some point, someone stopped active heather management. It is also thirty-seven years during which the RSPB has been in charge. One might think it unreasonable to assume that they stopped the management, which has now resulted in the parlous state of affairs described in their application for £3.3 million from the HLF. Surely it would have been someone else. But, as they were in charge of managing the place, it is difficult to imagine whom.

Just to reiterate the scale of the problem, without the grant of £3.3 million, match-funded to bring the total to over £6 million, the RSPB was clear that the reserve's habitat, and the birds it supports, were on their last legs.

Contrast this tragic mess with what they said could be found there four decades ago. Healthy populations of red grouse; large numbers of breeding curlew and whinchats. Less common, but still breeding, and not in any way endangered, were golden plover, hen harrier, merlin and stonechat. This is not a glitch, it is not a blip, it is not something that happened overnight. This is evidence of long-term systematic failure and incompetence on the part of the people who have appointed themselves as guardians of the Lake Vyrnwy reserve.

Then there is the confusion around the area that will be restored as a key part of the expenditure of £3.3 million. The statement in the *Farmers Guardian* refers to 'thousands of hectares of blanket bog and upland heath'. That sounds like reasonable value for money. What appears in the HLF bid is far more limited. The stated outcomes are:

> By raising the water table on 90ha of blanket bog conditions for tupilid larvae (Daddy Long-Legs) will be improved.
>
> 360 ha of ridge top bog systems will be covered in short natural bog vegetation rather than deep heather.
>
> 90ha of gully systems will be shallow flooded with at least 50% sphagnum cover.
>
> 35,000 metres of eroding and drying peat exposed in the form of peat hags will be completely covered in natural vegetation.

That's it. Whatever way you look at it, it does not appear to be 'thousands of hectares'. Assuming that the two 90-hectare areas are different locations, that adds up to a total of 540 hectares. But there is the bizarre appearance of a linear measure, 35,000 metres, for what must be an area, as peat hags are not linear features. What can it be? Well, it can't be a mistake, where metres are substituted in error for hectares or acres, as if either were the case the whole reserve and much of its hinterland would be one giant peat hag, easily visible from space. The likeliest explanation is that the author of the £12,000 application, simply missed off the 'square' before metres. An easy mistake when you are being paid so little to fill out a form. Even so, 35,000 square metres sounds a lot. Happily it isn't; if the guess is right, the total area of the peat hags will be a much more manageable 3.5 hectares. This will bring the total that we can find in the bid to 543.5ha. This seems a little short of the thousands of hectares the RSPB claimed in the *Farmers Guardian*.

The Welsh Government, or at least someone in it, is clearly impressed – and has been for many years. At least that is the only conclusion one can draw when looking at the amount of public money that pours into the RSPB for a variety of important conservation functions. The vital biodiversity intervention of renovating the RSPB car park, cafe, and toilets at the seabird cliffs at South Stack on Anglesey got them £230,000. Preparing the application for the HLF bid for Lake Vyrnwy cost the Welsh taxpayers £12,000. But the funding most relevant to the grouse moors is the £637,359.32 that the RSPB, received as a Single Revenue Support grant from the Welsh taxpayer between 2015 and 2019. This is, in part, to enable them to work with the private individuals who own the moorlands of North Wales and explain to them the principles of sustainable upland management. It is uncertain whether the private landowners would welcome advice from an organisation with the RSPB's record of failure, but what is certain is that the Welsh Government was not interested; they simply continued to give money to the RSPB without even inquiring what, if anything, was being achieved.

The need to do something about the upland bird populations of Wales is indeed pressing. They are largely gone. One of the classical examinations of the outcome of the end of grouse shooting relates to North Wales. Called the Berwyn Study, it looked at breeding bird populations before and after the ending of grouse shooting and it tells a story of uniform loss, with curlew, black grouse, golden plover, lapwing, red grouse and snipe all in catastrophic decline.[4] In North Wales there is one shining example of an exception to this tragic story – Ruabon Moor. This heather moorland also happens to be the only habitat in the region where active grouse moor management is taking place. The landowner has a small syndicate of friends who together meet the costs of managing the moor out of their own pockets. They shoot perhaps two or three times a year and so far make fairly modest bags, but they are aiming to improve. Their subscriptions enable them to employ two gamekeepers, who manage the moor and carry out legal predator control with considerable efficiency and effectiveness.

There is only the slenderest chance that they will ever have access to any Welsh Government funding. The first problem is that, unlike at the RSPB's Lake Vyrnwy, there are lots of upland birds. There are quite a lot of red grouse; hundreds of them. Curlew, far from being functionally extinct, are thriving, as are lapwing, redshank and snipe. There are even golden plover nesting there. However, the jewel in the crown is the black grouse: a bird for which Vyrnwy was noted, and which now is effectively extinct there, is thriving on Ruabon. Numbers fluctuate, affected primarily by the weather in the weeks following hatching, when chick mortality can be high if it is cold and wet. But even after a run of bad springs, the number of lekking blackcock counted in 2020 was well over a hundred – or, to put it another way, well over a hundred more than on the whole of Lake Vyrnwy.

Another problem is that, unlike the RSPB, the people who own and manage the land are not a rich NGO, employing a cadre of grant application specialists. Nor do they benefit from years of working with Welsh civil servants and politicians as a result of receiving the Single Revenue Core Grant, which ensures they get early warning of any grants coming down the pipeline. Finally, they are very unlikely indeed to be funded by their friends in the Welsh Government simply to fill out an application form to get a grant from someone else.

It is surely beyond shameless that an organisation, which has had total control over one of Wales' great grouse moors for decades, that has received huge sums of public money to further its chosen management of the place and has overseen a catastrophic decline in the birds it set out to protect, has the temerity to put itself forward to advise Welsh moor owners on how to manage their land and has happily and unblushingly received huge sums of public money to do so. All the while this was going on, a small private grouse moor comprehensively outperformed them on the only factor that really matters, the conservation of upland birds. But of course they focused on outcome and not process, so it doesn't really count.

In summary

- *Grouse moor management is not perfect but it has resulted in the survival of beautiful landscapes supporting some of the greatest assemblages of ground-nesting birds in mainland Britain.*

- *The planting of commercial forestry on and around heather moorland has been an ecological disaster.*

- *The principal critics of grouse moor management have proved to be wholly ineffective when faced with the task of managing these moorlands despite being supported by millions of pounds of public money.*

- *Their inability to produce outcomes comparable to private moor owners does not stop them putting themselves forward as experts in the areas of their greatest incompetence.*

- *Huge sums of public money are being absorbed by the conservation industry without any interest being taken in the value for money.*

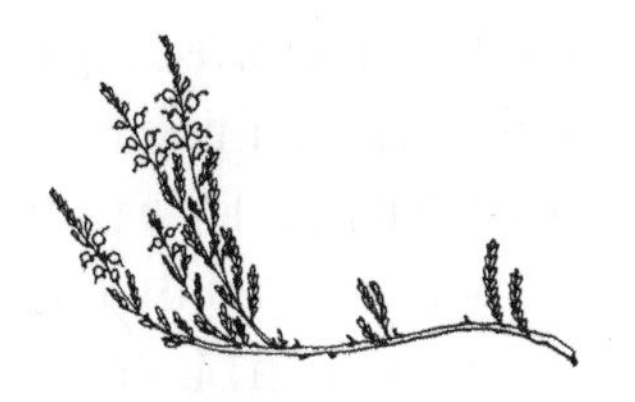

5. Curlew calling

The RSPB is planned to be the only beneficiary in the project, as it has the guaranteed capacity and experience to deliver it. It has run several previous EU LIFE projects on a sole-beneficiary basis and has completed them all successfully.

Importantly, however, we will involve numerous other organisations in the project as partners in a more general sense. Many of these organisations will be brought under the 'umbrella' of the UK and Ireland Action Group (UKICAG). This group brings together five statutory agencies (NE, SNH, NRW, the Northern Ireland Environment Agency (NIEA) and the Joint Nature Conservation Committee (JNCC)) and various NGOs, RSPB, Wildfowl and Wetland Trust, BTO, GWCT, the National Trust and BirdWatch Ireland. Its aim is to shape and drive a co-ordinated programme for curlew conservation and to help the UK meet its international obligations for this species. It will play a key role in developing the UK-level After-LIFE Plan (AEWA Species Action Plan) and provide an effective for engaging the governments of all four countries in the project.

Extract from the RSPB's EU LIFE
Curlew in Crisis Project statement

THERE ARE ELEVEN pages like this. That is what is needed to be successful in getting the EU to provide 60% of the €4,601,472 that the project costs. Nowhere in the list is there any reference to the people who have most of the curlews on their land, that are still breeding successfully. For goodness sake, don't mention the people whose management ensures that their curlews are doing very well. To paraphrase Kipling, 'To keep your curlew, when all about are losing theirs and blaming it on you.'

The shooting community labours under a profound misapprehension. It is widely, and not unreasonably, believed that if we can demonstrate that estates managed for shooting are rich in biodiversity, that they provide safe havens for rare birds and other wildlife and they protect beautiful landscapes, the RSPB will be delighted and tell the world that we are good boys and girls, who should be treated as the dedicated conservationists we undoubtedly are. Nothing could be further from the truth. Based on long personal experience I believe that it would be difficult to find anything that enrages the RSPB strategists more than the news that a properly managed shooting estate is an exemplar of good conservation practice.

The reason for this is simple. They rely for their funding on the public believing that, without them, the UK's wildlife is going to hell in a handcart. That they, and they alone, know how to fix things, and, if only they are given enough money, all will be well. There is nothing they cannot fix. If that is the way you raise the £140 million you need to run your organisation in the manner to which it has become accustomed, the last thing you need is some ghastly shooters achieving far better results, funded out of their own pockets.

If you don't believe me, consider the curlew. To say that it is loved is a profound understatement. I have never met anyone who is not a fan of this remarkable bird. Those who spend their time on our estuaries and grouse moors could be excused for thinking that these wonderful, enigmatic birds are doing well, perhaps as well as ever – but they would be profoundly and tragically wrong. Over much of its traditional British range the curlew is in dire straits, if not already locally extinct. Places where people took for granted that the spring would be enriched by the sounds of curlew returning to their ancestral breeding meadows and moors are now silent. Generations are arising who are not even aware of what has already been lost. The species is slipping into history. The world's curlew species are not in good shape: the Eskimo curlew and the slender-billed curlew have not been seen for years and are probably already extinct. The UK's own bird, the European curlew, is disappearing from huge swathes of these islands, being virtually extinct in Eire and Ulster, hanging by a thread in Wales, and with only a couple of hundred pairs in England south of the Peak District, while the annual Breeding Bird Survey shows that in Scotland the population declined by 61% between 1994 and 2017. Taken as a whole, the British population of breeding curlew has halved since the mid-1990s. To make things worse, unlike some species that could do better in the UK (capercaillie, for example), they are not underwritten by huge successful populations elsewhere. We have nearly 30% of the world's breeding population of curlew and it is doing no better abroad than it is here.

These birds face a loss of suitable habitat and, in areas of improved grassland, their eggs and chicks may be destroyed by silage making, but neither of these factors is their biggest problem on and around moorland. There is no silage cut on prime habitats like Dartmoor, the Irish peat bogs, the New Forest heaths or the Welsh moors. Predation is far and away the largest threat. Over a decade ago the GWCT demonstrated in the Otterburn Study[1, 2], one of the most robust and elegant experiments of its kind, that in perfect habitat, but without gamekeepers, curlew breeding success was insufficient to maintain their population. Conversely, with effective gamekeeping, curlews produced a healthy surplus of fledged chicks and over time the number of breeding pairs rose steadily.

The malign influence of predation on the curlew population was demonstrated with less scientific rigour, but perhaps greater force, by the project in Shropshire named Curlew Country. This monitored the fate of eggs and chicks in what is the last redoubt for curlew in a county where they were once widespread. The Onny and Camlad catchments west of the Long Mynd held twenty to thirty pairs and every effort was made to find nests and monitor their success. In the event, there wasn't any success to monitor. In the first two years of the study, virtually all the nests were destroyed (mainly by foxes, badgers and corvids). The few chicks that hatched in the second year, thanks to electric fences thrown round them to keep foxes and badgers at bay, were all predated before they could fledge. Predator control in subsequent years resulted in an improvement but it meant that getting funds from the usual sources became next to impossible. Such money as was forthcoming often specifically excluded dealing with the very issue that was driving the birds to extinction.

Obviously, as the largest and richest bird protection charity in the world, the RSPB is aware of the peril faced by the curlew. It is fully aware of the Otterburn research and what happened in Shropshire. It knows that, whilst modern farming has been a major problem in some areas, it is not a problem over huge swathes of the uplands, which historically held large numbers of curlew and now hold none. Faced for over a decade with the unpleasant reality of the scientific evidence, the RSPB reacted by running their own little experiments, comparing predator control with habitat manipulation. These were not, by their own admission, in any sense akin to the elegant and incontrovertible science of Otterburn. They were 'suck it and see' attempts at finding a way of avoiding what every unbiased person already knew – that, without efficient legal predator control, curlew have little chance of long-term survival as a British breeding bird.

When I say that the RSPB ran the experiments, obviously they needed to be subsidised by public money. In their world it would be unthinkable for an organisation with an operational surplus running into tens of millions of pounds to be expected to bear the whole cost of research into a rare and declining bird. Happily for them, NE was on hand to subsidise the research and this undoubtedly helped when they set out to acquire far more resources later.

However, if you look at the issue from another perspective, the situation appears bizarre. I would suggest that if the state wishes to have more curlews the obvious people to approach are those who have a track record in producing more curlew. This does not seem a particularly radical idea. If you ran a football team and wanted your side to win more matches, it would seem logical to acquire a manager who had an excellent record of winning rather than, as NE decided to do, get a mate from a non-league side to do a bit of practice and take charge.

The RSPB is very guarded about their ability to increase curlew numbers on their reserves, despite the fact that they have been managing high-grade curlew habitat for years. So poor is the insight that RSPB allows into its performance that we must return again to Lake Vyrnwy, one of few places where their wish to access money resulted in an unusual degree of frankness. When, some forty years ago, they took control of the huge expanse of moorland and pasture at Lake Vyrnwy, they said that, 'Because of the regime of burning and despite grazing the moorland, there is still a fairly healthy population of red grouse and large numbers of breeding curlew.'

That was long ago. By the time NE gave the RSPB the money and created the situation that gave them a route into acquiring effective control of the

UK's curlew recovery, the population on Vyrnwy had collapsed. Conversely, when the deal was done, GWCT had already conclusively demonstrated at Otterburn that they had the ability to completely turn the fortunes of the curlew around. It is fair to ask why a supposedly unbiased NE decided that the RSPB and not GWCT should do the research and lead the recovery. Had they taken a different course, the previous decade would not have been wasted and there would undoubtedly be more curlew.

It is also fair to point out that predator control means different things to different people and that, to make a value judgement as to its importance in curlew conservation, it is essential that it is done to the highest level of effectiveness. We know that what the RSPB calls predator control would not satisfy a competent head keeper, as it excludes reducing the population density of, for example, stoats. Thus what has probably occurred is comparing habitat manipulation with not particularly effective predator control – a near perfect definition of a waste of time and money.

It is, of course, worse than that. There are places where curlew, and a host of other ground-nesting birds, are doing really well. Places where they breed with such success that they produce sufficient fledged young to see local populations maintained and increased. These places are producing surplus curlew that could repopulate the landscape. They have a technical name – they are called grouse moors.

To say that the RSPB do not like this fact is a huge understatement. Their vice-president, Chris Packham, talks dismissively of grouse moors 'curlew farming', and claims that their success on grouse moors is irrelevant.[3] The RSPB itself is also in denial, claiming that grouse moors are 'industrial landscapes', devoid of life and biodiversity. The fact that most grouse moor keepers can see more curlew out of their kitchen window than you can find on the whole of the 3,250 hectares of moorland at their Lake Vyrnwy reserve bothers them not a jot.

As I said at the outset, it is the success of grouse moor management that enrages them but, to be fair, they probably do not need to worry. Their capacity to access huge sums of money has now reached levels not previously seen, even in the conservation industry. The fact that privately funded grouse moors can produce better curlew outcomes, and that the RSPB cannot evidence anywhere to compete in terms of curlew conservation, is irrelevant. They can still draw in huge sums of public money on the back of the poor benighted curlew. The worse they do, the more money they get. Poor Curlew Country, one the very few curlew projects to actually produce some fledged curlew, can't get a bean, while the RSPB continues to be showered with cash.

The HLF's £3.3 million grant for Lake Vyrnwy was partly based on the impending extinction of the curlew; the same applies to the €7 million for killing stoats on Orkney. But the most striking came to light in 2020 when the EU Life Fund gifted the RSPB the lion's share of €4.6 million (over £4 million) for work at five historic curlew locations. As this sum is only about a third of the RSPB's operating surplus, an unkind person might ask why they didn't do something earlier, but at least the fortunes of this lovely bird will now improve. They ought to, for over £4 million on just five sites. The RSPB has been given more money in one hit than it costs to run most conservation charities in their entirety. So what is the target to be achieved by all this money?

Twice as many curlew? Perhaps two hundred additional pairs? Three hundred? Were there to be four hundred additional pairs at the end of the project that would be £10,000 a pair. By conservation industry rates, a very good deal. Well, no – not four hundred additional pairs; not three hundred or even two hundred. How many then? None. The target for an expenditure of over £4 million is, to quote from their own document, 'that the number of pairs at these sites will be at least as high at the end of the project as at the start'.

This apparently modest, or arguably disappointing, outcome for the expenditure of £4 million, is seen by the promoters as such an outstanding achievement that 'The project's sites will be actively promoted as centres of curlew conservation excellence.'

Their English site is Geltsdale, which, when it was a grouse moor, was alive with curlew. Now the population is sadly so reduced that apparently only vast additional resources can stem their decline. To quote the RSPB's description of the site, 'Geltsdale, which lies in the heart of the Pennine Region ... is by far the most important part of England for curlew.' Would that be the Pennine Region that is one of the most important parts of England for grouse shooting and where any grouse moor can produce more curlew than RSPB? Well, yes, it would be.

But, as ever, the RSPB need not worry about the obvious fact that a moorland keeper with a bad leg and a fear of the dark could outperform them. They need not worry that they have a record of success with curlew akin to my success at indoor hang-gliding. No one will ever know why NE decided to select an organisation, which had run a moorland reserve in a manner that saw curlew go from large numbers to effectively none, to lead its curlew project. No one will know why they selected an organisation that is deeply uncomfortable with predator control, and can show little evidence that it does it effectively, to trial predator control interventions. No one will ever know why the nation's grouse moor managers have been excluded from the process.

But, what we can be sure of is that the nature of the problems and the actions needed to solve them have been known for years by anyone who took the slightest interest. The relationship between keepered grouse moors and the breeding success of curlew and other waders has been repeatedly and clearly demonstrated. The refusal of the RSPB to reference these facts, or to even mention grouse moors or gamekeepers in the context of the desperate need to conserve curlew and extract a huge sum of money from the EU and others, is not an oversight. It is a deliberate and reprehensible decision made in full knowledge of the facts.

In case of doubt, this is what Ian Newton, a former chairman of the RSPB, has to say on the subject:

> Overall, the evidence for predation impacts on wader numbers includes: (1) recent catastrophic declines of Curlew and other species in various regions where studies revealed high nest predation (Grant et al. 1999, Bolton et al. 2007, Newton 2017a, Colwell 2018); (2) higher breeding success and density of waders on land managed for grouse than on land not managed for grouse, due at least in part to predator control by gamekeepers on grouse areas (Tharme et al. 2001); (3) positive effects of predator control on wader breeding success and population change (Fletcher et al. 2010, Parr 1993, Newton 1998, Jackson 2001, Bolton et al. 2007, Merrick 2010); (4) declines in breeding waders following the removal of gamekeepers from moorland areas, or increases following the reinstatement of gamekeepers (Warren and Baines 2014, Whitehead et al. 2018, Ludwig et al. 2019); and (5) the lack in some studies of any influence of other factors capable of affecting the nesting success and population change in waders, such as grazing pressure, habitat and topography (Douglas et al. 2014).

I've taken the step of including the references to make the point that a large number pre-date the decision by the RSPB and NE to spend five years trying to prove that water flows uphill. Everyone knew what reality was and is.

Ian Newton returns to the subject with:

> Nowadays, waders breed with greater success on grouse moors than almost any other habitat in Britain, and such moors are some of the few places where wader numbers are being maintained. This seems to have affected the regional occurrence of waders in Britain, with some of the highest densities in regions where grouse-moor management is prevalent, and some of the lowest where it is absent (Dartmoor, Exmoor, and North Wales).

It could hardly be clearer, but such is the RSPB's determination to see an end to grouse moors and their communities, not a word has come from them.

In summary

- ❖ *It has been beyond doubt for years that the efficient legal control of common predatory mammals and birds is an essential prerequisite of curlew conservation.*

- ❖ *The grouse moor community has outperformed the conservation industry in producing sustainable wader populations for decades.*

- ❖ *Where conservationists have achieved comparable results (e.g. Merrick) they have used equivalent predator control techniques.*

- ❖ *The ability of the RSPB to take the lead in an issue as crucial as saving the British curlew population when their own record is so poor is at best regrettable.*

- ❖ *In such circumstances, the RSPB's refusal even to allude to the importance of grouse moors in relation to curlew conservation is unworthy of a once-great organisation and stands in stark contrast to the honesty and frankness of their former chairman.*

6. There must be an alternative

We went to this meeting organised by the bird-watchers club to listen to this enormous bloke who had written a book attacking grouse shooting. His talk was interesting but annoying. Everything we do was wrong. The moors were appalling places. Everything he said was theoretical. That was hardly surprising, by the look of him he'd spent more time in pie shops than on grouse moors. When we got to the questions, he got off his script, broke into a sweat and waffled about. I was really surprised how he didn't seem to have thought much beyond his own theories. The real shocker was when he was asked what would replace grouse shooting. Apparently the owners will be required to leave the land to revert to woodland. When the moor is covered in trees, pine martens will come back, wipe out the grey squirrels, they will be replaced by red squirrels and eco-tourists will pay to watch the pine martens chasing the squirrels. As far as I could see he was stone cold sober. Sober but mad as a rat.

D.T., Lancashire

THOSE WHO DO not like grouse shooting and want to see it stopped are faced with a serious question. In the absence of grouse shooting – which ensures that the upkeep of the moors and their wildlife is paid for by the landowners and their sporting tenants – who keeps these places looking as the public likes to see them and still contributing significantly to the local economy and culture? The taxpayer?

It is clear from the Lake Vyrnwy experience that the richest and most powerful conservation organisation in the land cannot compete in terms of conservation outcomes with even a small, isolated grouse moor. There are endless examples of forest planting in the uplands doing huge damage to moorland eco-systems, water quality, and carbon storage, of which the Southern Cheviots is just one. So what are the other possibilities?

There are, in practice, very few. Alternative uses are energy generation, pastoral agriculture, tourism and enhanced eco-tourism following some sort of rewilding. The first point to bear in mind with all these options is that they are not binary choices. All of them can take place on fully functioning grouse moors.

To pretend, as those opposed to grouse shooting generally do, that there is only a binary choice – energy or grouse, sheep and cattle or grouse, tourism or grouse – is simply a deceit. All of these can co-exist and already do. There are a lot of places where all of these 'alternatives' are integrated into the management of a single estate and where speculation can be replaced by direct observation.

It is, in fact, entirely normal for large estates to integrate grouse moor management with sensible and sensitive forestry, arable and pastoral farming, deer stalking, sport fishing, tourism, energy generation, water supply and rewilding. One of the great advantages of the private ownership of large estates is that it allows long-term integrated planning to be coupled with personal accountability. If the owners get it wrong, they can't just get another job – they have to live with it for the rest of their lives. That accountability is one of the most important factors missing in the authoritarian, process-driven model beloved by the NGOs.

If you examine the CVs of most of the growing band of advisers, monitors, regulators, policy people and 'managers', who drift across the uplands from board to partnership, and partnership to project, you find that there is an extraordinary degree of staff interchange. It is perfectly normal – indeed expected – to find someone working for NE who has worked for the RSPB, NT and a County Nature Trust. It's a bit like playing cards; you can shuffle the pack as much as you like but the cards themselves don't actually change. They are the same fifty-two, whatever you do.

Most of the time the locals are not aware of the intimate nature of the relationship of the RSPB, NE, NT and the rest. But what they do notice is that when things go wrong, it is they, the locals, who have to clear up the mess, live with the consequences and get the blame, while the people responsible get a better job in another organisation, move elsewhere and start all over again. This is not an option if the land is yours, and this is why, with a few exceptions, private estates provide some of the best examples of integrated, multifunctional land use, coupled with excellent conservation outcomes, to be found anywhere in the British Isles.

If, however, you want to do away with grouse shooting, then the object is not to integrate but to replace. So the question is: can these activities replace grouse shooting? Well of course they can. You can replace a salt marsh with an airport, so it is obviously possible to replace grouse moor management with tourism, grazing, or energy generation. But that is not the point. The real question is whether these things are so much better in terms of their conservation, economic, societal and cultural outcomes, that it is justified to force people to adopt them on their own land, by the simple means of rendering grouse shooting impossible?

Tourism and eco-tourism

Tourism and eco-tourism are relatively straightforward to deal with. They currently contribute virtually nothing to management of the landscape and the wildlife it supports, outside of a very limited number of honey pot locations managed by NGOs. Even there, many of these locations are subsidised, either from the organisations' core funds or from periodic external grants. Furthermore, it is very difficult to see how they could ever make a significant direct contribution to landscape management, for the simple reason that tourists, including the eco-variety, will pay for travel, accommodation, food and drink, but they will not pay for access.

If you want to shoot grouse on heather moorland, you have to pay. The people who want to walk there or watch birds there would be completely outraged if they were asked to pay a penny. There is no chance whatsoever of this situation changing, even if the offer is improved. Some extraordinary claims are made for the imagined riches that would flow as a result of the presence of whatever species is being promoted as the key to triggering the pent-up surge of eco-tourists. These are based on the assumption that the results of one or two early experiences can be repeated *ad infinitum*. This is, of course, both nonsense and irrelevant to the central issue. Whilst it may be true that the sea eagles on Mull had a positive effect on tourism (although the actual scale of the effects may be disputed), it is highly unlikely that this provides a model that can be endlessly and profitably repeated all over the place and with a mass of species. What is certain, however, is that the additional funds, whatever they were, made no contribution to managing and maintaining the landscape these birds exploited.

The idea that because one species in one place has a positive impact they or some other creature will have a similar effect anywhere or everywhere, is simply risible. If you open a fishmonger's shop in a Yorkshire village, people may be so impressed and so starved of access to good-quality fish, that they will travel from miles around to shop there and the business will succeed. Only an idiot would take this as evidence that you could open lots of fish shops in every village in the Vale of York. There is a limited demand for anything, including eco-tourism.

This is also illustrated by what occurred on Langholm Moor during the project to integrate large numbers of the scarce and beautiful hen harrier into a successful grouse moor. Hen harrier is not the nicest name for a bird implying, as it does, that they might harry hens – something they have indeed been known to do, as they feed their chicks largely on baby birds and small mammals. So, the RSPB prefers to call them 'sky dancers' and, as such, they are said to be one of the most popular birds in the country. They are certainly as good an eco-tourism draw as can be imagined.

At its height, the gamekeepers on Langholm Moor were so successful at protecting the ground-nesting harriers from predation by foxes and stoats that there was a greater concentration of these wonderful birds on the moor than anywhere else in the UK, or in the whole of Europe. They were so abundant that, when I made one of my regular summer visits, there was not a single occasion when I failed to see one from the road that ran across the moor. Often I saw several in the air at once. A genuine wildlife spectacle.

What I did not see was anyone else. Nor interestingly, did the gamekeepers. They saw the occasional person or two with a telescope and there was a man in a white van who came some weekends. But hordes of eco-tourists, filling the coffers of the shops and pubs in nearby Langholm? None. There was no secret about the project or the presence of the sky dancers; Langholm is a short distance from the M74 and you didn't even have to walk.

This is not to say that eco-tourism doesn't exist. It does and it can have positive financial outcomes in some circumstances, for some people and organisations. But it is not a panacea and it will not replace the income generated by grouse shooting, because such money as it generates does not go to the landowners who manage these magnificent landscapes – even though it is the landscapes that facilitate the eco-tourism.

The final problem with a tourist-based solution is that it tends to destroy both culture and community. The almost unique feature of the grouse moors is that they are part of a living, functioning landscape, where communities thrive doing real jobs that have local cultural significance. Compare the vitality and self-reliance found in the villages amongst the grouse moors with the hollowed out, second-homed, theme parks of parts of the Lake District. You are comparing a living person with an inflatable doll. From a distance it may look alive but close up there is no mistaking that it is plastic.

Energy generation

Energy generation in the heather moorlands would necessarily be from wind or small-scale hydro-power. Solar might work in some places, but somewhere that has rain on more days than the sun shines may not be an ideal location. We know that wind generation can take place on what are currently grouse moors, because it already does, without the grouse moor ceasing to function. But once again, those who are opposed to the very existence of grouse shooting are not interested in a multi-functional landscape. They want replacement.

If it is replacement, it is fair to compare the impacts of seeding a moor with wind turbines with its management for grouse. The first and most obvious impact is on the landscape. There hasn't been much research into whether people prefer an apparently natural vista of purple heather and cotton grass, to one dotted with wind turbines, towering above the landscape. There may be other reasons why large sums of money have not been spent researching which view the public prefer, but the obvious one is that anyone asking the question would risk being certified. It is obvious that they are an eyesore and an intrusion into the landscape, albeit one forced on us by climate change, and it is equally obvious that they are likely to have a profoundly deleterious impact on tourism. The sentence 'Come to the wind farms, they're so lovely', is unlikely to feature in many holiday brochures.

Another issue is their size and the need for them to be anchored by standing them in immense blocks of concrete, coupled with a network of roads and tracks needed to move the materials to construct them and allow regular inspection and maintenance. These impacts dwarf the issues for which grouse moors are criticised, and it is surprising that the intrusion of these structures, into what are effectively wilderness areas, is not opposed more robustly by the critics of the minutiae of grouse moor management.

The final issue is the toll they take on the wildlife that flies around them. They can be a very effective way of killing birds and bats. The tips of the turbine blades are moving at immense speed in a circular motion that no bird or bat will have ever encountered in nature. Unsurprisingly, they can kill the best of flyers. When a rare spine-tailed swift turned up in the Western Isles a few years ago, it caused great excitement and there was a general rush to see it, with plane schedules being combed to get there as quickly as possible. The rush ended when news broke on Twitter that it had met its death on the tip of a rotating wind turbine blade. Spine-tailed swifts are amongst the fastest flyers in the world. If a wind turbine can get them, nothing is safe.

In countries other than the UK, those interested in conservation have done a considerable amount of research into the impact of turbines on natural systems, such as the killing or excluding of birds, in particular raptors. In the USA it has been shown that large numbers of eagles and even larger numbers of harriers are killed by turbines as they migrate along the Rocky Mountains. One study refers to the bodies of no fewer than 67 golden eagles, 188 red-tailed hawks, 348 American kestrels and 440 burrowing owls killed in a single large wind-farm complex.[1]

In Germany, research into the impact of 337 turbines found the bodies of 36 sea eagles, 101 red kites and 121 buzzards. These figures were not collected by some pressure group keen to attack wind energy, but by the State Bird Observatory of the Brandenburg Environment Agency.[2] They were at pains to point out that the data had been collected haphazardly, thus 'making the total number of collision victims in Germany likely to be far higher than officially listed'. Other species found killed by the German turbines include short-eared owls, ospreys, harriers, merlin, eagle owls, rough-legged buzzards and lesser-spotted eagles. Further to this, a wind farm on the Norwegian island of Smola consisting of only 68 turbines killed 38 sea eagles[3], while in Spain another study showed the turbines killing 16 short-toed eagles, 23 kestrels, 13 lesser kestrels and 138 griffon vultures.

In the UK? Nothing apparently. Eagles and hen harriers are very likely to carry a geolocation tag and if anything untoward happens to them their RSPB handlers can find the body and will surely tell the world – won't they? As far as can be ascertained virtually none of these tagged birds has ever had even a mildly unpleasant experience with a wind turbine, or so we are led to believe.

With bats there is a similar anomaly. In other countries bats are killed in very large numbers by wind turbines. They are in a worse situation even than birds. Not only can they be killed, as birds are, by being struck by the rotating blade, they can also be killed outright or fatally injured by barotrauma, the effect of a catastrophic change in air pressure on the internal organs and eardrums of a bat passing close to the rotating turbine blade. In other countries this is recognised as a significant cause of mortality and concern. In Germany, for example, it is estimated that turbines are killing over 300,000 bats every year.[4, 5] But in the UK, who knows, or perhaps, who cares?

The RSPB, which is happy to comment on virtually any mammal issue related to upland management from voles to red deer, seems strangely uninterested in finding out if a similar carnage of rare, declining and protected bats is taking place in the UK. It is not difficult to avoid finding dead bats. They are small and readily scavenged and the ones with perforated eardrums will take some time to die of starvation and so will never be counted, even if they were looked for. But apparently it is not a problem here.

The RSPB has a wind turbine of its own at The Lodge, its headquarters in Bedfordshire, and the organisation receives significant support from several businesses involved in wind energy. As the largest and most assertive business in the conservation industry, the RSPB would obviously never enter into a financially beneficial arrangement if there was even a remote chance of a turbine killing an eagle, a hen harrier or a rare bat – would they?

Yet it is curious that the approach of the UK is so different from Germany or Norway or Spain or Canada or the USA. It is, of course, true that if you do not look, you will not find, but that explanation, whilst it might work for bats or buntings, can hardly be used to explain the raptor anomaly. Here, so many raptors are tagged and their fates determined apparently precisely that there can be little doubt that someone knows. That someone is obviously the RSPB and its acolytes, who tag these birds and who decide which ones they will tell the world about and which ones they will keep secret.

Thus replacing grouse moor management with wind turbines would be likely to result in significant environmental damage, a massive loss in landscape value and, judging by the experience of countries such as Germany, Spain and elsewhere, the deaths of large numbers of bats and birds, including many raptors. It is not a risk-free option.

Increased pastoral activity

The final issue on the list of potential replacement for grouse shooting is increasing pastoral activity. In fact the grazing of sheep and cattle already takes place on grouse moors and historically, before the EU headage payments scheme created the chaos that it did, moorland managers had no difficulty accommodating larger numbers than are currently allowed on many moors – but it took skill and understanding to make it work without serious habitat loss. Such skill as remains is, of course, currently disregarded in favour of the opinions of people who know virtually nothing about sheep and may not even personally approve of their use as food.

Any attempt to increase the grazing of stock significantly would run into difficulties. First, on designated sites, the behaviour of farmers and graziers is just as likely to be subject to draconian controls as grouse shooting. Second, sheep in the uplands are hardly profitable as it is and, if you are losing money, increasing the number of sheep simply risks you losing more. Third, sheep are the only creatures that hardcore rewilders dislike more than grouse moor managers. Finally, this is a classic example of people who have no practical knowledge telling people who do how to live their lives.

Cattle are generally less objected to by the conservation industry and they, just like sheep, and even native pony breeds, may have a potential role in the detailed management of any heather moorland. But while they can fit comfortably into the plans and management of grouse moors, they cannot replace the economic, biodiversity and cultural losses that would occur if, instead of working with the grouse, they were expected to replace them.

In summary

- *Grouse moors are already multi-functional landscapes. They already accommodate native woodland, pastoral farming, energy generation, tourism and much more.*

- *The binary choice presented by those who wish to see an end to grouse shooting is false. It is already 'grouse shooting and ...', and there is no need for 'grouse shooting or ...'*

- *None of the alternative uses proposed provide the cultural and economic benefits of grouse shooting whilst simultaneously maintaining the existing biodiversity.*

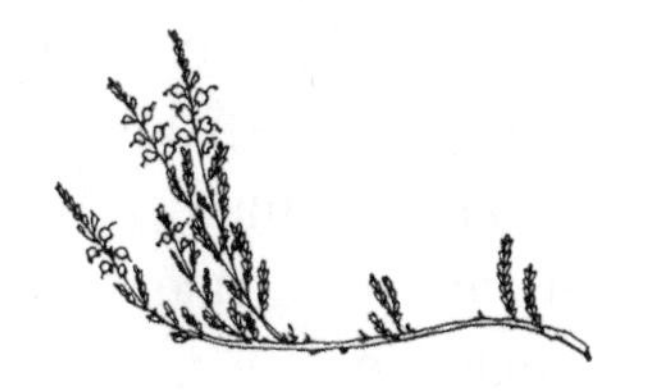

7. Let's just leave it to nature

Nature reserves don't look after themselves. If we were to leave them alone, they could soon deteriorate and lose their value for wildlife. At reserves with reedbeds, such as Minsmere and Radipole Lake, we have to remove scrub vegetation or they would turn into woodland.

RSPB *Places to Visit*

REWILDING IS LIKE love. You can hardly be against it, but it is just as blind, and like love can lead to some strange and potentially disastrous situations. Because it is difficult to define, rewilding has the knack of being whatever you want it to be and it is likely to change in form and intent during the course of a single conversation with one of its proponents, as they discover exactly which description is most likely to get your support.

Despite these problems, the underlying theory is clear enough, that all conservation problems are caused by human beings and if we all just got out of the way everything would sort itself out. All the problems would go away and everything would be wonderful, just as nature intended it.

The idea appeals to the perhaps universal feeling that there was a golden age, and if we could just find the key we could put things back just as we each think they were. Furthermore, there are examples of various rewilding projects and approaches that have had beneficial outcomes. But our key question is, does rewilding offer a better way of retaining heather moorland and the wildlife it supports than the system of management that is currently in place?

Most grouse moor managers are small rewilders, as indeed are most people who shoot more generally. While grouse moor management does intervene in order to keep a dynamic landscape in a stable state of perpetual change, this is not significantly different from the way in which reed beds or alder and willow carr – all dynamic landscapes – are managed to preserve their unique characteristics. One of my favourite quotes that illustrates the value of the management needed to maintain wild places came from the manager of the RSPB Old Moor and Blacktoft Sands Reserve, who posted on Facebook in 2019:

> There's nothing like the crackle of the fire when you are controlled burning out here along the Humber on Blacktoft. Here's a bit of footage from today's in beautiful weather with the team keeping the home fires burning well for the benefit of bearded tit, marsh harrier, reed warbler and so much more ...

Most people who shoot will agree with the general idea that turning something back to nature or, all too often, simply stopping a piece of wilderness from being wrecked, is almost always a good thing. Virtually from its inception the GWCT has been telling anyone who would listen that saving or creating bits of wilderness, within the wider landscape, is almost invariably of benefit to wildlife. Some have gone further and saved or created entire chunks of landscape. The famous wetlands of Minsmere and Leighton Moss were farmland that was converted to duck shooting marsh before they were acquired and developed into RSPB reserves. When were they at their wildest in that progression is an interesting question. My own view is that it was when they were only visited by humans a dozen times a year and were, for the rest, private, unvisited and trackless. I may be biased but I have to say that the large car parks, hides, hard paths, shops and toilets that have intruded into the landscape for the public's convenience tend to detract from any sense of wilderness, for me at least.

Heather moorlands were protected from destruction because their owners valued them as beautiful wild places, as well as for their shooting potential. Now we have the idea that human beings can simply walk away from these landscapes, and nature will take care of itself. It is becoming increasingly popular, especially with people who are uncomfortable with continuing to take responsibility for the landscape and its wildlife if that involves having to make decisions that do not suit their sensitivities and prejudices.

Although full-blown rewilding is rare, there are examples where it has been successful and examples where it has not. The two best-known are the Dutch rewilding project at Oostvaardersplassen, a 5,600-hectare fenced nature reserve established on reclaimed land outside Amsterdam, and Knepp Castle in the south of England near Arundel.

The Dutch project consisted of releasing small numbers of red deer, domestic cattle and horses (to act as pretend wild ones) and leaving them to get on with it. It was said to be an outstanding success. Chris Packham wanted the same to be done on the Kent Marshes, to create our own Garden of Eden. Unfortunately the wheels came off in the winter of 2017/18 when the weather returned to what was historically typical for winter in the Low Counties, with prolonged frost and snow. The number of red deer, cattle and horses had by then reached 5,230. The forage had been exhausted long before the really bad weather set in, and large numbers of animals of all three species, began to starve to death. Those in charge of the project were neither surprised nor dismayed by this turn of events, as it was, after all, apparently natural. Unfortunately, or fortunately, depending on your commitment to rewilding, the main railway line to Amsterdam ran alongside this latter-day Eden (or charnel house, again depending on your viewpoint). Lots of people, previously relaxed about rewilding, reacted badly to the spectacle of thousands of animals starving to death, so the project managers were eventually forced to allow the inevitable 'trained marksmen' to shoot huge numbers of animals on the point of death and now the numbers are capped at 1,500 for all species, which makes the area a ranch rather than a wilderness.

Interestingly, the far more sustainable approach at Knepp Castle avoided this catastrophe by never giving up killing the 'wild' animals in the first place. Knepp's wild animals are red deer, supplemented by Tamworth pigs, longhorn cattle and Exmoor ponies, acting as surrogates for wild boar, aurochs and tarpan. The management have avoided the Dutch problem by harvesting their livestock. They have been successful in creating a very different landscape from the agricultural one that preceded it, with far greater biodiversity than was to be found on the unprofitable heavy arable land it replaced. To be fair, it could hardly have been worse, but the same does not apply to grouse moors, which are as far removed from undesignated agricultural land as you can get.

There are, of course, examples of large-scale rewilding in other parts of the world. In southern Africa huge swathes of degraded range land have been fenced and now, instead of producing unsustainable beef, provide entirely sustainable plains game meat in habitats that have reverted to approximately their original state, supporting extraordinary levels of biodiversity when compared to the semi-desert that was created by the cattle. Unfortunately, the economic model is underpinned by harvesting the game. This allows people to call the process trophy hunting, although it isn't, and obviously makes it unacceptable to most rewilding enthusiasts in the UK, but it cannot be denied that it works.

Whichever it is, whether it is the Oostvaardersplassen evolution by starvation project, promoted by Chris Packham, or the 'red in tooth and claw' Knepp model, or even the African system, the outcome is a change from what preceded it. In the context of grouse moors, you do not have to speculate what the outcomes might be. They already exist, where moors have been abandoned or, in the case of supposed blanket bog, management has simply stopped. Excluding genuine blanket bog, where it is too wet for most trees to grow – at least initially – the usual pattern is for the heather to grow long and rank and increasingly combustible. The landscape will be progressively infiltrated by trees, bushes and bracken. If you are lucky this is a progression into native species such as birch; if you are unlucky, you get spruce, rhododendron and various pines – elsewhere bracken and scrub will dominate. Given time, as the fuel load increases, there are likely to be horrendous wildfires, after which the whole thing may change again, becoming vast swathes of purple moor grass and sedge. Obviously, the bird assemblages, for which the moors are almost their last refuge, the curlew, redshank, snipe, grouse and lapwing, will disappear as the mosaic landscape of bilberry, cotton grass and heather they depend on itself vanishes and predator numbers increase in the absence of legal predator control.

Furthermore, we live in a small country with a population of nearly 70 million, not in a post- glacial paradise with a few thousand hunter-gathers wandering about chasing mega fauna. What is gone is gone, and cannot be re-created, however hard it might be wished for. Even the places which appear as wide, wild and empty, as grouse moors do, are in reality small, altered and crowded. There is a balance to be struck between keeping the precious things we still have and gambling them against what might be if we walk away.

If, for instance, we stop managing the vegetation and wildlife of the Peak District moors and simply walk away, letting nature take its course, what will happen? No one really knows, but on the basis of what has happened elsewhere and what is happening in parts of the Peak District already, the outcome will not be what is currently there, an important part of our stock of one of the world's rarest and most threatened habitats. Ironically, one likely outcome of simply walking away is that this internationally rare and valued habitat will turn into bracken, scrub or birch woodland, habitats that are widespread and abundant on a global scale. This is one of the reasons why international observers are so shocked when they discover that the great idea of the people who seek to control the destiny of one of the world's rarest landscapes is to let it degenerate into one of the commonest.

There is the view that this is only a problem because we are not bold enough. If we just grasped the nettle, and reconstituted the nation's lost fauna, everything would be all right. Bison, red deer, elk, beavers, wild boar, lynx, wolves and bears would do for a start. Obviously, the farmers and shooters would have to go but just think of the tourist income. The first problem is that, even at that level, you have still not re-created the original ecosystem – no aurochs or tarpan, no mammoths, woolly rhinos, or other extinct mega fauna. So what you have created is not just an unsustainable mess, it is a mess that cannot ever approximate to the fully functioning primeval reality that was promised.

Furthermore, these real and substitute animals naturally range or forage over huge areas, and require large, interconnected populations if they are to avoid the problems that are the inevitable consequence of a restricted gene pool. Even at the low numbers currently wild in the UK, wild boar and beavers, probably the most robust and least problematic of the proposed reconstituted fauna, are causing problems to farmers and the environment.

The farmers who point to the problems these animals cause are not selfish Luddites. They are just faced with a practical problem that is of someone else's making, and would rather grow food on their best patch of land than watch it disappear under water. Furthermore, relocation only works for so long. The small state of Latvia now has around 100,000 beavers. Simply to deal with the problems they create for everybody – not just farmers – they have to kill around 20,000 every year. It would be interesting to see what happens should we get to that stage in the UK. The licensing of the very small-scale lethal control operated by the Scottish government is already generating outrage from many of the usual suspects, so imagine what 20,000 a year would result in.

There are, of course, benefits from having these interesting species back in the country but any rational person who is aware of the power of social media will be very concerned about letting anything out that might subsequently need lethal control. Probably the main reason why so many country people are against these introductions is that they have the learnt the power of the irrational.

Skilful rewilding has its place in the conservation tool-box. That is hardly surprising; it has been part of these island's land management strategy since William the Conqueror cleared the New Forest of most of its human inhabitants. But it is difficult to see why it should be applied to rare landscapes that are amongst the wildest we currently possess. The maximum benefit comes from the greatest positive change. Turning a heather moor into a bracken bank and birch wood would be the equivalent of turning gold into base metal – worse than pointless, little more than an act of vandalism.

There are, however, huge swathes of land where positive change as a consequence of rewilding can be virtually guaranteed. This struck me years ago when an inevitable row broke out about a proposal to build on a fragment of Birmingham's green belt. The usual argument about the use of brownfield sites being preferable was immediately and understandably deployed. Before anyone gets overexcited, let me say that it did not go ahead, but I did go and look at the field in question. It would have been very difficult to find any of Birmingham's brownfield sites then in existence that had less biodiversity interest than that field. In fact it would have been difficult to find a supermarket car park that couldn't have given it a run for its money. If you want to rewild – and I can understand that people do – go where you get greatest biodiversity gain, and that will not be the grouse moors.

If you want to abandon your own land, no one should force you to manage it. Equally, if you want to manage your land, no one should force you to rewild it. Rewilding can take place on a vast scale without touching a grouse moor and would have a much greater impact if it didn't replace any heather moorland. Grouse moors are already wild places. They are managed, but they are managed to be wild. They have greater ecological value than almost any other land use from which an upland landowner can derive an income. They are less impacted by pollution and chemicals than almost any other land, including commercial forestry, so the net gain from rewilding is far less than was the case at say, Knepp Castle, where land used for modern arable and grass production was allowed to become far more biodiverse through a process of managed wilding.

To all this can be added the confusion about what a National Park actually is. The name leads people to believe that the land within it belongs to the nation and is public property, but this is completely wrong. In the UK, National Parks are an administrative designation, and have no bearing on the ownership of land. This misunderstanding, based on their name, is compounded by the fact that in other countries, for example the USA, National Parks are federal property. That was possible there because, when it was decided to designate them thus, no white Europeans owned any land within them. Obviously, the lands were occupied to a greater or lesser extent by the Native Americans who had been there for thousands of years, but it was thought that those who hadn't already been killed could be removed and dispossessed. This cynical process is definitely not the case currently in Britain, where the last person to take a similar line with the locals was William I post-1066. Thus the fact that Yellowstone National Park in Wyoming is quasi wilderness does not mean that the thousands of people who own property and land in the Peak District or the North York Moors, can simply be told, 'Get out, we're rewilding'.

The inevitable conclusion regarding rewilding is that it does not provide a viable alternative to the existing systems of moorland management. It does not preserve the unique eco-systems and wildlife assemblages they support. Thanks to the size and density of the human population and the huge infrastructure needed to support that population, large-scale faunal reintroductions are, in the main, a convenient distraction for those who would prefer to avoid the difficult stuff. When it consists of simply walking away and leaving moors to look after themselves, the outcomes can range from replacing the rare with the commonplace to the wholesale destruction of a landscape and the rare fauna and flora that depend on it for its survival.

In summary

- *Rewilding is intended to change the landscape and, when it does, it is often a matter of unpredictable chance whether the outcome is better or worse.*

- *Heather moorlands are one of the rarest habitats in the world. When they have been abandoned, they commonly revert to bracken, scrub woodland, or rough grassland depending, in part, on the frequency and severity of wildfire.*

- *Why would anyone want to abandon what is precious and rare simply to watch it revert to what is commonplace?*

- *A prelapsarian paradise cannot be re-created in a small, overcrowded country by releasing a few missing mammals, just to see what happens.*

- *Successful rewilding schemes have involved management and the harvesting of herbivores.*

8. Predation and its control

Non-lethal methods, whilst always our preferred way of doing things, are not always practical. Lethal vertebrate control is only considered where the following criteria are met:

- *That the seriousness of the problem is established.*
- *That non-lethal measures have been assessed and found not to be practicable.*
- *That killing is an effective way of addressing the problem.*
- *That killing will not adversely impact on the conservation status of the target or other non-target species.*

Martin Harper, RSPB Director of Global Conservation

I am sure no serious conservationist would claim that we could or should, at all times, and without exception, protect all species. That is simply unrealistic.

Tony Juniper, Chairman of Natural England

IT IS VERY difficult to talk about predator control without sounding mad and fixated. This is because the need to control pests and predators is the unavoidable element of conservation that the big mainstream organisations do not want to talk about. Many years ago the great farmland ecologist Dick

Potts formed the view, based on years of very high-quality field research, that the conservation of most if not all species was based on what he called his three-legged stool. The first leg was suitable habitat for nesting, rearing and adult life; the second was adequate food supplies throughout the year; the third was freedom from excessive levels of predation.

Conservation organisations talk endlessly about the first two but rarely want to discuss the third, less palatable, but equally necessary leg. As a result, the people who do, seem obsessed with killing things. Saying that here is a third leg and that it is important does not diminish the importance of the other two. It simply faces the inevitable fact that without all three the stool falls over.

Killing sentient creatures to protect the interests of human beings and to conserve species that we value has been going on for a long time and continues on a vast scale. It is definitely not limited to grouse moors. All of our nation's local authorities will have overloaded and under-resourced pest control departments responding to complaints from their residents about rats, mice, pigeons, gulls, squirrels, feral cats, foxes and corvids. These complaints will often result in lethal control, resulting in the deaths of millions of mammals and birds across the UK every year.

The lethal control of both carnivores and herbivores is also commonplace on land owned and managed by the conservation industry. The RSPB, the NT, the Wildfowl and Wetlands Trust and County Wildlife Trusts carry out lethal control, although they tend to avoid discussing the subject. They also enter into partnerships where they are fully aware their partners will kill predators as part of the programmes they have agreed.

The RSPB, almost alone amongst the major players in the industry, is honest enough to admit that it kills quite large numbers itself. Taking a random year's bag return, in 2014/15 they shot over 1,100 deer of various species, more than 400 foxes, and killed, by various means, nearly 300 carrion and hooded crows and large gulls. They also destroyed 140 eggs of 'large gulls'. To this can, of course, be added the far larger number killed by partner organisations as part of projects the RSPB is involved in and, whilst they make no attempt to draw these to anyone's attention, they are to be congratulated on their honesty and courage for at least making it clear by their own actions that such lethal control is often essential if conservation of some species is to succeed.

What pest control occurs on grouse moors is normally limited to foxes, corvids, stoats and weasels, and some rodents such as rats and grey squirrels. There may also be a need to control deer, rabbits, hares and large gulls and, obviously, some people have killed raptors, but as that is already illegal and a big subject in its own right, it is dealt with separately in a later chapter.

The list of species is not a very long one and all are subject to control rather than extermination and, although the latter might be considered a desired outcome in relation to brown rats and grey squirrels, it is unlikely to be achieved. Furthermore, all of these species, apart from stoats and weasels, are on the list of those controlled by the RSPB and even the stoat has recently become one of their target species because it is now common on the Orkney Islands, where it is not native, and is wreaking havoc. The reason why this control is essential is the considerable impact these predators have on the breeding success of a range of species, particularly ground-nesting birds.

There is no doubt about the importance of this intervention. There is ample evidence that even low numbers of foxes, stoats and corvids can have a devastating effect on species such as the curlew, whose numbers have crashed in areas remote from grouse moors, whilst holding steady or even increasing on them. Interestingly, the predator control carried out legally on grouse moors easily meets the RSPB tests set out at the start of this chapter. The problem is serious, non-lethal methods don't work, the control does work and the conservation status of the controlled species is not impacted adversely.

The above-mentioned curlew is an excellent example and can stand proxy for many other waders and ground-nesting birds. A project called Curlew Country in western Shropshire, intended to save the species from impending local extinction, began by monitoring curlew nests during the summers of 2015 and 2016. In 2015 not a single egg hatched, primarily as a result of predation by foxes, badgers and crows. In the following year, three nests that were protected by temporary electric fencing were the only ones to hatch, but the chicks from those nests were all subsequently predated before they could fly. Thus, in two summers, more than thirty nests produced not a single fledged chick. In 2017, with some limited predator control over a part of the area, at least three chicks fledged successfully.

In Northumberland, the GWCT ran a double-blind trial, known as the Otterburn Study[1,2], over a period of eight years, to examine the impact that predator control by gamekeepers had on the success of ground-nesting birds. A project of this standard and duration is very expensive and was considered by many country people to be a waste of money as it was obvious what the outcome would be. It was self-evident to them that it is necessary to carry out legal predator control if you wanted thriving populations of ground-nesting birds. It had to be explained to them that the conservation industry was in denial and it had become necessary to demonstrate scientifically what they themselves imagined was simply common sense. In fact the doubters were more wrong than anyone thought. When the results emerged nearly a decade later, even they were surprised.

The experiment took place on four extensive moorland sites, which had very similar habitats but were far enough apart to ensure that populations and interventions did not overlap. One site was left alone for the full eight years (2000–2008) and merely monitored, with no interventions at all. One was keepered continuously for the full period of the study. One of the other two was subject to effective legal predator control by gamekeepers for the first four years and the fourth left without any predator control for the same period. This was followed by a complete reversal of the keepering for the second four-year period: the ground that had been keepered for the first four years was left without predator control, and the gamekeepers were moved to the previously unkeepered site to control predators there.

This long time-frame was necessary to find out if the predicted improvement in breeding success translated into more pairs breeding. As curlew do not breed until their third year, it was necessary to keep the project going long enough to see if the breeding population increased as well as the fledging success.

The results were surprising. On the areas where there were no keepers, an average of 15% fledged at least one chick. On the areas where there was predator control this rose to 51%. But the real shock was that on the areas where predators were not controlled there was a 17% decline in breeding curlew, whilst with predators controlled this decline was turned into a 14% increase, a net difference of 31%. In other words, without the gamekeepers and legal predator control, the curlew were sliding towards local extinction. This simple fact applies to many rare ground-nesting birds. Without the control of generalist predators such as foxes and crows, they are going to disappear. Most people had assumed rightly that the curlew would do better with predator control, but what they had not expected was that, without the keepers, curlew would be extinct as breeding birds in a few years, despite them having access to excellent habitat and virtually no disturbance.

A simpler example was provided by the Elmley Marshes in Kent where a remarkable farmer and conservationist, Philip Merrick and his family, own a huge grazing marsh, created by them from a more orthodox farming landscape with the intention of providing a haven for declining waders, especially lapwing. The site is divided into two more or less equal sections by a freshwater dyke, which is both deep and wide, and creates a natural barrier for mammalian predators. One side was managed by the RSPB; the other Philip managed himself. The only difference in management was that while Philip practised legal predator control, the RSPB did not. The productivity of the lapwing on the area where predators were controlled was 1.1 fledged chicks per pair, well above stability. The area managed by the RSPB where no predators were controlled was 0.11 fledged chicks per pair, way below the level needed to sustain the population. To sustain a stable population, lapwings need to fledge an average 0.7 chicks per pair. The RSPB system had created a 'lapwing sink', where birds are attracted to breed by excellent habitat but fail to produce enough young to maintain their population and the breeding pair numbers are maintained by immigration.[3]

Another way to look at this is through the eyes of an intelligent and unbiased non-shooter, who has taken the trouble not only to research the subject but has also looked at the reality on the ground. People fitting that description are rare, but by chance just such a person exists in the case of the curlew: a journalist, radio producer and author called Mary Colwell. She took the remarkable step of walking west to east across Eire, Wales and England, finishing at Boston on the east coast, and looking for curlew along the way. She visited the Curlew Country Project in Shropshire and an RSPB-managed moor in the Peak District, amongst many other sites, but she didn't see what was really possible until she met Tom Orde-Powlett in Yorkshire and was taken onto his family's grouse moor at Bolton Castle. There, in the midst of humane and effective legal predator control, she saw something she had not seen before; real live curlew chicks, all over the place. She has subsequently had the courage to make it publicly clear that legal predator control is essential for the conservation of curlew and other waders.

Just to be clear, there is no doubt whatsoever that if you want to have sustainable populations of ground-nesting birds, you need to control generalist predators. That this repeatedly demonstrated fact is unpopular within the conservation industry is obvious, but it doesn't stop it being true. The discomfort is understandable. The large conservation businesses have huge infrastructure costs and need to raise millions of pounds every year, much of which comes from people who may well be unhappy about facing what has to be done to conserve wildlife. It is entirely understandable that they like to keep quiet about the fact that they have to kill things, or rely on their neighbours doing so. The problem is even more acute for the smaller businesses as they might rely on a small number of funders, who may prefer to fail with a clear conscience rather than have to kill a crow or a stoat to succeed. This also applies to many grant-giving bodies. The mere mention of predator control, even when it is obviously essential, means waving goodbye to any chance of a grant.

Why is this? It is caused by several factors. First, the fact that most of the nation's 67 million inhabitants have no contact with the reality of rural life and go to considerable lengths to avoid even smelling it, let alone understanding what has to be done to keep it as they wish it to be, whilst simultaneously producing food, clean water, energy and wildlife. Second, there are plenty of individuals (some of considerable celebrity) and organisations who are happy to claim that none of this is necessary and everything can be solved by habitat improvement or, in the more extreme cases, by simply walking away. Third, even the organisations, who know full well that efficient predator control is an essential conservation tool, are careful to keep as quiet about it as possible because to do otherwise can have disastrous personal and organisational consequences, thanks to the malign impact of social media as manipulated by single issue groups.

As a consequence of this craven behaviour, a small number of organisations are left to make the case for predator control while the others scatter for cover mumbling about habitat and food supply. This has left those brave enough to tell the truth taking all the flack and appearing ever more peevish and fixated on killing things. In fact people who manage grouse moors are very clear about the importance of habitat and food, as the provision of these ingredients is an essential part of their recipe for success. It is just that they are also clear that if you get the conditions right and attract large numbers of birds to your nature reserve, the least you should do is try to stop them being eaten at such a rate that it would have been better for the species not to have nested there in the first place. What exactly was the point of the RSPB managing their part of the Elmley Marshes in a way that attracted large numbers of lapwing to settle and nest, when the result was the wholesale loss of eggs and chicks? It would have been better if they had gone somewhere else where the habitat was less perfect but there was less certainty that their offspring would end up a tasty snack.

There are people who call themselves compassionate conservationists, who object to killing for any reason and believe that it is simply wrong to kill one animal to protect another. Nothing can be done with this group, but at least they have an honest position. They would rather curlew became extinct than someone killed a fox to stop it. They understand what is happening, but simply believe that the end does not justify the means. In a free country they are entitled to that view and we should all defend their freedom to hold it.

This puritanism is extended to any and every situation, no matter how extreme. It includes, for example, the response to the RSPB's plans to exterminate the giant mice that eat baby albatrosses alive on Gough Island in the Tristan de Cunha group in the south Atlantic. The mice shouldn't be there in the first place, being descended from escaped house mice. They are eating nearly two million eggs and chicks every year and exterminating a very rare bird, the Tristan albatross, in probably the worst way imaginable, by being eaten alive by mice. Faced with these appalling and unarguable facts, I have to say that people who believe that the mice should be left in situ to eat as many baby albatrosses as they like, and have the bare-faced cheek to call themselves both compassionate and conservationists, should be prosecuted for wrongful description. While I (and the albatrosses, if you could ask them) consider these people to be neither remotely compassionate nor conservationists, they have a right to hold whatever views they like. What is not right, however, is when they seek to force this view on others by direct action and intimidation, such as stealing and breaking legal traps and threatening gamekeepers. Such action is now increasingly commonplace in the British countryside and is not only illegal but must surely be unacceptable when what is at stake may be the local extinction of a rare species.

There is also the widely held view that predator control is unnecessary because all these problems can be solved by improving the habitat. Well, the science says that is not the case. Improving the habitat is always a good idea and it can reduce predation, but it cannot get rid of the problem. The Otterburn Study shows that even in first-rate habitat, without the keepers doing effective predator control the ground-nesting birds were drifting into oblivion. But why now? How can these birds have survived at all if this were the case? The answer is because we have changed the countryside in a manner that favours generalists, such as gulls, foxes and crows. We also have large and increasing numbers of predators that cannot be controlled because they are legally protected, such as badgers and buzzards. The colonisation of cities and towns by foxes, magpies, crows and large gulls has produced dense populations of these predators, who forage widely in the countryside or disperse into it under the territorial pressure created by the large, uncontrolled populations. To these can be added the fact that places like grouse moors and nature reserves, possessing as they do much higher concentrations of potential prey than the surrounding countryside, act as honey pots for predators looking for their next meal.

When the countryside was a mass of over-wintering stubble, fields left fallow, hedgerows and hedge banks, when every estate had a team of gamekeepers and farming was low input, and there were 'only' forty million people in the country and virtually no cars, the world was a very different place and things were easier but, even in those halcyon days, everyone knew that the control of predators was necessary and did it. The need to control predators is not new; what is new is the desperate search for someone to blame and a reason for not doing it.

There are, indeed, ways of reducing the impact of predators that do not involve killing the predator. In the context of moorland bird assemblages, the most obvious and immediately useful is to push back any forestry adjacent to the moor and remove any self-set trees that are colonising the heather. The forestry provides shelter and breeding places for generalist predators and the trees create energy-free lookout stations for predatory birds, in particular crows, magpies and buzzards.

Another, increasingly popular, non-lethal intervention is the use of electrified fencing to surround key nesting areas. These are increasingly used by the RSPB, not least because, in addition to excluding foxes, which could otherwise be controlled, they exclude badgers and otters, which cannot, but are serious predators of ground-nesting birds given the opportunity. There is little doubt that electric fences have their uses, whether small temporary ones protecting individual nests from badgers and foxes during incubation or permanent ones for small localised populations of waders, at least for part of the high-risk breeding season.

Unfortunately, there are problems with this method. First, if the fencing is permanent, it is costly and intrusive. An electric fence protecting just two fields on a Welsh reserve is 2km long and about1.5m high, mounted on large, heavy and regularly braced posts. Second, they need regular inspection, as any grass or stick can short-circuit the entire system. Third, to work they have to be big, and as a consequence they cannot run on batteries and must be powered by mains electricity. A wet otter's day can be seriously upset if it puts its nose against a mains electric fence. Fourth, predator control has to address a suite of predators, otherwise they simply replace one another. You can stop nest predation by nocturnal mammals, and substitute daytime chick predation by birds such as crows, ravens, buzzards and kites. Finally, and fatally from the point of view of replacing legal predator control on a grouse moor, is the impossibility of accommodating the necessary scale. By 2017 the RSPB had, at considerable cost, installed electrified anti-predator fencing on twenty-eight reserves, protecting a grand total of 874 hectares; an average of 31 hectares per site, enough to make a nice little market garden, but insignificant when confronted with protecting the ground-nesting birds on the North York Moors or the whole of Swaledale. If our ground-nesting birds are to be preserved in perpetuity, it will not be by establishing *'Stalagwader'*. From the point of view of protecting whole populations of vulnerable ground-nesting birds in the wider landscape of a heather moor, the use of electric fencing is simply a non-starter.

There is, of course, the idea that predation is a consequence of shooting itself. An important theory, promulgated by the conservation industry, is that recent increases in the numbers of released pheasants and partridges has resulted in a huge increase in the number of foxes. This, the theory goes, means that predator control is forced on them in order to protect ground-nesting birds and, if releasing game birds stopped, the need for predator control would disappear. It is easy to dismiss this as a piece of self-serving speculation, but it needs dealing with or it will, like many myths, become Holy Writ. Furthermore, there are bits of what looks like science starting to appear, intended to promote the theory and, as the peer review system is inevitably biased towards what the big players in the conservation industry want, there will be more to come.

The theory is based on three assertions. First, that the fox population is increasing. Second, that the increase is caused by the availability of released game birds and, finally, that the impact of predation on species of conservation concern is related to the increase.

Have fox numbers increased during the last twenty-year period of the rapid increase in pheasant releasing? The first problem is knowing how many there actually are. The basic technique is to make an estimate for small areas and multiply them up. If you substitute the word guess for estimate, you are probably nearer the truth. It is far from easy to count birds accurately, even though they fly about in plain sight, are mostly diurnal and make noises. Mammals are secretive, nocturnal and mostly silent, a far harder proposition. So when someone says there are X or Y foxes in the UK, always ask how they counted them. You can multiply a guess, divide it, and obtain the square root of it, but it is still a guess.

You are on better ground with trends rather than totals, but there are still only two data sets good enough to allow a stab at population changes. These are the British Trust for Ornithology's (BTO) Breeding Birds Survey (BBS) and the GWCT's Game Bag Survey (GBS). Interestingly, these show apparently different trends. The GWCT indicates stability, whilst the BTO shows a 44% decline across the UK over the last twenty-two years. What is notable is that neither shows an increase. The BTO data is derived from field observations and has detail relating to region and to period. The 2019 data shows a decline of 16% on the preceding year, and a 49% decline over twenty-two years for England, with the steepest fall in the southwest, being a drop of 58%.

In fact, the two data sets may be less conflicted than they appear. Foxes may well have declined. The GWCT data is derived from the numbers of foxes culled by estates. There has been a technological revolution in the control of nocturnal predators; first the development and refinement of the equipment for shooting at night using lamps, and then the use of thermal imaging rifle sights. These make fox culling far more efficient. The ending of foxhunting with hounds also removed the *de facto* close season operated informally in areas where foxhunting was popular and allowed greater access to fox cullers over longer periods. If one couples this with the tendency of foxes to move into areas left vacant, this should, if you are killing foxes more efficiently, lead to more foxes being killed, not stability. It appears possible that the apparent stability of cull numbers could actually mask a more general decline.

The RSPB has sought to use national population density estimates to prove its point, but even this raises more questions than it answers. Their data shows that Italy has a greater fox density than the UK, without any released bird shooting worth the name, whilst Scotland, with some very substantial released bird shooting, has one of the lowest fox densities in Europe.

Could increased food supply increase the number of foxes? Yes, of course it could. Is there any evidence that it has and that the increase is caused by releasing pheasants? Not on the basis of the best trend data available, produced by the two organisations with the best record for accurate assessment of wildlife trends in the UK. One might, therefore, assume that this assertion is of no interest as the basic premise that fox numbers have increased is not true, but you would, of course, be deemed wrong. The theory is too convenient and too comforting to go away.

What all ground-nesting birds need is not complicated. They need somewhere to live, something to eat and not to be eaten themselves. Without all three they will not survive, let alone thrive, and neither would you.

This leads into the reason why we now have to be harder on those predators that can be legally controlled than might historically have been the case. The fact is that there are so many more predators that you can't control than there used to be. To look just at avian predators, a combination of the disappearance of some agricultural chemicals, successful reintroductions and the virtual disappearance of persecution, has seen an amazing explosion in numbers of raptors. The BTO data shows that, in the last twenty or so years, ravens have increased by 49%, buzzards by 226% and red kites by nearly 22,000%. It should be understood that none of the common predators are *reliant* on the eggs and chicks of ground-nesting birds; they simply take them as and when they can. Thus their predation pressure does not decline as their prey declines. If they decide to target ground-nesting birds – and they do – there is nothing that can be done to arrest further decline other than to exercise control over the number of predators. However, the chances of anyone outside the conservation industry getting a licence to cull them is zero, and the conservation industry would not countenance such a thing.

Whilst it is true that population estimation is not an exact science, it is far better with birds than with mammals, and it is all we have, and so we must use what is available. The scale of the challenge faced by ground-nesting birds is huge. The aggregate breeding population of protected raptors in the UK is 146,000 pairs and rising rapidly. There are over 4.5 million pairs of egg and chick-eating corvids (some of which can be legally culled but are the subject of a campaign to remove them from the general licence) and there are 250,000 pairs of lesser black-backed and herring gulls, both voracious predators of eggs and chicks, for which only two conservation culling licences were issued in 2020. The current best guesses for mammals are that foxes are declining but there are still over a quarter of a million individuals, badgers have doubled since the 1980s to nearly half a million and stoats and weasels together probably total around a million. That is nearly ten million predatory birds and almost two million predatory mammals at the start of the breeding season. That is without counting pet cats killing millions of birds every year, 2.5 million grey squirrels, millions of rats, and out-of-control dogs running amok. Frankly, it is a miracle that ground-nesting birds survive at all, let alone thrive, as they do on well-managed grouse moors. Without the legal control operated by gamekeepers there would be little left, and bizarrely some celebrity conservationists are actively campaigning to stop what remains of legal predator control.

It is fair to ask, faced with these numbers, how even the best gamekeeper can make any difference? They can, because they seek to control local predation problems, not national populations of predators. To reduce corvid predation on eggs and chicks you do not need to worry about the 4.5 million, you only have to deal with the ones that are working your moor.

If gamekeepers produce such outstanding results, why don't organisation within the conservation industry employ them and why does the predator control work carried out by the contractors, who are employed from time to time by these bodies, not achieve the same results? If you ask them, the reason they give is that gamekeepers are too expensive. All they can afford is to pay contractors on an hourly rate and, as they don't want predators killed all year round, having someone full time is a waste of money. This misses an important point. If you go to a large estate, which has within it a successful grouse moor, you will find that one of the most consulted employees is the head keeper. This individual will be a key member of the team that makes the decisions, and the boss's eyes and ears. The role also requires engaging in negotiations with the regulators, suppliers, contractors and the local community and, in addition, the control of predators. Of all the estate's employees, the head keeper will represent the best value and will not be treated as the contractors are, as an unpleasant necessity, of significantly less importance than the person running the shop and cafe, and far less likely to be involved in the decisions that are key to success.

This is also one of the reasons why some research into the benefits of predator control indicates that it does not work. Catching wild animals is a skill, just as playing tennis is. Some people are naturally adept and, with practice, become world class. Others, who have little aptitude and less interest, are never able to master it. If you want it done well, get a top of the class gamekeeper, not a disgruntled bird-watcher.

If you have a moor like the one at Lake Vyrnwy, and over the years you spend millions of pounds on all manner of things from the shop and car park to building paths and occasionally hiring someone to shoot a few foxes, and employing all sorts of people, except a full-time gamekeeper, and you finish where the RSPB now is, do you never even wonder why the moors with gamekeepers outperform you every time? Sadly, apparently not. It is far more likely that the criteria used to judge success will be changed to accommodate failure. Some NE staff are now talking about there being too many waders on grouse moors and the NT saw a decline in golden plover as an acceptable price to pay for stopping rotational burning.

If you want the ground-nesting birds, whose last great refuges in mainland Britain are on or around the grouse moors, to survive and prosper, it is essential that effective legal predator control continues as it is currently practised. The conservation industry can make its own decisions about the way it manages its own land, and it can live with the consequences, but it would be hugely helpful if it told the truth about the importance of predator control and the vital role that honest and law-abiding gamekeepers play in the survival of some of the UK's most challenged bird populations. If they do not, it is perfectly possible that all this may be lost, or become regulated to the point of impossibility. Telling the truth should be neither too painful nor too expensive.

Let me conclude by quoting a Dutch conservationist, Eddie Van Marum, who works tirelessly for the conservation of waders, such as the black-tailed godwit, in Holland, a country with virtually no released bird shooting, no grouse, hundreds of miles from the nearest UK grouse moor and who has no interest in grouse shooting:

> Every penny of public money put into the conservation of ground-nesting species will be in vain, if further legal protections are given generalist predators and, for example, you ban fox snares and Larsen traps. I would love to tell politicians in the UK what they have now and what they risk destroying, based on what we have lost here in Holland. Predation is something that can be managed and must be managed or we will lose the battle to prevent the extinction of waders. We cannot leave it up to nature; we need to make an active choice and if we decide to save our beautiful birds, half-measures are no good.

In summary

- ❖ *The effective and humane control of common generalist predators is essential if ground-nesting birds are to continue to thrive in the uplands.*
- ❖ *Whilst in some small areas other methods such as electric fencing may help in reducing predation, they and other non-lethal solutions cannot provide a sustainable solution in the wider landscape.*
- ❖ *Despite a reluctance to discuss the subject, most organisations within the conservation industry recognise privately that predator control is necessary and frequently attempt to control predators themselves.*
- ❖ *The aggressive and confrontational tactics of the more extreme elements in the debate has suppressed the willingness of many to publicly support what they admit in private to be necessary.*
- ❖ *Shooting has not created a need to control predators by increasing their numbers. The need has always been there and has become more pressing because of the huge growth in predators that cannot be controlled.*

9. The road to hell is paved with regulation

Good regulation is not about process – what some call red tape – but an outcome: a greener world. So all good regulation must be outcome focused, stipulating what needs to be achieved rather than focusing only on the means to achieve it. And the ultimate aim of environmental regulation should not be to slow the decline of nature or even just protect it; it should be to enhance it.

Good regulation is not about eliminating risk – almost all worthwhile activities carry some risk, and most risks can never be removed – but about managing and reducing it.

It (regulation) also needs to be proportionate.

Good regulation is business friendly, with simple processes, clear goals that make it easy for operators to do the right thing, and rewards for those who do and painful consequences for those who don't.

Extracts from a speech by Sir James Bevan, Chief Executive of the Environment Agency 13/1/21

IT IS SAID by the RSPB, both loudly and often, that grouse shooting and grouse moor management are 'unregulated'. In a free country, most activities that take place on private property involving consenting adults are indeed unregulated, but the RSPB clearly feels that this universal freedom should be withdrawn from people who manage grouse moors.

By a happy chance, they can rest content as, despite their assertion, the activity is already heavily regulated, almost to the point of destruction. If you manage a grouse moor and employ people to help you do it, there is a long list of legislation with which you and your staff are required to be familiar and to obey. I asked a grouse moor manager who runs a moor in Scotland what were the statutes he had to observe and he kindly supplied the list set out below. It is not exhaustive and the lists for England and Wales would be no shorter.

Wildlife and Countryside Act 1981
Wildlife and Natural Environment Act 2011
Protection of Badgers Act 1991
Hill Farming Act 1946
Deer (Scotland) Act 1996
Deer (Firearms etc.) Scotland Order1985
Nature Conservation (Scotland) Act 2004
Conservation (Natural Habitats etc.) Amendment (Scotland) Regulations 2001
Snares (Training) (Scotland) (No 2) Order 2012
Conservation (Natural Habitats etc.) Regulations 1994
Food Safety Act 1990
Food Hygiene Regulations 2006
Game Act 1831
Ground Game Act 1880
Health and Safety at Work Act 1974
Town and Country (General Permitted Development) (Scotland) Amendment Order 2014
Planning (Scotland) Act 2019
Land Reform (Scotland) Act 2003
Land Reform (Scotland) Act 2016
Welfare of Farmed Animals (Scotland) Regulations 2010
Water Framework Directive
Forestry Act 1967
Conservation of Habitats and Species Regulations 2017

The gamekeepers will also need to be trained to operate to the standards dictated within their own codes of practice and the law in relation to game meat hygiene, corvid control, heather burning, snaring, medicated grit, use of rodenticide and first aid.

There are probably some that have been forgotten, but there are enough mentioned above to understand why claiming that grouse moor management is unregulated is complete nonsense. It is very difficult to believe that the RSPB is unaware of the mass of legislation that those who own and manage grouse moors are faced with every day. It is equally difficult to believe that, when they state, as they repeatedly do, that grouse moors are unregulated, they haven't got their fingers firmly crossed behind their backs.

Their position is that, because grouse moors are supposedly unregulated, they want them to be licensed by the state, and to provide bag returns to the state regulator of everything they shoot. These demands which may, because the RSPB is very rich and very powerful, come to pass (and indeed are promised in part by the Scottish Government), need to be considered in detail, partly because at first glance they don't seem too unreasonable.

The suggested changes are not based on an honest assessment of the mass of rules and regulations with which grouse moor managers have to conform. They are based on a quick look across the Channel at the nature of hunting legislation in some European countries, coupled with a visceral desire to make things harder for people they really don't like, because they have persuaded themselves that they are all killing raptors and this is the way to stop it.

The logic of this is that it is difficult to obtain sufficient evidence to bring people to successful trial for the illegal killing of raptors. Obviously, the idea that people might be innocent can be rejected by the RSPB as absurd – so something that doesn't need evidence or proof would be ideal. After all, there are successful precedents for this approach: in the French Revolution's Reign of Terror, most people had their heads cut off on the simple basis of accusation, without the need for any boring old evidence, and not one of them subsequently complained.

The idea is that, if shoots needed a licence to operate, the licence could be removed 'on suspicion', without the tiresome need for proof, thus stopping any risk of interference with raptors at a stroke. Indeed, it might go beyond suspicion of an actual crime, as mere absence is regularly cited as evidence of criminal activity, in which case the inability to meet your quota of say, merlins or kestrels, could see your way of life proscribed. If none of that worked, there are people available who can periodically photograph a dead raptor where needed, and that, plus a few photographs of illegally set traps, ought to do the trick.

In case such behaviour seems preposterous, the August 2009 RSPB's *Birds* magazine contained a photograph of an apparently illegally killed buzzard swinging from a fence post. Unfortunately, from their point of view, the landscape was recognised by the entirely innocent owners of the estate. In the February 2010 edition of *Birds*, under the heading 'Dead Buzzard: an apology', we read, 'This photograph was staged and not a genuine illegal incident. While the location was not specified, someone with local knowledge could have recognised it. We have apologised to the landowner and the immediate neighbour.' So, it is perhaps understandable why the landowning community might feel less than enthusiastic about the RSPB's plans for guilt without evidence.

The favourite refrain is that grouse shooting in the UK is an unregulated free-for-all, compared to the situation in Europe, where the individual states license shoots, and everything is so much better for conservation generally, and birds in particular. If you know little or nothing about shooting or the situation across the North Sea or the English Channel, this sounds a potentially powerful argument and many politicians might have taken it on trust. The Scottish Parliament decided instead to take a look for themselves and commissioned a subsequently published study, *A Review of Game Bird Law and Licensing in Selected European Countries*, the results of which are now in the public domain and have proved to be extremely interesting.

The first thing that strikes anyone on reading the review is that the attitude of all the countries examined and that of the EU to their hunting communities appears strikingly and universally positive. There are lots of statements making this clear but one will suffice to give their tone.

The French Environmental Code says the following about hunting:

> The sustainable management of faunal heritage and its habitat is in the general public interest. Hunting, an environmental, cultural, social and economic activity, forms part of this management and thus contributes to the balance between game, the environment and human activities, ensuring a true agricultural-fishing-hunting balance.
>
> The principle of rational thinning of sustainable natural resources is imperative to the way these resources are used and operated. By their action of management and regulation of species the hunting of which is

> authorised, and by their operations in favour of biotypes, hunters contribute to the balanced management of ecosystems. They thus participate in the development of economic and ecological activities in natural environments, notably in rural areas.

The second thing that is obvious is that each country's approach to the rules and regulations relating to hunting reflects the nation's approach to regulation in general. Anyone who has had dealings with Germany will not be surprised by emphasis on citizen responsibility; those who have done business with France will not be disappointed by the large amount of paperwork involved.

Strangely, none of the countries covered in the review actually license shoots. They license individual shooters, mainly as a form of taxation, and may license shooting clubs and associations but, in the latter case, it is in order to give them additional powers over and above those enjoyed by individual shooters. For example, in France, members of recognised shooting clubs can hunt on private land without the permission of the landowner.

The process of an individual obtaining a hunting licence varies between countries from effectively on demand to an examination like the British Deer Society certification process. This reflects both the importance of large mammalian game on the Continent and the fact that most European hunters are operating alone and without supervision, often on land owned or controlled by the state. The balance of advantage seems to fall, in most of these individual licensing systems, perhaps surprisingly, to the licensee. Because of the high regard in which hunting is held, the money raised is used to improve hunting and reduce poaching and not siphoned off for other purposes. In France the licence fees are ploughed back into employing an anti-poaching police force and, additionally (the income from licences alone being insufficient), the state provides an annual additional stipend of between €30 and 40 million to ensure that hunters have the services they expect.

The total annual cost of France's Hunting and Wildlife Agency is €120 million and it employs 1,700 people so, based on an annual licence fee of €30, the licensed hunter is getting a pretty good deal, especially considering that, if they are a member of an Association Communale de Chasse Agree (ACCA) they have the legal right to hunt on private land without the permission of the owner so long as they don't shoot within 150 metres of the landowner's main residence. Bag one wild boar and you've got your money back.

For many years the UK had a system of taxing game shooters via the need to possess an annual game licence, but eventually decided that the cost of collection and enforcement made the practice a pointless one and it was abandoned. The French and many other European nations went in a different direction, but they have made sure that, as the cost and complexities have risen, so have the benefits to the hunters. They appear to have followed the important principle of policing by consent, a concept highly valued in UK urban contexts but almost entirely absent from the British countryside.

The review shows that quite a lot of countries operate bag limits and have systems of reporting bags of wild game killed by individual hunters or clubs. This is the other element that the RSPB has suggested could be usefully imported into UK grouse shooting practice. In fact, it is already standard practice in the UK in relation to circumstances where it has value and relevance. If you run a grouse moor and keep meticulous bag records, these records are of interest and value to you but irrelevant to the state. If you go wildfowling on Crown Land you are expected to make equally meticulous bag returns to the agents of the Crown Estate, and what you may shoot is constrained by any bag limits they may set. No one can reasonably complain about rendering unto Caesar the things that are Caesar's.

However, what would be worse than pointless would be having to make bag returns to the state from shoots on private land. Not only would it cost time and effort and generate no benefit for the landowner, it would cost the state a fortune just to receive and store the data, whilst any analysis would increase that cost exponentially. This fairly obvious fact is unsurprisingly reflected in European practice. In France, whilst there are bag limits and reporting arrangements in place for species such as capercaillie and black grouse when they are hunted on public land or under the ACCA system, the state does not demand bag returns for released French partridge and pheasant. In Norway we are told, 'the state does not interfere with game bird management on privately owned land'.

Bag limits may be necessary where hunting is managed by the state, but not when the hunting takes place on private land managed by individual landowners who have a vested interest in maintaining sustainable stocks in perpetuity. A typical grouse moor will conduct transect counts in the spring to calculate the breeding stock and again in July to ascertain how many chicks have fledged. From this they can calculate what the optimum harvest will be, and plan the shooting days accordingly. What on earth has that got to do with a politician sitting in Westminster or Holyrood? State-imposed bag limits, if they were to generate as high a degree of sustainability as existing systems, would be expensive to run, difficult to enforce and provide no conservation advantage over the existing successful system, which has ensured healthy stocks of game in perpetuity, at no cost to the taxpayer.

Of all the countries examined by the review, it must be said that the state of affairs existing in Spain was, and may well still be, exceptionally severe, in relation to raptors, the group of birds RSPB is most interested in. The claim for reductions in raptor persecution appears to relate to raptor poisoning, which would seem to occur on a scale unimaginable in Britain. Whilst some wild birds and mammals can still be poisoned legally (for example, the RSPB, entirely legally, poisoned the last remaining colony of black rats existing in the UK), and whilst many local authorities use poison to control rodents, pigeons and gulls, it is simply inconceivable that any member of the UK's rural population is unaware that raptor poisoning is a crime. Incredibly, the review makes it clear that this was indeed a common misconception amongst Spanish country people.

There is absolutely no doubt that the Spanish authorities take raptor persecution seriously. The state employed 500 environmental police to prosecute, between 2010 and 2014, more than thirty significant cases of bird crime. What is not at all clear is whether this immense effort has produced outcomes significantly better than those existing in Britain.

On the basis of the anecdotal evidence provided within the review it would appear that, compared to Spain, the current UK approaches are something to be proud of. Here, a combination of education, firm law enforcement by the existing police force and some inexpensive and relatively minor adjustments to legislation have resulted in the level of raptor poisoning reducing at a rate that may see it completely eradicated as an intentional act. Meanwhile in Spain the situation is such that only now is it dawning on people that wholesale raptor poisoning is illegal, it is deemed essential to employ 500 specialist police to deal with it (more than are used to police cities the size of Glasgow or Birmingham), and people are still being caught poisoning scores of imperial eagles. Given the choice, any rational person would opt for the British system.

This leads to what is probably the most significant flaw in an interesting study. The document fails to explain the regulatory systems and societal and cultural constraints which already impact on hunting in the UK. Whether this is because they consider them so obvious and well known that they have no need to refer to them, or that they are themselves unaware of them, is unclear.

Unfortunately, the absence of such commentary risks perpetuating the myth that grouse shooting is an unregulated free-for-all. In fact, as has been demonstrated, nothing could be further from the truth. A grouse moor is one of the most regulated of landscapes and, moreover, standard management practices go beyond what the law demands.

Perhaps a better test of the different systems used to manage hunting in Europe is the actions and reactions of the many European hunters who come to the UK every year to shoot. They are amazed by the landscape, the abundance of game and the quality of the sporting experience. It is unfortunately true that some people in the UK still persecute raptors but so, according to this review, do people in Germany, Sweden, Bulgaria, Slovakia, Hungary, Romania and Spain. It may be that some people will always break the law, just as there will always be murderers, thieves and dangerous drivers. The question is, what is the most effective way of reducing wrongdoing to the absolute minimum? On the basis of this interesting review it seems that the system currently operating in the UK has made more progress to date than 500 Spanish environmental police, and should be celebrated as the developing success story that it undoubtedly is.

It is fair to ask why, in the UK, game shooting is so sustainable and successful without state intervention. This is the result of an ancient decision that made game the property of the person whose land it is on. This simple fact means that every landowner with a shoot has a vested interest in ensuring that the season ends with enough stock to repopulate their ground in the breeding season. It is worth their while to ensure that at least some of their land is managed in the interests of the game and it will be to their advantage to employ people to manage the land and the generalist predators to optimise the harvest they can take in due season. All of that disappears if game is the property of the state, or a resource held and exploited in common. Why spend the money or leave the breeding stock when somebody else is going to have a free hand to benefit from your hard work and expenditure? This is known as the curse of the commons, and a curse it surely is.

But the mere fact that shoots are not licensed anywhere in Europe and that there is more game in the UK than anywhere run by the dead hand of the state, did not stop the drive to license grouse moors. Nor does it explain why people who claim to be honest citizens are so set against what appears to be a minor matter. What is so wrong with licensing driven grouse shooting?

The first thing is that to license something, you first need to make it an illegal activity without a licence. For example, it is only possible to license the sale of alcohol because it is illegal to sell alcohol except from licensed premises. No sane person interested in preserving grouse shooting and its manifest biodiversity, economic and cultural benefits wants to see what they love made illegal, even if some transient politicians makes promises that they will do the right thing.

Next is the problem of trust. Why would anybody who shoots grouse, or any game for that matter, trust the RSPB and their fellow-travellers? Any sensible person can share their frustration at the continued existence of raptor persecution, but close contact with what is going on leads many to believe that that organisation's depiction of the *status quo* includes a fair helping of what is now known as fake news.

Then, what standards would be used to assess fitness for licensing? One promoted enthusiastically is setting numerical targets for breeding raptors. This is an appalling idea. It is perfectly possible to have expansive areas of heather moorland, do no harm to any raptor ever, and still not have the birds that people think should be there. On the vastness of the RSPB Abernethy moors there are no breeding hen harriers. In their application for Lake Vyrnwy's HLF grant, the RSPB made it clear that they were about to lose merlins and that hen harriers might soon follow them. Does that mean that the RSPB is secretly killing these birds? Of course it doesn't. But a grouse moor owner could see his life's work and an important source of income disappear because he couldn't do what RSPB couldn't do. How can it be reasonable to set targets for others that you can't reach yourself?

Finally there is the obvious issue of dirty tricks. We are all protected by the law's commitment to evidence and its corroboration. You and I cannot be convicted on hearsay. That is not the case with a licence. It is a simple matter to plant fake evidence. So many Fenn traps have been stolen by so-called Moorland Monitors that there must be hundreds, if not thousands, available, just waiting to be put out in illegal and compromising situations to provide photo opportunities for the darker side of the abolitionists.

The supposed need for licensing was based on the premise that raptor persecution is increasing, when it is in fact at a historically low level and likely to go lower. It is, according to the Scottish Government's own review, at a lower level in Scotland, with grouse shooting, than in many European countries where they have never heard of grouse.

It is possible to go on a grouse moor and not see a raptor, but it is very difficult, and I find it very hard to believe that RSPB spokesmen can go to these places and see nothing. In 2019, as an example, on the few days I shot, I saw sea and golden eagles, kites, buzzards, peregrines, merlins, kestrels, sparrowhawks, hen and marsh harriers and short-eared owls. I have to admit I didn't see a goshawk, but as they live in woods that is hardly surprising. Away from these 'awful' grouse moors I mostly saw kites and buzzards, plus the odd kestrel. If I didn't know better I might think that the RSPB spokesman was making things up for political effect.

But the RSPB will have its way. The pressure on the Scottish Government to license grouse shooting was in no way reduced by discovering that, contrary to their claims, shoots were not routinely licensed in Europe, nor by the fact that persecution was reducing, nor yet that other countries had more raptor persecution than Scotland. So they set up more enquiries: one to examine the claim made by grouse moor managers that they made significant contributions to their local economies, the other to review the need to deal with the assumed joint sins of grouse moor management – exterminating mountain hares, killing raptors, burning heather and putting out grit containing a wormer to prevent the grouse from dying of disease.

The wormer is another example of how a carefully regulated activity is portrayed as unregulated. There is a tiny parasitic worm that lives in the caeca of the grouse and, when present in large numbers, can debilitate or even kill its host. On moors where this nasty little parasite thrives it was shown to cause periodic crashes in the grouse population. The worm is susceptible to the standard worming chemicals used in almost all livestock, but the problem was how to get it into the grouse. The answer was provided by the birds' need to consume lots of grit. This is because, as birds have no teeth, the food they eat is ground in their gizzard, using grit that the bird has swallowed. The grit wears over time and needs to be regularly replaced, and as the food of grouse is largely heather, it needs to re-stock its gizzard with grit very regularly. By mixing the wormer with the grit the birds can be given enough wormer to kill the parasites and prevent the birds from suffering a miserable life and, and in many cases, a slow death. On some moors, where the worm may be a problem, a veterinary surgeon can prescribe the use of what is called medicated grit to reduce the losses. The process is controlled by the vet and the treatment must cease far enough before the start of the season to ensure that any birds eaten by people are free of the wormer, as is the case with other meat animals that are wormed.

Unsurprisingly, the people who do not like grouse shooting are unhappy about this, but in reality it is a very minor matter: many animals reared for food are medicated in broadly similar ways and to date no significant adverse effect of medicated grit has been identified. This is not surprising. As a licensed animal medication, the chemical was only permitted for use after a lengthy and arduous testing regime designed to investigate any possible effects on non-target species and the wider environment. Had any problems been found, its use would not have been permitted. Thus an allegedly unregulated activity turns out to be heavily regulated and demonstrably safe.

The first report was clear. Driven grouse shooting was an important source of revenue in the areas where it took place. As the money it attracted was entirely from private sources, it outperformed every other possible land use. Claims that other uses for the land would make more money, even when marginally true, were based on large taxpayer subsidies. Grouse shooting was alone in drawing large amounts of private money into the upland communities.

The second report, the Werrity Review, made a list of recommendations, none of which supported the position advocated by the RSPB and its allies. The nearest they got was that if there was not a significant improvement in raptor persecution in five years, steps should be taken to attempt to bring in a licensing system.

The Scottish Government thought about it and largely ignored the findings. They announced that they will license driven grouse shoots, mountain hare culling and heather burning. They appear to have no idea how this might work in practice, but they certainly hoped that this huge reward for years of campaigning will get the RSPB and its friends off their backs.

They will, of course, be disappointed: those who pay the Danegeld never get rid of the Dane. From the point of view of the campaigners, the purpose of licensing was not to stop raptor persecution. Raptors are the ultimate weapon, not the end. The real value of licensing is to mire the grouse moors in ever more red tape. This will create endless opportunities for finding, or creating, misdemeanours which, one piled upon another, can be used to crush the grouse shooting community and clear the way for the acquisition of devalued land, simultaneously getting rid of those infuriating comparisons between the biodiversity success of managed moors and the failure of their own land management.

In summary

- *Grouse moor management is not unregulated. It is subject to a greater burden of regulation than many other land uses.*

- *Licensing shoots is not, as the RSPB claims, based on a successful European model. In European countries the shooter is licensed, not the shoot.*

- *European bag limits are necessary for shooting that takes place on public land. Where shooting on privately owned land occurs, as is the norm in the UK, bag limits are not normally set.*

- *Ever more regulation, licensing, and nationally collected and analysed bag limits and returns would be costly to everyone, including the state, and achieve nothing of value for conservation.*

- *The people who own and manage grouse moors are as respectable and honest as any other British citizens. They should be treated as individuals and judged, as we would all wish to be, by their own actions. They should not be discriminated against on the basis of generalisations, which are frequently found to have no foundation in fact.*

10. A licensing department and how not to run one

In Douglas Adams' The Hitchhiker's Guide to the Galaxy, a fleet of space ships arrives to destroy the earth to make way for a hyper-space bypass; these are under the command of the Vogons, one of the most unpleasant, bureaucratic, officious and callous species in the Galaxy.

Their commander's announcement to the earth's stupefied inhabitants will come as no surprise to those who have to deal with the various manifestations of officialdom which now beset our moorlands.

'People of Earth, your attention please ... As you will no doubt be aware, the plans for development of the outlying regions of the Galaxy require the building of a hyperspatial express route through your star system, and regrettably your planet is one of those scheduled for demolition. The process will take slightly less than two of your earth minutes.

'There's no point acting all surprised about it. The planning charts and demolition orders have been on display in your local planning department in Alpha Centauri for fifty of your Earth years, so you've had plenty of time to lodge any formal complaint and it's far too late to start making a fuss about it now.

'What do you mean you've never been to Alpha Centauri? For heaven's sake mankind, it's only four light years away you know. I'm sorry but if you can't be bothered to take an interest in local affairs

that's your own look out. I don't know, apathetic bloody planet, I've no sympathy at all.'

Based on Douglas Adams,
The Hitchhiker's Guide to the Galaxy

From simplicity to chaos

In Britain the approach to the protection of birds was practical and pragmatic. The rare ones were protected all the time. Some, game birds and wildfowl that were harvested for food, had close seasons to allow them to breed in peace. Others, that were pests and abundant, could be taken at any time. This approach worked, as most simple and logical things do. You had to be really stupid not to understand it and obviously of criminal intent if you decided to ignore it.

Then we joined the EU. Our legislation prior to this was simple, effective and cheap to run. It had better outcomes than those obtained in many countries and there was no pressure or need to change it. That was, of course, deemed irrelevant and the European Commission put a group of civil servants to work, assisted by lobbyists from the conservation industry, to produce a one-size-fits-all system of bird law.

What came out of the other end of the Brussels sausage machine, the Birds Directive, was different. All birds were protected. Then some birds were unprotected and the grounds for this reversal were listed. At the same time the Habitats Directive was drafted, giving the state regulator power to designate sites on the basis of the presence of specified bird species, including species that may have been protected and then unprotected. The whole lot was then exposed to the decisions of the European Courts of Justice and we began the long trek from simple and practical to chaos.

Initially and creditably, the British Government dealt with the problem in as simple a way as possible. In relation to pest birds like crows, wood pigeons and large gulls, it issued simple general licences, which allowed authorised persons to control them in the usual way. There were no problems. Then, in 2007, the task of issuing wildlife licences was passed from the ministry to NE and the descent into chaos began.

As it happens, I know about the demands on a licensing function because I was responsible for one. I was told one bright and sunny morning that I had to manage one of the largest local authority licensing departments in the country. It was not a job I wanted. In fact it was not a job that anyone wanted. It was a battleground, with solicitors' letters and threats of judicial review arriving almost daily.

When I met the staff, I found them entirely delightful. They were hardworking, well informed, committed and had a far greater knowledge of licensing law than I had or ever will have. When I met the customers, they were frustrated, confused, angry and convinced that the licensing department's staff were being paid by their competitors to make their businesses impossible to run.

The reason for this remarkable dichotomy was complexity. The solution was simplicity. We went through a simple process of asking why a particular activity needed to be licensed, and how simple we could make the process without compromising its purpose. We learnt together, from each other and from our customers, what it takes to be a highly regarded licensing department. The principles are the same whether you are licensing hackney carriages or the control of cormorants. Here they are.

Successful licensing departments treat the licence applicants as customers or service users, and remember the injunction from the *King James Bible* to 'Do unto others, as you would have them do unto you'. The staff need to be gently reminded that it is the people applying for licences who ensure their continued employment. They should, whether they get a licence or not, feel that the staff were helpful and polite, not dismissive and patronising.

Successful licensing involves viewing the applicant's problem as your problem. If they need extra information, there should be an explanation as to what and why. Do not, as has often been the case, only tell them that they needed more information when it is too late.

If it is necessary to say 'no', it should be done as soon as possible. Delay causes applicants to waste resources, draw up plans that will have to be discarded and not to engage in other solutions, albeit less satisfactory ones, whilst living in hope. If you are going to say 'no', have the decency to do it directly, and explain exactly why that is your decision.

It is absolutely essential to strive constantly to simplify. It is in the nature of licensing to complicate. For reasons no one has ever satisfactorily explained, when faced with a problem caused by unnecessary complication, it is usual to try to deal with it by increasing the complexity that caused the problem in the first place. This is almost always the wrong thing to do. The fact that something can be in existence is emphatically not the point. Must it be there? If not, get rid of it. Every extra phrase, or even an extra word, leaves the licence more open to challenge and pointlessly infuriates customers.

It is essential to be aware that the staff, like all human beings, may be subject to prejudices. Do not be surprised if someone is inclined to be less helpful to a Duke's head keeper than they are to the RSPB. Of course, they may in fact be perfectly even-handed, but you are not managing the process properly if you do not have procedures in place to check on both quality of service and discriminatory behaviour, either personal or institutional.

It must be made clear to the staff that any licensing department exists to issue licences. These licences enable people with real problems to solve them within the law. It should be a department where success is judged by the percentage of satisfied service users and the number of sound licences issued, not the department for the non-issue of licences.

It is extremely desirable to have system of appeal against the non-issue of a licence that approximates to independent and accessible. In a local government context this service is provided by a licensing committee. This is beneficial to management and customers alike. It provides an automatic check on competence and institutional discrimination and provides management with an additional insight into the working of the department. The establishment of such an independent appeals process, even an informal one as an aid to quality control, is always a good idea. Without it the only challenge is through the courts and that is expensive for both sides, usually a waste of somebody's money and discriminates against the less well off.

The foregoing are not novel concepts, thought up on the spur of the moment. They are common practice in successful licensing departments across the country and have been for many years. I know that NE is aware of them because I have had conversations with senior staff in which I explained how it was done. I have even offered to help sort out their problems. It is therefore clear that the only reason that NE are not working to these standards is that they decided not to. In what follows you can judge for yourselves how closely the service provided by NE approaches the industry norm.

As soon as NE took over licensing, the general licences went from two pages to five. They were now stuffed with conditions that had nothing to do with European law and everything to do with their personal opinion. They defined 'serious damage' as excluding 'normal business risk' and said that, in the case of game birds, normal business risk was not exceeded until half of your stock had been killed. These conditions were simply made up by people sitting in an office.

In addition to the general licences, which dealt with the common pest species that had never been protected in the UK, there were individual licences available to deal with damage caused by species that were otherwise protected. These presented another set of problems. How do you prove that something is going to damage the survival of a rare bird? Perhaps by showing that it did last year? Not necessarily. What you saw may not be evidence. By showing that they kill them all over the place perhaps? Not necessarily. They may not kill them where you are. For a gamekeeper or farmer, the process was like the old song 'Soldier, soldier will you marry me'? Every time you answer the question, they think up another one. Just as you think you have done it, the person you have been dealing with disappears and you have to start with someone else. If you get a licence it is usually too late. It then runs out before the next breeding season and you start all over again.

Years ago, people who work in the countryside, outside of the conservation industry, had already formed the view that, as far as individual licences were concerned, one being granted to a farmer or a gamekeeper was seen as tantamount to failure and granting anything to do with common raptors to anyone not from the RSPB was likely to be career limiting.

This was all confirmed by a judicial review, *McMorn v. Natural England* (2015), which examined the persistent refusal by NE to issue a licence for the very limited control of buzzards by a gamekeeper on a small shoot in Northumberland. The applicant had done everything that had been asked as alternatives to lethal control over years of applications. He had demonstrated repeatedly that his small business, his only source of income, was being seriously damaged by the impact of a very common and increasing bird. The bird, aptly named the common buzzard, was classified as of lowest conservation concern and the limited and carefully targeted control proposed would have no adverse impact on their status either locally or nationally. Had the business been a trout lake and the species a cormorant, he would have got a licence. Had the business been a nature reserve and the species a lesser black-backed gull, there would have been no problem, but as it was a shoot and as the species was a raptor, albeit the commonest in the country, the answer was no, no and no again.

The judgment when it arrived was excoriating. NE, and their enthusiastic supporters in the RSPB, were found to be at fault on seven points at issue and the judge could not have been clearer in his condemnation of the conduct of the NE licensing department. The impact on the issue of licences was miniscule. Things continued in their joyous mixture of secrecy, incompetence and malice until Wild Justice challenged the entire operation of general licences in the spring of 2019.

Wild Justice is a 'Lawfare' organisation formed by three people led by Chris Packham of the RSPB. They sought to take NE to judicial review on the basis that they were issuing general licences incorrectly. This caused NE to withdraw the general licences with immediate effect, and consequent pandemonium, as it occurred at the most crucial time of the year, when lambs, the chicks of rare birds, and seed beds and tender crops most needed the protection afforded by the general licences. The impact of this panic-stricken decision was so ghastly that even the people whose actions had caused it claimed that instant withdrawal had not been their intention. Leaving aside the fact that when it was announced they had been beside themselves with joy and only adjusted their stance when they saw what the consequences were, it does illustrate the shambles NE had created.

NE said they would correct the situation by rapidly issuing new general licences. When they used the word 'rapid', it was obviously not in the normal sense, and the licences, when they started to emerge weeks later, were a classic of their kind. Each species would have its own licence and each purpose would have a separate licence. Initially, if you applied for a licence to control crows on a farm in Durham, your licence bizarrely empowered you to kill crows anywhere in the UK and to delegate anyone to kill them anywhere on your behalf, effectively turning the individual licence- holder into a *de facto* licensing authority.

The licence, which had originally been two sides of A4, and recently grown to five, now became eleven pages. There were to be licences for each species and each purpose, and a farmer or keeper could have finished up with dozens of eleven-page licences at the end of a soul-destroying application process, all to avoid defending a robust, logical and simple system, which worked perfectly well before they started tinkering with it.

In an attempt to stop bad from becoming worse, the secretary of state temporarily took the licensing function back under his direct control and reissued licences, more or less in their old form, and things started to calm down, but sadly far too late for the eyes and tongues of lots of lambs and the chicks and eggs of thousands of birds – but it is never too late to do the right thing.

The only places where the new temporary general licences did not apply were designated sites, and these included many grouse moors on the basis that, as these sites had special designations, there would need to be a Habitat Risk Assessment (HRA) undertaken to ensure that the 'project or plan' proposed would not damage the site's status. Naturally this did not seem to make sense to the owners of these sites. Far from being some sort of novel project for which they were speculatively applying, they were only asking to continue doing something which was a long- established management practice, without which the species they were seeking to protect (and for which the site was often designated), would suffer serious damage. But this was as nothing compared to the mystification that followed the announcement that there would be a 300-metre buffer zone round each and every site, and in those buffer zones the general licences did not apply. Any control of the species listed in the general licences, such as carrion crows or jackdaws, would need an individual licence if it took place within 300 metres of a designated site.

For reasons known only to NE, they were extremely reluctant to share the rationale behind this decision but eventually, months later, they were forced to share the documents with their service users. The reason given for the buffer zones related entirely to bird species for which the site was listed and was based on the idea that no project or plan should be allowed without a full HRA if there was any possibility that a sensitive species (one of the bird species for which the site was designated), might be induced by the project or plan to take flight. The issues they were specifically concerned about, which supposedly justified the buffer strip, were the consequences of the use of firearms (a bang), associated human presence, companion animals and scaring measures.

If you unpick this it is beyond ludicrous. The issuing of an individual licence to kill the species listed in the general licences on a grouse moor designated site because it has thriving populations of golden plover, curlew and redshank, is said to be a 'project and plan', and treated as though this is the first anyone has heard of such an idea, only because NE says so. On any rational view it is no such thing. The same people will be doing the same thing in the same place. They have always killed crows and they propose to continue doing what they have always done, which happens to be one of the main reasons why the 'sensitive species' are there in the first place and why the site is listed. However, according to NE, something which is beyond all doubt a continuation of an existing practice is, for the purposes of the NE licensing process, a 'project' and everyone has to behave as though no one has ever killed a crow before.

Not only that, but what exactly is wrong with a bird taking flight? That is what birds do. There is no evidence that merely taking flight has any detrimental effect on any of the species for which such a site is listed, for the simple reason that what is proposed is merely a continuation of management that has been in place for decades. If shooting or trapping crows had a detrimental effect on the golden plover and curlew, it would have been obvious long ago. Of course shooting a crow might make a curlew take flight but the consequences of not shooting it would be far worse. If you could ask the curlew, it would unquestionably say, 'Shoot the crow'!

Perhaps the most extraordinary consequence of this is that it could apply to anything and everything that occurs within 300 metres of one of these sites. Try to think of anything that any human being can do that could be guaranteed not to make a bird fly. As birds fly when they see people, I can't think of anything, and apparently neither can NE, as the alleged problems include 'associated human presence'.

So we were left with an absurd situation. You have a site designated because of the abundance of species A. One of the reasons why species A is abundant is that there has been control of species B, a process that has been going on for over a hundred years. The regulator now prevents the control of species B in case the control process disturbs, to the slightest degree, species A. The fact that the population of species A has been maintained at a sufficiently high level to justify the site's designation, in the presence of the control of species B, is completely discounted, by the simple expedient of ignoring it, and calling what is now proposed a project, which requires an HRA. This, by the way, may require the applicant to prove that what is proposed will not disturb species A, which may be impossible, as shooting a crow probably does make a nearby lapwing fly for a second or two. As a result species B is free to eat species A and the site owner is castigated by the conservation industry and, God help me, NE, for not maintaining the site in its required state.

Of course, it shouldn't have been a problem; there were months before the control of common predators like carrion crows became crucial in the spring of 2020. The idea was that generic HRAs could be turned round rapidly with the help of potential licence applicants and there would be no difficulty in getting the individual licences out in good time and in a sensible form to meet the practical necessities of stopping the eggs and chicks of rare 'red listed' birds from being eaten by common predators.

In the event, 2020 was another utter shambles. There were, to be fair, a lot of applications for individual licences, but that was the predictable and predicted consequence of making everyone apply for them. The first licences did not begin to appear until late April, by then, half the time they were needed for had already gone, and much damage had been done. Even at that late stage, if the outcome had been competent licences that were fit for purpose, there would be some hope that NE was finally getting a grip of the situation. In the event it was as bad as ever. Some people got no licence in spite of being informed they had one, others got licences intended for someone else, yet others were asked to re-send information which had been lost, and no one at all was licensed to cull rooks, jackdaws or jays, apparently because of concerns about their conservation status. This was despite the fact that the same farmer or keeper could kill them once they were 300 metres from where they were doing the damage, and that the buffer zone was to protect the species the rooks, jackdaws and jays were predating, and emphatically not the rooks, jackdaws and jays.

Conservation status is an interesting point to make in relation to the control of corvids, such as jackdaws. The latest best estimate for the number of jackdaws in the breeding season is 1.55 million pairs. This is higher than rooks, estimated at just under a million and even higher than carrion and hooded crows, which taken together come to 1.3 million pairs. In total there are well over 4.5 million pairs of corvids breeding in the UK in a typical year. The control proposed is to protect species that are far, far rarer. The curlew has a total breeding population of, at best, 66,000 pairs; its numbers have halved in the last twenty-five years and are continuing to fall. The UK currently holds 29% of the total world population of curlew, but you cannot stop jackdaws eating their eggs and chicks because of NE's concerns about the conservation status of three million jackdaws.

To be fair, even NE recognised that this shambles would cause real problems for the conservation of rare ground-nesting birds. When cornered they suggested that applicants who had yet to get their licence could rely on what is known as a 'section 4 defence'. Essentially, this relies on the idea that things were so bad that they justified immediate action, that could not be delayed for the arrival of a licence. There are three problems with a gamekeeper relying on NE's advice and this defence. First, that there is no case law to allow an understanding of how it might work. Second, that the burden of proof is reversed, so you are guilty until you can prove yourself innocent, which is not a comfortable place to be. Finally, and extraordinarily, it does not apply to control for conservation purposes, so had a gamekeeper followed NE's advice he would have had no defence in law.

Gulls and the advantages of countryside living

> It was a lovely day, so at lunchtime I went down to a pub by Gas Street canal basin, where President Clinton had a pint at the G8, and bumped into some of the women from the office having sandwiches by the canal. There was a great big gull hanging around looking for a free lunch. I said something derogatory about gulls in general and they all leapt to its defence.
>
> A few minutes later a mallard duck with half a dozen ducklings came paddling along, to be greeted with 'oohs' and 'aahs' from my little group. The gull spread its wings and let the breeze lift it into the air. It swung gracefully over the canal and snatched a duckling. The duck went frantic splashing about trying to distract it but all that did was attract loads of gulls that piled into the ducklings. Within seconds they were all gone. The old gull that had started it all drifted back to our bank with the duckling head-first down its throat. By now there was as much pandemonium on the bank as there was in the canal. My gull lovers were shouting at me to do something, but obviously it was far too late. To make matters worse the duckling's legs were thrashing about and the gull was having a job getting it down. It was one of the least successful lunch breaks I've ever had, but it was at least educational.
>
> **P.M., West Midlands**

Until recently, herring gulls and lesser black-backed gulls were included on the general licence. This was because of the damage they can cause to ground-nesting birds, the danger they pose to public health and safety, and their propensity to attack livestock. In 2019 they were then moved, because of concerns about their conservation status, to individual licences.

The thinking behind this is set out in an HRA which runs to thirty-two pages of such prolixity that it would warm the heart of a bureaucrat from Byzantium. Careful study reveals, so far as can be ascertained from a document apparently designed to be unintelligible, that the reason why a lesser black-backed gull cannot be killed to prevent it eating golden plover chicks in County Durham in June is that to do so might impact on the numbers of lesser black-backed gulls breeding in Suffolk or in the southern end of the Lake District. This gull is not 'amber listed' because it is rare; it has that status because it breeds in very few places. That is not because it is forced to do so. It breeds like that because that is how it likes to breed. The places these gulls choose for their massive colonies are selected because they are close to a large food supply. If the food supply goes, or if the number of predators increases to too high a level, they will go somewhere else.

Unfortunately for everyone concerned, but especially for the golden plover chicks, this entirely reasonable exercise in freewill does not sit well with NE's interpretation of the EU's Habitats Directive. If a colony, based say on the exploitation of a huge landfill site as a food source, becomes big enough to be designated, the NE interpretation of the law is that everything must be done to maintain the site at the population level that allows the site to maintain its designation. If the landfill site closes, as they eventually do, or if the fishing fleet changes its grounds or methods, this becomes the avian equivalent of pushing water uphill. The lesser black-backed gulls have the good sense to go where they want, but NE see their duty as making them continue to nest where they don't want to be. This would be crazy if they were a species like geese that eats grass, but hungry lesser black-backed gulls are prepared to eat anything – including each others' chicks – so in this instance, trying to push water uphill might result in fewer rather than more of the species.

So, NE have used calculations involving, as ever, estimates and assumptions, otherwise known as guesses, to justify curtailing the total number of lesser black-backed gulls that can be culled for any purpose in rural England to 900. This is despite the fact that there is no evidence that the population as a whole, or at the breeding colonies, is affected by culling for the purposes of conservation in areas remote from breeding colonies. This is also in spite of the fact that during the time they could be killed in large numbers under the general licences, the population increased by 29% from 1970 to 1988, and by 40% between 1988 and 2000. That large numbers of individuals can be culled from a population whilst the species remains stable, or actually rapidly increases, should surprise no one. The RSPB has, itself, made clear that, based on current evidence, the millions of birds killed by domestic cats in the UK every year have no population impact on the species predated. Studies of raptor predation on songbirds quoted by the RSPB show that the prey species can still increase in the presence of high levels of loss to raptors. Killing individuals of species like lesser black-backed gulls, whose numbers fluctuate with the available food supply, will have no effect as, just like the cats and the raptors, what you are removing is what is called the 'doomed surplus'.

It cannot be stated often enough, because it is the source of much misunderstanding, that culling to prevent damage is entirely different from culling to control a population. Stopping predation is about removing the individuals that may cause the problem, usually in and around where the problem occurs. Preventing levels of predation from rising to a point at which vulnerable populations of rare ground-nesting birds are eliminated from sites designated for their conservation is time-consuming and expensive, but it is within the capacity of the owners of these sites to achieve the desired outcome as part of the work they do to manage a grouse moor. Killing enough lesser black-backed gulls to impact on the national population is not something they could do, even if they wanted to.

To give an idea of the total change in population, something that the NE paper fails to do, the current over-wintering population of these gulls is around 130,000 and the breeding population is 120,000 pairs. In 1953 the total winter population for England and Wales was 165 – that's not thousands – that's individual birds. There has been a decline in rural areas and a drop of around 30% in the breeding population since 2000, but it is still huge compared to historical norms, and large numbers have moved into towns and cities, where they are causing problems, albeit mostly at the level of nuisance, stealing chips and ice creams from children, attacking pet cats and dogs, ripping open rubbish bags and, of course, leaving the consequences of their digestive system on people, street furniture and buildings.

Urban lesser black-backed gulls are causing a lot of problems but they are not going to attack the chicks and eggs of rare birds on sites designated specifically for their protection in towns and cities because such sites don't exist. However, there is just as much pressure to control their numbers in towns as there is in the countryside. Faced with all this, and made far more complicated by their own arbitrary decision to limit the total cull in the whole of rural England to 900, the NE licensing department decided to get the secretary of state to approve a system to prioritise licence allocation.

The agreed system is that the first call on the rural quota is human health and safety. After that everything else is lumped together, including the protection of rare birds on sites designated for their conservation long distances from the nearest declining lesser black-backed gulls' breeding colony. In towns and cities, where there is ample evidence of the presence of birds that have emigrated from declining rural colonies, often very close at hand, there is no numerical limit or quota at all.

In the nesting season of 2020, the entire rural quota was predictably taken up by human health and safety concerns. As a result none should have been issued to cull the gulls to protect rare ground-nesting birds. The people who took the priority system to the secretary of state for his approval had reviewed the previous year's licences and will have known that the quota would be taken up with health and safety issues. They will have known that the secretary of state was being sold an entirely different scenario from the one described. Far from allowing prioritisation, what he was agreeing to was the ending of the control of lesser black-backed gulls for conservation purposes. It would be interesting to know if this inevitable consequence of his action was explained to him when the decision was being made.

So if you want to stop chips and ice creams being stolen in a town twenty miles from a declining lesser black-backed gull breeding colony you may well get a licence to kill them. If you want to stop a gull killing every curlew chick on a moor a hundred miles from a breeding colony, you can forget it. This is in spite of the fact that there are thousands and thousands more lesser black-backed gulls breeding and wintering in the UK than was the historical norm. It is also in spite of the fact that what controls their numbers and the location of their breeding colonies is primarily food or predator pressure, not culling in places remote from where they breed. It is also in spite of the fact that they increased hugely in number at a time when they were subject to much greater levels of control than is currently being requested, and in spite of the fact that without the capacity to deal with the predation of these common birds the status of European sites designated for a multiplicity of ground-nesting birds will be fatally compromised. Frankly, you couldn't make it up!

The capacity of large gulls to inflict catastrophic damage on rare ground-nesting birds is real enough. Faced with the frustration of having to stand by and watch the massacre of the innocents, the upland gamekeeping community determined to at least record what they saw in April and May 2020. In those two months, which exclude the peak curlew month of June, they witnessed 815 predation events resulting in the loss of a minimum of 1300 eggs and chicks of lapwing, curlew, golden plover and other species. Although the keepers spend most of daylight out on the moors, this must only be the tip of the iceberg as they cannot see more than a fraction of such events.

Just when everyone thought that NE's handling of gull licensing could not descend further into farce, it did. Having used all the rural quota for health and safety issues and refused every request to cull lesser black-backed gulls for conservation purposes because the rural quota had all gone, it decided to break its own rules and issue a licence to kill these gulls to protect a hen harrier nest on a grouse moor. The real lunacy is not breaking their own rule; it is a stupid rule and should be thrown away, not simply broken. It is the conditions attached to the licence which pushed farce into madness. It said that lesser black-backed gulls merely flying over the site must not be shot; that shooting must only be used in conjunction with shoot-to-scare and gas bangers, and that, 'head shots should be avoided due to the risk of causing non-lethal injuries'. This has to be read in the knowledge that there is another condition that no one is allowed to approach within 750 metres of an occupied hen harrier nest.

To protect a shy rare bird's nest from predation by lesser black-backed gulls the licence- holder must set up gas bangers and fire scaring shots. This madness is required by the same organisation which has put a 300-metre general licence exclusion zone around every designated site in case a farmer's companion animal caused a bird to fly. What do they think the hen harrier's reaction would be to a gas banger or someone hidden in the heather firing scaring shots whenever a lesser black-backed gull hove into view?

If you can't shoot these birds when they are flying, when can you? Presumably you have to wait until a gull has actually landed and is trying to eat an egg or chick. Large gulls don't need to land to take small chicks and, if they do, it is for seconds, so the chance of any sort of shot would be vanishingly remote. If such a chance arose you would be shooting into an occupied hen harrier nest. But all this madness is as nothing compared to the 'Head shots should be avoided due to the risk of non-lethal injuries', as you can't shoot them, according to the other conditions, unless they are actually at the nest site, and you can't approach within 750 metres of that. At that range there is no risk of someone opting for a head shot, as most people, myself included, would have difficulty hitting a parked car at 750 metres, let alone a seagull's head.

Stoats, just when you thought it couldn't get worse

> I've always liked stoats. I know they have to be controlled because of the damage they do but they are such ruthless little devils that you have to admire their tenacity. I was fishing the Cromweil pool on the Tweed very early one morning and there is a huge cliff on the left bank under Scott's View. I saw what I thought was a large stone come bouncing down the cliff, then seconds later a stoat could be seen peering over the top a good fifty yards up. A minute or two later, and the stone became a groggy half-grown rabbit, that had evidently thrown itself off the cliff to avoid the stoat. I watched it stagger away down the fisherman's path that runs under the cliff and returned to my fishing. A couple of casts later and the stoat came bounding downstream, having made a massive detour round the cliff. He found where the rabbit had fallen and went away down its scent trail. Half a dozen more casts and the squeals of the rabbit brought this extraordinary little drama to its end. I have to say I felt sorry for the rabbit but you have to give that stoat first place in the remorselessness stakes. That's the problem, they can clear anything out if they set their minds to it.
>
> **A.C., Melrose**

The stoat is a common and widespread predator and has been subject to control by gamekeepers and farmers for hundreds of years. The normal method of catching them is to use what is called a Fenn trap, which works on the same lines as the rat or mouse traps you can buy in an ironmonger's or a DIY store, but Fenns are a lot more powerful.

In the UK no animal is trapped for its fur but the British Government signed up to an international convention, the Agreement In Humane Trapping Standards (AIHTS), which controls the trapping of fur-bearing animals. Since then, the convention has decided to change the specification for traps used for stoats, which are trapped for their winter coats (ermine) in colder countries. As a signatory, the government needed to ensure compliance, and the process began in 2018 with a consultation exercise. Following that consultation the government determined that the measures would be implemented in the least burdensome way possible. This would be by making regulations and issuing a simple general licence, which dealt only with the specification of the traps to be used for catching stoats.

The regulations were passed in 2019 and, as NE only had to produce a general licence of transcending simplicity, and had a year to think about it, what could go wrong? But something did. Nothing was done until a few weeks before the deadline for the issue of the general licences set, with stunning irony, for April Fools' Day 2020. It is now clear that NE consulted Defra on what they meant by least burdensome and were told very clearly that it meant least burdensome. So, no problem there.

NE chose not to engage with their service users, the people who needed the licence, although the potential licence-holders' representatives tried repeatedly to engage, or at least find out what was happening. Finally the licences went public on the day before the deadline and were met with horror and dismay. They were complex when they were supposed to be simple. They added new burdens. They removed entire classes of birds from protection. They limited the use of traps by farmers. Evidently, least burdensome has a different meaning to NE from the one commonly understood.

Eventually, the instructions from Defra to NE were obtained and this is what was said:

> The purpose of the 2019 Regulations is solely to regulate the use of traps for stoats to ensure that only those which comply with AIHTS can be used. The regulations do not introduce a general prohibition on killing or taking stoats. Their purpose is not to conserve stoats, which are common in England, or to

> otherwise reduce the number of stoats that are trapped.
>
> When considering a general licence for trapping stoats the context is fundamentally different to licences for species, such as birds, which are protected for wider reasons. A licence for trapping stoats should not curtail the trapping of this species; nor should it place new burdens on the licence user other than to restrict the types of trap.

That could not be much clearer, but it might as well not have been written. A few examples illustrate how out of control the licensing department of NE is.

1. The secretary of state said, *'Nor should it place new burdens on the licence user other than to restrict the types of trap'.*
The licence says that, *'Any person using this licence must be able to show, if asked by an officer of NE or the Police, what wild bird or livestock any action under the licence is protecting. Licence users are advised to keep a record or a log.'* Had the secretary of state's clear instruction been followed the only thing anyone would be interested in would be the trap.

2. The secretary of state's instruction was that a licence *'Should not curtail the trapping of this species'.*
The licence excludes the protection of the nests and eggs of any bird species that does not nest on the ground, from the reasons for trapping stoats, bizarrely ignoring the fact that stoats are climbers and frequently predate species which nest in or on trees and in holes in cliffs or in the ground.

3. The secretary of state makes it clear that, *'Nothing should be done to reduce the number of stoats trapped'.*
The licence makes it just as clear that anyone protecting livestock will only be permitted to use it if they are subject to serious damage. This, we are told excludes, *'Mere nuisance, minor damage or normal business risk'.* The potential licence user is left to work out for themselves what these categories may mean to the NE officer or police officer or indeed presumably the court if their log is found to be defective and they are judged to be in breach of the licence conditions.

What has happened is beyond all reason. The requirements of the AIHTS, the regulations and the secretary of state could have easily been met to the letter. Any competent civil servant could have drafted the licence in an afternoon. The secretary of state's instructions could not have been plainer, simpler or more in keeping with the AITHS requirements and the outcome of the consultation. It is surely inconceivable that they were misunderstood, since a section is actually quoted in the licence. The only rational conclusion is that what has occurred goes beyond incompetence. Taking two years to get it wrong is one thing: taking two years and deciding not to follow your instructions is something else entirely.

The end of the road

> They should run a mystery customer exercise. Where Sally works they do them and they find out some real howlers. She's always been OK. It is obvious that some of the people at NE think that giving a gamekeeper a licence for anything is the last thing they want to do. I don't want to control the national population of lesser black-backed gulls and I couldn't if I tried. I just want to cull a few to stop them wiping out all the waders and grouse. They're not stupid, if you shoot a few they clear off; if you don't shoot any they all turn up. But you need evidence that they eat eggs and chicks. When you give them it, it is only anecdote and not evidence. What I see is not evidence. On that basis what is evidence and how am I supposed to collect it? Then just because it happened last year, that's not evidence that it will happen this year, so it doesn't count. Then when you think you've seen the last of the patronising lunacy, they tell you that the allocation has all gone so apply again next year. I wish they would come up here and see what I have to watch. It is heartbreaking. Just because I'm a gamekeeper, it doesn't mean I have no feelings. Watching a mob of lesser black-backed gulls piling into a brood of lapwing chicks is a miserable thing.
>
> **J.S., Yorkshire**

In fairness it has to be recognised that the issue of licences for the lethal control of some species and for some reasons is perilous. Anyone having to deal with a request to issue a licence, with which the RSPB may disagree, has to have any reasonable person's sympathy. The officer can expect to be named and shamed on social media, with the usual death threats and spurious attacks on their character and relationships. They, and any decision, may be the subject of an online petition which may or may not be based on reality, and if they have the courage to carry on, and if they have the temerity to issue a licence, they face the months of worry and stress leading up to a full-scale judicial review. In the circumstances it is not surprising that individuals are defensive, and no one should blame them.

The willingness of otherwise apparently respectable organisations to use whatever means they deem necessary to prevent the issue of a licence with which they do not approve was demonstrated in the case of *McMorn v. Natural England* (2015), mentioned earlier. This, as you will remember, related to an application to remove a small number of common buzzards to prevent the destruction of someone's livelihood derived from pheasant shooting. One of the objections to granting the licence was that there was no evidence that it would work. The reason there was no evidence was that such action had never been licensed, so no one could have ever seen the consequences of such action. Such was the extraordinary significance attached to this relatively minor matter (buzzards are very common birds and what was proposed would have no impact on their conservation status), that the secretary of state had become directly involved and he agreed to support an experiment to catch some of the suspected birds and keep them in captivity during the period when the damage was occurring as a short, one-off experiment to ascertain if the problem was reduced by their absence. The idea was that they would be released unharmed after the trial was over.

The applicant and the people owning the land where the problem was occurring agreed to stay the application whilst the experiment took place, but the idea of getting the answer to the question they were posing, when it seemed possible that the answer would not suit them, did not endear itself to the RSPB, as is illustrated by what was made clear in Mr Justice Ouseley's judgment.

> The RSPB had been part of the group considering the research. But comment in the media had reached such a stage that on 24th May 2012, Defra felt obliged to put out a statement denying that it was to cull buzzards or to implement a new policy to control their numbers. 'We work on the

> basis of sound evidence. That is why we want to find out the true extent of buzzards preying on young pheasants and how best to discourage the birds that may cause damage to legitimate business. This would only be in areas with a clear problem using non-lethal methods.'

This statement accurately set out the position, as the RSPB well knew. They had, after all, been on the group considering the research. But it did nothing to stop the attacks on Defra, NE and against the secretary of state, personally. The consequences were set out in Mr Justice Ouseley's judgment.

> It only took until the 30th May 2012 for an email campaign led by the RSPB to see off this modest research. It invited the public to email the Minister to protest at an 'illegal, scientifically illiterate and unethical trial'.

Further on in the judgment, Mr Justice Ouseley makes it clear that he dismisses NE's reliance on its lack of knowledge about buzzard predation on poults as a justification of its refusal to grant a licence.

> This argument is circular. NE's attitude in effect requires the Claimant to prove without licensed disturbance or control what the effect of licensed control and disturbance would be. The Claimant, the National Gamekeepers Organisation, NE and Defra had all been prepared to co-operate in research on the effect of buzzard predation and counter-measures, research which it appears would have involved some licensed disturbance of the birds. Defra changed its mind, shrinking from some RSPB-led public opposition to the grant of licences. Defra research, with licensed disturbance or control, could have informed or resolved the debate. That route is closed.

Is it not extraordinary that one of the biggest and richest organisations in the conservation industry is happy to use what is akin to brute force to ensure something as benign as research, intended to clarify a difficult licensing issue, is crushed, for no better reason than they don't want to hear the answer? In the circumstances, individual licensing officers can hardly be blamed for wanting to avoid being the personal target of a social media storm. In a world where hugely powerful organisations, and their even rougher fellow-travellers, make it clear what they want and what is likely to happen if you stand in their way, it is perhaps surprising that things are not worse.

The performance of NE's licensing function is not all bad. It makes some brave and sensible decisions under difficult circumstances and it contains some good people who want to improve things, but the consequence of the actions of the function as a whole has been to create a breach with much of rural England, the people who own and manage the countryside, which will, if something is not done quickly, widen beyond repair. It has allowed the licensing and consenting processes to become an impassable barrier to most people outside the conservation industry and, whilst it has undoubtedly been, to an extent, cowed by external pressure from the RSPB and their fellow-travellers, that cannot excuse what is currently happening.

The problems set out above are only examples: there are many more that could have been chosen. They are the result of NE's approach to licensing and it cannot be a coincidence that wildlife licensing only became a problem after the task passed from central government to NE in 2007. It is also telling that, faced with the self-inflicted chaos around the general licences in 2019, the government took the function back in-house and sorted the mess out in days. Even more damning is the fact that, having given the repaired system back to NE, with the best part of a year to get it right for 2020, NE managed to create a different sort of chaos all over again. Surely this cannot continue. Government has a duty to ensure that there is a system that works. If NE cannot provide it – and on present evidence they are unable or unwilling to do so – then government should take the function back again, until such time that it can be delegated to a body that is fit for the purpose.

It is also within the power of government to use our recent separation from the EU to return to a simpler and more robust system for the protection of birds, whilst facilitating the control and management of common species that cause problems to conservation, health and safety and food production. It would not be difficult to create a system far easier to understand and implement than the existing morass, which was designed by authoritarian bureaucrats in Brussels for the delight of authoritarian bureaucrats in Britain.

It should, of course, be made clear that the foregoing takes into account the obvious fact that some of the applicants are ill-informed, or rude, or plain mad, or all three. That is what some of the public are like, and if you work for NE, or any other licensing function for that matter, you are a public servant, and you are paid to deal with it. I know – I was a public servant myself for over forty years. But there are far more service users who are facing what to them are important problems, and who need help to solve them, and that is what the licensing function exists to do. NE's licensing department could have become an exemplar of good practice if it had wanted to, but it cannot continue as it is.

In summary

- *The approach of NE and some of the other UK regulators to issuing licences and consents bears only an occasional resemblance to licensing best practice.*

- *The experience of those who use the system is that it is unnecessarily bureaucratic, complex and restrictive. They are left with the reasonable impression that they will not receive approval whatever they do.*

- *The European legislation on which the licences are based and the precedents set by European courts and Commission are difficult to apply sensibly, but their effect is made worse by a tendency to gold-plate and complicate, which is entirely home-grown.*

- *There is evidence that NE, at least, considers the government's wishes are to be viewed as merely suggestions.*

- *The actions of RSPB and Wild Justice have cost the regulators a great deal of money and, although these challenges have mainly been found to be without merit, they have made the regulator even more nervous and risk averse.*

- *What is needed is new simple legislation, and an approach to licensing which is user friendly. The simpler and clearer the process is, the less likely it is to be challenged.*

11. Raptors

We found the nest when we went to look at the butts, to see if they needed any work before the season started. We were walking by a bit of long heather between two 3- or 4-year-old burns when the hen appeared out of nowhere and started to mob us. We got out as quick as we could and that was pretty fast and when we got home the boss followed the protocol and told the landlord. We just kept well away after that. It was all supposed to be secret, and we never told a soul until it was all over, but they obviously did because the next thing we knew, there was a thing on social media, a video of a local hero, sitting outside a blue tent in a clough below the nest, telling the world that he was guarding a hen harrier nest at a secret location. If you knew anything about the area you could tell exactly where he was and, if you didn't, you only had to look for the tent.

Then the boss got a phone call to say they were going to ring the chicks; he asked if they couldn't just be left alone but there was no chance of that. They also told him that there were 4 chicks and disturbance would be kept to a minimum. Next he got another phone call to say that they were going back to put big rings on them so they could be recognised from a distance. I think he was a bit clearer about his feelings that time but they do whatever they want. We went up and sat on a ridge half a mile away and watched the hen screaming her head off at the ringers. They say the hens vary in their willingness to mob intruders, but this one was very determined, but of course she was getting a bit of practice.

We stayed a bit after they had left, just chatting in the heather, to make sure everything settled down, which it did, with the buzzards and ravens soaring about, when we spotted one of them, in a white shirt for God's sake, come sneaking back and sit himself down in the heather. I don't know how long he stayed, because the boss said he couldn't stand any more and we left. I can't be sure how close he was sitting to the nest but we were half a mile away hidden and he was a lot nearer the nest than he was to us and wearing a bright white shirt. You couldn't make it up.

Then the boss got another call to say they were going back to put satellite tags on them. This time, I think, he told them what he thought, which was basically, 'Can't you just leave the poor little buggers alone?' But they do what they do. In the event they had left it a bit late. Apparently they can't put the harness on until they are very nearly full grown otherwise it will kill them. So, they can nearly fly and catching them can be a bit difficult. These didn't fancy it one bit and they could only catch and harness one.

All this time the bloke in the blue tent had been keeping the world up to date with his heroic stand against people like us, who were determined to destroy these wonderful birds, ironic really. After a few days they found that two were dead and eaten by buzzards by the nest site and the one with the tag on was dead not far from the bloke in the tent. No one really knows what happened to the last one, I hope the poor little bugger made it. They did autopsies and all were found to have died of natural causes but I suppose they were never going to put pestered to death on the report.

K.G., Derbyshire

THERE IS NO doubt that raptors have been killed by gamekeepers and there is equally no doubt that some still do sometimes kill them. This is illegal and should not happen, but if it does it behoves everyone to find practical ways to make it stop. The illegal killing of any raptor is unacceptable but the species that is particularly important in the context of grouse moor management is the hen harrier.

The hen harrier is at the centre of a bitter conflict. The birds love grouse moors, ironically because these supposedly impoverished landscapes, according to grouse shooting's critics, have far more prey per hectare than almost anywhere else. During the winter they wander all over the country and often travel south into France and Spain, but when they want to breed they go back to where they grew up, which is, often as not, a heather moor.

They feed themselves and their offspring on small mammals and the chicks of ground-nesting birds and this obviously risks conflict with keepers who want to keep the chicks alive. A pair of hen harriers is not a major problem but, unlike many birds of prey, they are not territorial, and their habit of nesting in loose colonies allows numbers to build up to levels that result in the loss of grouse chicks being so great that the moor can become unviable. This, in turn, could result in the collapse of grouse shooting, the disappearance of gamekeepers and the end of the control of foxes and stoats. These then kill the chicks of the ground-nesting hen harriers, whose population consequently dwindles and may even eventually disappear. Thus, in the worst case, everybody loses. No grouse, no employment, the slow death of one of the world's rarest eco-systems and, ironically, potentially no hen harriers.

That said, there are many reasons why what appears to be a suitable piece of moor or heath has no nesting harriers, most common and widespread being recreational disturbance, and it is disingenuous to claim that their absence is evidence that they have been slaughtered by gamekeepers. Making somewhere a National Park and encouraging millions of people to walk, camp, mountain bike, hang-glide and bird-watch, will undoubtedly be good for the people. It may not be an unalloyed blessing for wildlife, especially those, like hen harriers, that like a quiet life.

An enormous amount of thought and effort have gone into trying to find how this mutually catastrophic outcome can be avoided. Millions of pounds have been spent on research to find a solution that can ensure healthy and sustainable hen harrier populations whilst, at the same time, keeping the manifest economic and biodiversity benefits provided by properly conducted grouse shooting. After over a decade of discussion and debate a plan was agreed with government that was designed to find a way to get more hen harriers in England – the imaginatively titled Hen Harrier Action Plan (HHAP).

The HHAP included three elements that everyone agreed on: better enforcement, better monitoring and what is known as diversionary feeding, where the gamekeeper provides alternative prey to the nest, so that the parent birds do not need to hunt for the chicks of grouse and curlew. Unfortunately it also contained two elements that caused continued controversy; brood management and the southern reintroduction. The reason they are controversial is simply that the RSPB and their fellow-travellers do not like them. The antipathy towards brood management is so great that it has resulted in a judicial review, and the southern reintroduction was condemned at a meeting in parliament by the RSPB's Head of Global Conservation as in clear breach of the guidelines for reintroductions set down by the International Union for the Conservation of Nature (IUCN).

So what are these awful things, which one side says will significantly increase the hen harrier population, and which the other side claims are the works of the devil?

In essence the technique of brood management is simply moving eggs or fledglings to a secure location where they can be hatched and reared until they are able to look after themselves, at which point they are then released back into their natural habitat. Far from being controversial, it is a well-tried technique, found in many countries and used for a variety of species by a wide range of organisations.

The RSPB itself is involved in a programme to help the spoon-billed sandpiper, one of the most endangered birds in the world. Its precious eggs are collected from nests in Central Asia, incubated in the UK and the resulting fledged sandpipers are flown back to join their wild cousins on their perilous migration. Hen harriers themselves are already brood-managed elsewhere in Europe, under the same legislative framework that applies in England, for no more pressing reason than to allow farmers to harvest their corn.

As the system works in Europe, the reasonable assumption was that it would work well with harriers here and happily that has proved to be correct. In 2019 a brood of five was reared in captivity, all fledged successfully and all were released on a Yorkshire grouse moor, with the enthusiastic support of the owners and much additional hard work by the keepers. Elsewhere, whilst it was a good year for hen harriers in England by our current low standards, it was, as ever, bedevilled in the wild by chick losses to predation and the weather, in some cases perhaps exacerbated by excessive attention from ardent harrier lovers enthusiastically attaching bits of kit to the nestlings.

It is important to remember that leaving a hen harrier's nest in place, rather than taking it for brood management, is highly likely to be lethal to the chicks. Despite how they look in photographs, they are a small bird: they are killed by eagles, peregrines, buzzards and goshawks and the chicks or eggs are also vulnerable to foxes, stoats, owls, gulls and corvids. In places where there can be no gamekeepers, they often fail to breed successfully; indeed, figures indicate that they might even do worse without gamekeepers controlling predators.[1, 2, 3] In 2018, thirty-seven of Scotland's 252 known hen harrier nests were on RSPB managed land. Only five (13%) of these nests were successful. Brood-managed chicks are likely to have a survival rate approaching 100%, far higher than would typically occur in the wild, even when cared for by RSPB, and as the birds are returned to the moors from whence they came, any reasonable person would consider the programme a laudable success. Unhappily the RSPB is by no means constrained by reasonableness.

Faced with the facts that brood management is a well tried and proven means of increasing wild bird populations, that the RSPB uses it for other species (albeit under a different name), that it has a history of being used successfully with hen harriers in Continental Europe and has now been proved to work in the UK, it is hard to imagine why anyone who wants to have more hen harriers could be against it, let alone seeking to use the courts to render it illegal.

Turning to the southern reintroduction, it is what it says. The idea is simple, and again, tried and tested with other species, including many raptors. You find extensive areas of suitable habitat, get the approval of key locals, import eggs and/or chicks from other countries that have a surplus, rear them in captivity and release them when they can look after themselves. The RSPB has repeatedly done or supported precisely this with other raptor species: Spanish red kites to the Chilterns and the Black Isle, Scandinavian sea eagles to the Western Isles and Fife and the Isle of Wight, and Scottish golden eagles to Eire are just a few obvious examples.

The current scheme is being managed, not by some NGO or a bunch of single-issue enthusiasts, but by NE itself. After a prolonged search they have found a perfect site from a long list of very good ones. They have checked that everyone in the locality is keen to see the birds thrive, and they are. The locals are used to living in harmony with them, because hen harriers already winter there. They have ensured that they have access to state-of-the-art facilities and possess the skills and resources needed to make it work. What's not to like?

Well, the RSPB does not like it at all. According to their Head of Global Conservation, the plan breaches the IUCN guidelines because the cause of their extinction is still extant. They are, the logic goes, extinct in Wiltshire because they were being killed by gamekeepers there over a hundred years ago. As they are allegedly being killed by gamekeepers hundreds of miles away, the cause of their extinction has not been removed. So you can forget any idea of releasing hen harriers in Wiltshire until it can be guaranteed that no keeper, or anyone else for that matter, anywhere in the UK, will kill a harrier.

The briefest of rational thoughts indicates that this position is hypocritical nonsense. How does this differ from the kites they released on shooting estates in the Chilterns or sea eagles they released in Fife? When the RSPB reintroduced these species, they were clear that they had been exterminated by killing and egg collecting and they were simultaneously campaigning against what they were also very clear was the ongoing persecution of raptors.

If it is against IUCN guidelines for NE to release hen harriers in Wiltshire because somewhere, hundreds of miles away, someone might kill a harrier, why was it all right for the RSPB to release kites in the midst of shooting estates in Hertfordshire or within twenty minutes flying time of a grouse moor on the Black Isle?

It is very interesting that this element of the HHAP is being treated differently from the brood-management scheme. The RSPB has not taken the reintroduction to judicial review and it is fair to ask why. There are two explanations that spring to mind. The first is, obviously, that they know that they would not just lose, they would be humiliated. The spectacle of the RSPB trying to explain under oath why, when *they* reintroduce a raptor species, it is different from when NE reintroduces one, would be something to behold. The second reason could be that they don't need to go to law to stop the scheme. Any hen harriers released in the south of England will have to be sourced in Europe. Whilst it might seem obvious to use the brood-managed birds from the northern moors, this is not allowed; they have to be released back onto moors near where they were born. France and Spain are the obvious choices; they have large hen harrier populations, and it would normally be considered relatively straightforward to get permission to take eggs or chicks for an important reintroduction scheme being run by the state regulator.

This is not how it has turned out. Repeatedly, initially in France, and then in Spain, everything started as well as one might expect, then without warning the 'Yes, how can we help?' turned to 'Don't call us, we'll call you'. Something happened. There were, of course, rumours of what that something was, but we could only really ponder what it might have been. Who would have the influence to have the conversation that brought about such a sudden and complete volte- face? Who feels strongly enough to take such an extraordinary step?

Obviously, given the circumstances, some people thought that the RSPB was involved. I sincerely hoped that they were wrong. They had ample opportunity to make it clear that there have been no negative conversations, direct or indirect, with those approached by NE to supply eggs or chicks for the southern reintroduction. However, they refused to be drawn, beyond cryptic responses such as: 'There may have been some misunderstanding.'

In the absence of such a simple step, no one could have been blamed for wondering if they might have been involved. They appeared to be the principal opponent of the scheme and to have the global reach and soft power to have such an effect. Their more extreme elements are now so opposed to grouse shooting that almost anything goes. It seemed not unreasonable to think that a significant increase in the range and numbers of hen harriers might make them less newsworthy and a less potent weapon to use against grouse moor management.

We come once again to the real conflict, which is a human one. The one side's position is that if the outcomes you want are less illegal killing of hen harriers and more hen harriers, here is a practical way to do both. The other side says, 'No! You must do it by the process we insist on. If that results in illegality continuing and fewer hen harriers, so be it. Our way or no way.'

Then, just as it seemed that no one would ever know what had happened, a series of internal Defra emails came to light. These indicated that the RSPB had not, after all, been the victim of a 'misunderstanding'. They appear to have cynically used their links with Europe to veto any attempt to source hen harrier chicks from France and Spain. Their claims of being misunderstood were simply a deceit, the equivalent of looking someone in the eye and saying 'prove it'.

The first email, only dealing with the French refusal, leaves a small element of doubt:

> The opposition (to sourcing French harrier chicks) may be in some way in order to support the RSPB's opposition to a brood management scheme being run by NE, which also forms part of the HHAP.

Those that followed left none. The night before NE's envoy met Spanish officials in May 2019, he was emailed by a senior Spanish official in Spanish Birdlife Partners (SEO) to say they were not supportive of the project. The Defra email says:

> We know RSPB has orchestrated this late intervention (the SEO simply cited the RSPB's standard position). The interference continues. The RSPB said that there 'may have been some misunderstanding'.

Simon Lee, the reintroduction project manager, whose feelings can only be guessed at, wrote:

> SEO stated they were acting on behalf of their friends the RSPB. The 11th-hour intervention had been prompted and in part worded by the RSPB.

Another Defra note says:

> Due to contact by RSPB with conservation groups in France and Spain NE has been unable to source chicks. Without the chicks the reintroduction cannot go ahead and we cannot stop the RSPB.

It is difficult to believe that this is a misunderstanding. The fact is that both Defra and NE clearly believe on the basis of conversations that they had with the officials from France and Spain that the RSPB, as was suspected all along, simply used its power to stop the successful reintroduction of a rare raptor.

There is not a single conservation argument for vetoing the reintroduction of hen harriers into suitable habitat in the south of England but they did it anyway, denied it was anything to do with them and said the equivalent of the playground bully: 'Yeah, and what are you going to do about it?'

I have been lucky enough to act as a trustee of several charities. I can hardly believe that any board of trustees of a respectable charity could agree to this extraordinary course of action, but it would have been arrogant madness for staff to do something as awful as this and then try to brazen it out, without at least the tacit support of the chairman and trustees.

It is difficult to imagine what a meeting would be like at which the trustees agreed a plan like this. Was there a paper explaining what was proposed laid before the trustees? If there was, it would make interesting reading. The sections on stabbing a compliant regulator in the back, and covering their tracks if challenged, would be especially enlightening.

What has conservation in the UK come to when the biggest and most powerful organisation in the industry, that constantly parades its 'values', apparently uses its power covertly to stop the successful reintroduction of a rare bird and then isn't even competent enough to cover its tracks?

The toxic problem of raptors, their persecution and their use as a weapon, is far wider than hen harriers. There are other issues that bedevil the attempts that honest people are constantly making to sort out the last remnants of raptor persecution. Two important ones are the special status of raptors and the special status of shooting.

If an important part of your estate or farm business income is generated by game shooting, this is seen by an element within the conservation industry as different from any other income stream your land might generate. The protection of that income, by the necessary legal culling of any birds under the licensing scheme operated in compliance with British and European law is, according to them, illegitimate. If it is suggested, whatever your business is, that you might use the provisions of the licensing system to protect your income by culling any raptor species, you can expect no quarter at all. You will be declared anathema.

Two examples will illustrate the point. The first is obviously the McMorn case referred to earlier, where it proved impossible to get a licence to control a common raptor (the buzzard, with up to 150,000 breeding pairs) to protect a small-scale shoot operator's sole source of income. Even when it was made clear in the court judgement that NE, egged on by the RSPB, had behaved completely illegally, the matter did not end there. It was claimed that shoots should be non-businesses and raptors should be removed from the licensing provisions altogether.

The other example is the regular, and entirely genuine, need for people who make their living selling access to fishing, in particular put-and-take trout fishing, to cull cormorants. In put-and-take fishing, captive reared trout are released in lakes and people pay to catch them, having a good day's sport and, hopefully, a tasty trout at the end of it. It is a well organised business with rules about how many can be killed and how many released and, just like released pheasant shooting, makes an important contribution to the local economy where it occurs. Cormorants are significantly less numerous in the UK than buzzards (8,000–9,000 pairs) but they have two lethal disadvantages. They eat fish, not pheasants, and they are not raptors. We should all (especially fishermen) be grateful that NE issues cormorant licences to fisheries on a very regular basis. Strangely, there is no evidence that the RSPB has ever declared fishing a non-business. There is no threat of judicial review and not even a hint of online abuse, something that the Northumbrian pheasant shooter soon got used to.

When Defra carried out a review of the impacts of cormorant on fisheries in 2013, the RSPB took part and expressed satisfaction in their magazine that the bird was not going on the general licence and the annual cull would be limited to 2,000 birds, but they remained 'concerned at the scale of killing already permitted'. Very reasonable and in stark contrast to their view of anything to do with a buzzard. Clearly, to paraphrase George Orwell, as far as the RSPB is concerned, 'All birds are equal, but some are more equal than others.'

It should be possible to reduce raptor persecution to vanishing point. The way to do this is the way you reduce any other sort of crime. The rules are always the same. You must, make it harder for the wrongdoers in any community to commit crime. You must support those within the community who want to do the right thing. The law enforcers must be honest and open in their dealings with everyone, even the potential criminals. Anything that can remove the incentive to commit crime by providing practical alternatives should be done.

In the UK, police forces, often working in partnership with local authorities and communities, have been very good at reducing crime in this way. Unfortunately, the system can be wrecked by the emergence of vigilante groups of amateur law enforcers. This is sadly the case with raptor crime. There are a range of organisations and individuals who are excited by the idea of bringing raptor criminals to justice. The largest and best resourced is the RSPB but there are a number of others, some of whom have sometimes demonstrated a relaxed attitude to the rules of evidence. The RSPB has an entire department that exists for nothing else, it has a large budget and equipment of the very highest quality.

Despite their resources and the freedom they enjoy, they are still very bad at catching people who commit these crimes and getting them successfully prosecuted. One of the reasons for this is that the courts sometimes take a dim view of the way the unit uses the freedom the RSPB management gives them. The fact that your employer is happy for you to trespass on private property, set up unauthorised covert surveillance cameras and, probably worst of all, be convinced a crime may occur, decide not to attempt to prevent it, but allow it to happen in the hope that you can catch the perpetrator, are all tactics that are unlikely to impress a judge, nor should they. Letting a cake thief you've been after for years steal one more cake so that you can catch him might be acceptable. Letting some idiot kill an eagle or a hen harrier, when you could have stopped it, is on an altogether different scale.

As you watch case after case collapse over the years, it is difficult to believe that intelligent people can keep doing the same things with the same negative result. But that assumes that having a case against a gamekeeper thrown out is a bad result. From the point of view of those whose aim is to change the law, it might not be the end of the world. You get the publicity you seek and appear to demonstrate that the existing law is incompetent so, far from being a total loss, the outcome may be almost desirable.

What could be done to improve the situation? The simple thing is to maximise efforts to prevent crime at the same time as trying to catch the wrongdoers. In a typical situation there will be layers of people who could, if they knew, do something about it before it happens. There may be the owner of the estate, the farming tenants, the shooting tenants, and the head keeper. As things currently operate, if the investigators suspect that, say, a hen harrier's nest might be in danger, they act as though all these people are party to the crime. They will obviously not ask permission of any of them to do anything that might improve the quality of their evidence, and the last thing they would do is discuss their concerns with them in an attempt – that would almost certainly be successful – to prevent the crime happening. If people behaved like that in an urban setting, they would get very short shrift from both the police and the community. Can you imagine the reaction to 'I suspected those men were going to beat and rob the pensioner, so I decided not to tell his family, his friends, his neighbours or the police but I got into a really good position to film it all'?

This feeds into another issue in the reduction of any crime, including raptor crime – that of supporting those within the community who are doing the right thing. There is virtually no attempt being made to do this in any way, in fact quite the reverse. If you were, say, the landowner or the farmer in the previous example, why would they have crept onto your land without your knowledge if they did not think that you were probably an accessory to the crime? What other logical conclusion could you be expected to draw? Presumably that they didn't feel it was important enough to bother you.

To this must be added the pernicious practice of arguing from the particular to the general. Something we should have given up with racism and sexism, but which is still used with monotonous regularity when attacking grouse moor management. The fact that a gamekeeper has been convicted of a crime, or even several of them over a period of years, does not justify statements like 'gamekeepers are wildlife criminals'. Think what the reaction would be if this casual defamation of an entire cultural minority was aimed at any other group. One prominent anti grouse shooting blogger actually ran a competition for the best collective noun for gamekeepers: all of the ones he aired were insulting and offensive. Which other minority could he have done that to and got away with it?

The vast majority of gamekeepers do not kill raptors. It is obvious that those who do, as criminals tend to, keep their actions secret. Despite this, if what is left of raptor crime is to be reduced still further – which is what virtually the entire shooting community wants – peer pressure is important. The lazy, casual and unpleasant generalisations, which seek to defame gamekeepers as an amorphous mass of raptor criminals, could not be more damaging. What is the point of being on the side of the angels if you are getting abused by the very people who should be celebrating your wisdom and honesty?

This tendency is also demonstrated in more subtle ways. In 2019 more hen harriers bred in England than for over a decade; in 2020 more hen harrier chicks fledged in England than in any season since the early 1980s, the best for nearly forty years. Where were the press releases from within the conservation industry saying that the majority bred on driven grouse moors, or that the gamekeepers on those moors had helped to make those breeding attempts successful? If you want to do basic crime reduction, you look for opportunities to celebrate those within the community who are doing the right thing. You don't look for ways to bury them.

That those who seek to enforce the law on others should be honest and open is, of course, obvious, and has been for a very long time. It was the Romans who first asked the question 'Who guards the guardians?' and with good cause. The whole point of the police force is put in jeopardy if there is any suggestion that they are not honest, and an important element of demonstrating this to the general public is that they are as open and transparent in their operations as practicable. The same cannot be said of the amateur cadre involved in the exciting business of catching real or imagined raptor criminals. Part of the fun is the cloak and dagger, covert surveillance, 'follow that car', buzz they get. That is why every responsible enforcement agency, from the police to trading standards, has rules, and worries more about overzealousness than almost anything else.

The temptation to use the law as a weapon against the 'enemy' is real and ever-present. It is difficult enough for the police to avoid claims of institutional prejudice: in the case of campaigning organisations prejudice is the whole point. The RSPB makes a decision to focus its efforts on gamekeepers, to the virtual exclusion of everyone else. It then reports, without a blush, that most of the people they catch are gamekeepers and that this demonstrates beyond doubt that gamekeepers are the source of all the crime. It *might*, but it *might not*. If you fish for trout, don't be surprised that the fish you catch are trout. Proper state-regulated law enforcers are expected to be able to show that they are dealing with different communities in a balanced and non-prejudicial manner. They are expected to conform to standards of impartiality and detachment that do not apply to campaigners.

Even things that could have no possible bearing on the detection and conviction of raptor criminals, and might further our understanding of the problems faced by raptors and enhance joint working, are kept secret. The most striking example of this is the tracking data from tagged raptors. The RSPB puts satellite tags on hen harrier and eagle chicks and then follows their movements remotely. If one disappears on or in the vicinity of a grouse moor, there are press releases, radio and television interviews and analysis. Not all of those that disappear, do so on grouse moors, or even near them, but you hear nothing about them. Why not? The tagging is licensed by NE, NRW, or SNH, but they do not require the RSPB to make the data public, ever. It might be acceptable if, as is claimed, the tagging is for scientific research, to allow it to be kept private for a period to permit the writing and peer review of papers, but never to make it public is extraordinary. It gives the tagger absolute control of the narrative and a veto over potentially useful insights by others, which might be of great importance to the future conservation of the species.

The more damaging consequence of this officially sanctioned secretiveness is that it makes even reasonable people think those involved are up to something. First, it is believed, not without evidence, that the tagging often has fatal consequences for the birds. They have to be more or less fully grown when the tag is fitted or it will be lethally constricting when they get to full size. With harriers, by that stage they are able to flap about and sometimes have to be chased through the heather and, because the chicks are all different ages, the older ones may actually fly away. This is all pretty disruptive and stressful – and if the weather is wet or cold, doubly so – and, as the hen may well be flying about screaming her head off in an effort to distract what she sees as predators, real predators may discover the location of a meal.

What the consequences of all this are, only the taggers know. Unsurprisingly, they say it's not a problem, but they would say that, wouldn't they? The chicks that die in or around the nest site after a tagging event are always recorded as dying of natural causes. There is never an admission that interference may have contributed.

An autopsy on a brood of hen harriers that had been interfered with twice for leg rings and once to be satellite-tagged found they had died of natural causes, in this case high worm burden exacerbated by disturbance by buzzards. In 2019, during a wet and cold summer, a brood of hen harriers had one fatality after another but it was decided to disturb them once again, to put a satellite on the survivor. Presumably to make sure that disturbance was kept to a minimum, the taggers took a television crew with them. There was the usual hushed commentary about the fear that this chick might be killed by an evil gamekeeper, which was a bit unkind as a gamekeeper had helped to keep it safe for weeks. Within days concern arose that the bird had not moved much. It was found a few yards from where it had been filmed and tagged, dead from 'natural causes'. Thank God it had nothing to do with the ringing and tagging, or the essential television opportunity.

Equally, how do we know if the tags make them more vulnerable to predation by making them more visible or slowing them down? A peregrine nest in Spain had a collection of tags from Montagu's and hen harriers scattered around it. How many die in wind farms? None, apparently, but how are we to know? How many get hung in fences? None, apparently, but how are we to know? The obvious question is, why on earth not? If you really want to reduce raptor crime, why don't you make common cause with the overwhelming majority of the shooting community who want the same thing? Why can't everyone be open and honest about the raptor data they possess and use it for the greater good? The RSPB has taken to itself the powers of a regulator without putting in place the checks and balances that apply in properly accountable law enforcement. As a consequence, far from enlisting the help of the overwhelmingly law-abiding majority, they seem content to alienate them whenever the opportunity arises.

It should also be borne in mind that, for all their failings, the RSPB are at the respectable end of this business. Some of the others are very shady indeed and are not above manufacturing 'evidence'. The mere fact that you are innocent of any wrongdoing will not keep you out of the news. In 2019 a dead badger cub, far too young to leave its natal sett, let alone go anywhere, was photographed outside a moorland sett by some heather that had been burnt a year earlier, and reported as a victim of heather burning. An adult road-killed badger was hung in a snare and photographed and reported as near to a named grouse moor. Traps legally set for stoats were moved and reset illegally in the open, actually on grouse butts, just to make sure everyone got the link. All became public, all were labelled as crimes. All were faked.

To this problem can be added the fact that, in some areas, this artificial generation of evidence is coupled with criminal damage, intrusive and covert surveillance, direct harassment and threats of physical violence. What makes the whole mix more toxic, is that the people responsible seem to drift in and out of otherwise respectable organisations at will and, despite their actions (some of which, in their more extreme forms, have resulted in custodial sentences), they are on cordial terms with senior figures in the conservation industry who appear happy to work with them without a blush.

The assumption that all gamekeepers are raptor criminals and that the persecution of protected birds of prey is endemic and universal in the game shooting world appears to be where the RSPB and its fellow-travellers want public perception to be and they are broadly succeeding. That this is the strategy can be assumed on the basis of the evidence of direct observation.

If the senior management and trustees did not want the public to believe something that they themselves must know is untrue, why do they persist in behaving in the way they do?

In May 2020 an interesting peer-reviewed study was published in the journal *People and Nature* by researchers from Exeter University. To quote Professor Robbie McDonald, who oversaw the study, 'We found that keepers were not particularly motivated by employer pressure but had diverse motivations, including a sense of custodianship for game and non-game wildlife.' The research had taken place in the south of England and every single gamekeeper disapproved of the killing of raptors and had never done it. This resulted in an article in *The Times* under the headline 'Gamekeepers felt under pressure to kill illegally', which is exactly what the report didn't say. How could this happen? The animal rights group called Moorland Monitors cut and pasted bits and pieces of the report and completely changed its findings, and a quote from the RSPB about raptor persecution gave the whole thing spurious credibility, despite the fact that it had not a vestige of truth. If this was a one-off, it might be forgotten, but, sadly, it is a long-standing pattern of behaviour.

Faced with all this, it is fair to ask if these organisations have any interest at all in working in partnership with the people who own and manage the land. If they have, why are they happy to treat an entire community as though it is part of a criminal conspiracy, and why do they not distance themselves from people who are engaged in acts of sabotage against the legitimate interests and activities of that community? The answer, as far as the uplands are concerned, is they almost certainly haven't. It suits them to keep people who are managing moorland, that palpably out-performs anything they can achieve in terms of upland breeding bird assemblages, well out of the way. Not having people at a meeting who know more than you about the successful management of these beautiful places is an advantage rather than a handicap. If you can use some real or, if necessary, alleged criminality to make sure that they are sidelined, so much the better.

Raptor persecution does serious harm to shooting in general and grouse shooting in particular. It does not matter that some of the species are now very common, or that other factors such as disturbance, egg collecting or rock climbing may be the real cause of local absence. It is of no significance that there are nature reserves with fewer raptors than many grouse moors. In fact nothing matters as long as, if there is one person breaking the law, everyone is blamed. For this reason, there is a great willingness to find ways to solve the problem on the part of the community most damaged by it. The granting of buzzard licences and the existence of brood management trials took away two of the last possible explanations for illegality and the community is genuine in its wish to work in partnership with serious and respectable people and organisations to solve any remaining problems.

Unfortunately, the same pressure to sort this out does not operate on the other side of the fence. There is no willingness to work in genuine partnership, no willingness to share information that is crucial to resolving the issue once and for all, no interest in finding innovative solutions or preventing these crimes before they happen, rather than trying to catch the perpetrator after the damage is done. The shooting community, and the police, do try to work with the RSPB and even some of the more extreme organisations, and there are protocols, painstakingly agreed, designed to sift the real crimes from the dross of misinformation and assumption, an essential first step in the process of creating an effective joint approach to weeding out the real criminal activity. Tragically, every time it seems that progress has been made, a television crew is taken to film something before the police are even informed, or figures for horrific levels of wrongdoing based on no more than allegations are released to the press, when they should have been subject to validation by the agreed protocol, which subsequently shows that many of them are not crimes at all.

Every dead raptor is either found 'near a grouse moor', which is the description applied to any rural location north of Sheffield or 'in a shooting area' which is everywhere else that isn't a city or a town. If someone says that a dead barn owl they have found outside Walsall might have been illegally killed, before anything else happens it is likely to become 'a raptor, reported illegally killed in a shooting area'. The facts that it was hit by a car, the nearest shoot is over twenty miles away and the entire allegation is based on having read previous, similar allegations, should make respectable elements in the conservation industry think twice about using such a report as a weapon, and, to be fair, many of them will say in private that they do not approve of what is going on. However, they are very wary about saying so in public, in part because it is obvious that some illegality continues, but also because there is no hope of a rational debate, and anyone who questions the imposed orthodoxy is unlikely to survive the social media storm that will be sent their way by the usual suspects.

If you relocate this extraordinary set of circumstances to any crime in an urban setting, you can see how ridiculous it is. You would have a huge charity employing experts in covert surveillance, watching crimes being committed rather than reporting them or having them prevented, ignoring protocols they have themselves agreed with the police, prioritising publicity over cooperation and conviction, and whose bungling compromises case after case. All the while, being supported by shadier characters, not averse to going a little further, and coupled with an orchestrated campaign of misinformation, designed to demonise a minority cultural community. In any town or city it would be unthinkable but it is apparently perfectly all right to behave like that in rural Britain.

Solving the problem relies largely on the police. It is difficult to believe that they would tolerate what is going on with any other crime. When the RSPB came out with a claim that over fifty cases of raptor persecution had occurred in six weeks of coronavirus lockdown, this was immediately and powerfully confirmed by the senior police officer concerned, who was 'sickened' by the level of criminality. This validation led to TV appearances and interviews and gave the story the legs it needed. What should have been said, and would have been with any other crime, is that these are as yet unconfirmed allegations, none of which has been subject to the agreed validation procedure, but which are the subject of ongoing assessment and investigation by the police.

This is especially so when the senior officer in question must have known that the percentage of allegations that eventually prove to be crimes is low. For example, the RSPB's own Bird Crime Report for 2012 shows that of 424 incidents recorded involving birds of prey that year, less than 25% were deemed to be confirmed, or even probable. That is still too many, but at least a firm basis for rational discussion. On this basis the lockdown figures would drop by 75% – still too many but perhaps not as newsworthy. Had the police stuck to what was agreed, the discussion would have been different, more focused and more likely to obtain results.

The other matter that only the police can address is the enthusiasm for letting crimes happen so that you can catch the perpetrator. This would hardly be tolerated if the police did it, would not be tolerated by the police with most other crimes, and must surely be unacceptable when the life of a protected bird is at stake. It is up to the police to provide coherence and rigour to the fight to eradicate raptor persecution; in the absence of such an approach the situation will not improve.

It is also the duty of those who shoot and the organisations that represent them to ensure that they can never be seen as apologists for illegal activity. This will be very much easier and more certain if the police treated raptor crime as any other crime, and similarly treated freelance law enforcers in this field as they would in any other.

The final element that would help solve the problem is having a practical alternative to breaking the law. Most raptor populations are in rude good health, yet there are probably no circumstances in which the RSPB would ever agree that a raptor should be removed for any reason. Their reaction to the hen harrier brood-management trial, the hen harrier southern reintroduction and the McMorn case all make it clear where they stand. Judged on their actions and statements, they believe that some birds are more important than others, and that raptors are more important than any. They are entitled to this view, of course, but it completely closes any legal avenue of removal, whatever the problem is, if it is caused by even a common raptor. This is also at odds with the legislation that allows the control of any species if the need is there, and it is important that the regulator has the courage to provide legal alternatives when the need arises, irrespective of the views of third parties.

Support for a position where legal alternatives exist and both sides of this debate compromise for the greater good of all, comes from an unexpected source. When he left the RSPB after twenty-five years, twelve of them as their conservation director, Mark Avery, now the arch anti-grouse moor activist, wrote an article in *The Field* magazine on this very subject. This was before he saw his future career as working with more extreme organisations like the League Against Cruel Sports (LACS) and Wild Justice. When he wrote the article, his time working for the RSPB enabled him, he said, to suggest what might be the best way to ensure that hen harriers were put onto a trajectory towards sustainable population increase.

It is a long article but sections of it are germane to the eradication of raptor persecution, in particular hen harriers. It starts with his thumbnail sketch of driven grouse shooting:

> The sport is so thrilling and singular as to bring in good money, which supports the local economy. As well as the economic and social benefits

> there are ecological benefits – management of moorland for red grouse favours other species such as some waders that are generally declining in the UK including curlew, golden plover and lapwing.

Later, Mark tells how he met with Colin McClean, the wildlife manager of Glen Tanar estate, who had hen harriers breeding on their grouse moor but whose numbers were probably kept in check by the golden eagles who also live there:

> We speculated about why there aren't more harriers on nearby estates and at Glen Tanar. Perhaps the presence of golden eagles in the area limits harrier numbers. Colin's description of Glen Tanar as almost a heather monoculture reminded me that meadow pipit numbers are lower on all-heather moors and it's the meadow pipits that attract the hen harriers to moors in the first place.
>
> I wonder whether we are all worrying too much about there being more at Langholm. After all, the RSPB nature reserves at Geltsdale and Abernethy don't have hen harriers nesting these days and nobody thinks the RSPB is bumping off hen harriers, so there must be precious few around in grouse moors. There never was a place as full of hen harriers as Langholm during the project there, and maybe there never will be again.
>
> Something else Colin said struck home. I'd heard it said many times before, I'd even heard it from a vocal ex-gamekeeper earlier that day, but it was when Colin said it that I really listened: the one thing that really annoyed him was when all gamekeepers were tarred with the same brush – as being the bad guys – because they included him and he was doing his best. I guess he meant the RSPB because my former employer is the most outspoken on the subject, and Colin might well have had me, personally, in mind as I have done my share of speaking out on the topic. He made me realise how it must feel for him, one of the good guys, to hear words which seem to damn all without exception. Fair point.

Finally, Mark came to his conclusion on the best way ahead. This would be a sort of sandwich:

> The bottom slice of bread, coming first, could be a restatement from the shooting organisations that illegal killing of hen harriers happens, that it

> is too often done by members of the shooting community and that those organisations will work to reduce the incidence of raptor-killing. Such a statement, if worded well, would remove a lot of the hypocrisy from the discussion and would mean there was no going back whatever happened next. And I believe such a statement would be seen as a significant move by raptor enthusiasts who don't like to be told that they are making it all up whenever they mention raptor persecution.
>
> Voluntary diversionary feeding would be the filling in the sandwich which would help grouse moors cope with low densities of hen harriers, as Glen Tanar does, and like many moors did in the old days. But another slice of bread is needed to top off the sandwich – what happens if, on some moors, harrier numbers rocket as they did on Langholm?
>
> The top slice of bread would be that conservation organisations would agree a safety net for the grouse-moor manager who did the right thing and allowed hen harriers to set up home on his grouse moor. This would require some form of quota system where hen harrier numbers could be capped (perhaps by egg pricking or translocation of young harriers) on individual moors if their numbers went 'too high'. Agreeing the quota figure would be difficult. Such a concession would not be easy for conservationists to make, and would require some clever brain work to be made legal, but could lead to the atmosphere of trust that would be necessary to move things on. And, of course it's only if persecution decreases, and harrier numbers rise, that quotas become even remotely relevant.

So there you have the considered opinion of a man who knew a great deal about the issues, viewed from one of the most elevated positions in the RSPB. He agrees that grouse moor management has economic, cultural and biodiversity value. He is a little ashamed about the generalised and undeserved abuse directed at gamekeepers and he thinks that, in the right circumstances, it would be perfectly appropriate to cap the numbers of hen harriers in a particular locality.

In the years that have passed since that was published, all the preconditions Mark set out have been met. The shooting organisations have established a zero-tolerance policy in relation to raptor persecution. While not accepting that every allegation made about a raptor-killing is automatically true, the organisations are clear that some people within their community do kill these birds illegally and it must be stopped. Shooting organisation are happy to pay for measures designed to protect hen harriers from persecution. Diversionary feeding of hen harriers on grouse moors does take place and hen harrier numbers are increasing and that increase is largely thanks to birds breeding on grouse moors.

The problem is that the other side, and Mark himself, have treated the actions Mark proposed, and which have been faithfully carried out, with open contempt. There is not a glimmer of trust or compromise. Far from following the sensible suggestions he made, the raptor enthusiasts, the RSPB and, bizarrely, Mark, are implacable in rejecting the idea of even discussing what he proposed as the best way ahead. Remember that the RSPB and Mark's own group Wild Justice took NE to court because they licensed the brood-management trial, something far milder than egg pricking and relocation. So is there any hope that the conservation industry is prepared to work with the people who own and manage these wonderful places on the issue of how to provide a legal alternative to what is going on, or even a partnership approach towards preventing the raptor crimes happening? On the basis of existing evidence, probably not.

Perhaps the last word should go to someone who will never shoot a grouse, who is very convinced that raptor persecution exists and has no time for raptor persecutors, and who is one of the most respected ornithologists of his generation. Ian Newton, a former chairman of the RSPB, recently wrote the following in his book *Uplands and Birds*:

> It has been suggested that banning grouse shooting would particularly improve the fortunes of Hen Harriers and other raptors. Although this would remove the main current constraint on their numbers in some regions, it might not translate into larger overall populations in the longer term. In areas currently dominated by grouse moor, a shift to alternative land uses could diminish the value of the land for harriers and other large raptors by destroying habitat or reducing prey populations. If the shooting of driven grouse were banned, so that heather moors were no longer of use to their owners, they would most likely be converted to sheep-walk or conifer plantation, and in conservation terms have much less value.[4]

Discussing the options that might be available to solve the current problems, he goes on to say:

> Progress requires continued dialogue between the main stake holders and more understanding of the costs, acceptability, legality and feasibility of these different approaches, as well as their environmental, economic and social consequences.

Amen, to all that. But as things stand there is no hope of dialogue. The biggest and most powerful stakeholder is the RSPB and they appear to have no intention of engaging in any meaningful dialogue with anyone who has any connection whatsoever with grouse shooting. Their Vice-President, Chris Packham, expressing views which elicited no contradiction from their executive, made the ending of driven grouse shooting in its entirety an essential condition of the truce he generously offered to the shooting community in 2020. The organisations that represent the people who own and manage the grouse moors and the people themselves want a resolution. They want to work in partnership to solve what remains of this debilitating problem. They are happy to engage in dialogue. There are two sides in a dialogue and, in the matter of finding a sustainable solution to the problem of raptor persecution, one of them has no intention of taking part.

It cannot be said often enough that raptor crime is unacceptable but the fact that it still exists does not justify the extraordinary way in which elements within the conservation industry are behaving. It doesn't even work. Why not try something else? Why not try something that works?

In summary

- *Any illegal killing of raptors by gamekeepers should stop.*

- *There is no crime that never occurs. The responsibility for a crime rests on the person who commits it, not on the wider community. This is as true for raptor crime as it is for robbery.*

- *The existing unofficial law enforcement activity is directed at catching perpetrators and generating publicity, not at preventing raptor crime.*

- *No statutory law enforcement agency would be permitted to behave as the RSPB and its fellow-travellers do.*

- *Prioritising publicity and policy manipulation over crime prevention and, on some occasions, convictions, is a characteristic of campaigning organisations' involvement in law enforcement.*

- *The shooting community has met all the criteria set by Mark Avery as the route to a better relationship and has been subject to even greater abuse as a result.*

12. The stoat's tale

The RSPB seems to have persuaded the National Trust to stop us controlling stoats. They say that they are natural and the birds evolved to live with them and so will have to put up with them. I pointed out that the RSPB had been happy to sign the Black Grouse Strategy, which was clear that controlling stoats is an important part of black grouse conservation, and that the RSPB were killing stoats on Orkney. Their reply was that the black grouse were already extinct, and Orkney was different. The black grouse went when the National Park took the keeper off their last stronghold and stopped controlling predators including stoats, and the curlew and lapwing on Orkney are the same as the ones around here, so what's the difference? But you might as well be talking to a log. They aren't going to break ranks. If the RSPB says stoats aren't a problem, none of the others dares to say they are. I was talking to a raptor worker who was looking after a harrier nest and he was worried that the stoats might get them, but he refused point blank to say anything. They don't take prisoners.

R.W., Derbyshire

LET US CONSIDER the conundrum of the stoat. A few years ago, before they withdrew all visiting rights, I had a pleasant dinner with the chairman and chief executive of the RSPB in, of all incongruous places, the OXO Tower on London's South Bank. The conversation turned to the chief executive's absolute refusal to consider controlling stoats. I had visited their flagship reserve at Minsmere in Suffolk and been amazed to find the artificial sand martin breeding cliff devoid of breeding sand martins but festooned with several different sorts of electric fence. This, I was told, was the result of a single stoat finding the thriving sand martin colony and eating it. This took quite a while, as there is a limit to how many baby martins a stoat can eat at one sitting, but with classic stoat tenacity it kept coming back until it got the lot.

When I suggested that it might have been a good idea to shoot one stoat to save an entire generation of sand martins, I was told that as the stoats and martins were both native they had evolved together and it would have been wrong to interfere. It was a question of values. It still seems strange to me that you create an artificial environment specifically to attract sand martins to nest in large numbers where they would not otherwise have done and, having lured them there, sit on your hands while they all get killed.

As has already been made clear, stoats are very common predatory mammals, and are routinely controlled by farmers and gamekeepers on grouse moors and elsewhere. The RSPB has, to date, firmly set its face against any stoat control on its land. Bizarrely, this is said to be based in part on the Otterburn Study. There, the numbers of stoats were naturally low and there was no evidence that control had any impact. Such a position is, of course, nonsense. The fact that something is not a problem where it is naturally scarce, does not mean that it will continue to be unproblematic when it is abundant.

The other reason unfailingly given is the one I got in the OXO Tower that, as it is a native animal, the birds it preys on will have evolved to live alongside it and it is therefore unnecessary to control the local population. Again, this is at best odd. Foxes are also native animals but that does not stop the RSPB killing them, so why is a stoat different? But, until recently, none of that mattered. It is a free country and if they wanted to let stoats eat their birds, that was up to them.

This all changed in 2010, with the news that stoats had reached Orkney. Until then stoats were absent from the islands, which were a haven for ground-nesting birds. The Orkneys were a mammal-free zone when the last glaciation ended some 10,000 years ago. Nothing without wings or fins could get there until, that is, human beings, that forever restless and inquisitive species, arrived in Neolithic times and decided that a few of their domestic animals might do quite nicely. Sometime later, a migrant boat, probably from the Low Countries, had another mammal stowed away on board and it, too, found the island conducive to its needs. These stowaways were common voles, a species widely distributed in Continental Europe, but absent from the UK, where we have field voles and bank voles and even water voles, but not the common vole. When, several millennia later, it was noticed that the unusually large voles found on Orkney were different from the mainland versions, they were christened, perhaps not very imaginatively, Orkney voles and are now seen as a 'native species'.

Being characterised as a native species is of vital importance in the modern conservation industry. Native species are far less likely to be subjected to lethal control by NGOs than 'non-native species'. The RSPB, for example, kills just about every mink it can lay its hands on but, as has already been said, will not kill stoats, irrespective of the damage they might do, because they are native and the things they prey on have evolved to live, if sometimes precariously, alongside them. At least, that was the position. It changed because the stoats had done what the Orkney voles' ancestors did, and what the black rat, the house mouse and the brown rat have all done when they got the chance, and stowed away on a ship bound for pastures new. No one is suggesting that anyone was mad enough to introduce stoats to Orkney deliberately. What seems likely to have happened is that one or more pregnant female stoats stowed away, probably in a consignment of round bales, and found, when they emerged, that they were in a veritable promised land, full of oversize voles, ground-nesting birds, no competition and no gamekeepers.

I first became aware that there was a problem (a very small one at that time) when I met with some senior RSPB staff at Abernethy in 2010. I soon learnt that many within the RSPB assume that, because I shoot, my knowledge and potential usefulness to them was limited to killing things. Accordingly, they raised three issues: hedgehogs on the Uists, black rats on the Shiant Isles and the problem of the Orkney stoats and how they might be exterminated. As shooter, red in tooth and claw, I ought to be able to help.

Unfortunately it turned out that my solutions were of little interest. I suggested the quickest way to catch hedgehogs was to go out at night with a good dog. They don't harm the hedgehog, which they quickly find by following its nocturnal wanderings by the scent trail it leaves behind, because it rolls up into a prickly ball. The handler can then wander up, pop it into a carrying bag, and move on to the next. I was told that was unacceptable because it would constitute hunting with dogs, which was something they would not do. Instead, they would use cage traps. I read seven years later that the programme had yet to achieve its aim of eradication. This was despite having cost until then £2.7 million and having caught and relocated on the mainland 2,441 hedgehogs, a rate of £1,106 for every hedgehog. The plan was to spend another £3.5 million over the next five years and this included the use of hedgehog dogs, so somebody had clearly decided that enough was enough. The aim is to catch the remainder, thought to be up to 4,000 and still breeding. If that is right the cost per hedgehog will have dropped to £875 each. A positive bargain. Hopefully the unfortunate hedgehogs would be released where there were no badgers, but in the face of this sort of behaviour I wouldn't want to guess.

My suggested solution to the stoat problem was considered so unhelpful as to be entirely unacceptable. My idea was that they ask the Scottish Gamekeepers Association (SGA) for the contact details of the best gamekeepers available and pay whatever it took to get one of them to come to Orkney. That done, they should give the keeper everything he asked for and promise a substantial bonus when he could demonstrate that the place was stoat-free. This would not be cheap, but it would probably have come in at a five-figure sum. I was told, not for the first time or the last, that I didn't understand. There was no need for lethal control, which would anyway be unpopular with their members, and instead the stoats would be live-trapped and released unharmed on the mainland.

Time moves on and, much to everyone's surprise and amazement, the plan to live-trap the stoats and relocate them on the mainland did not turn out to be an unmitigated success. After all, why would any sane person or competent organisation, faced with a serious and worsening situation, pick the least efficient technique to deal with it? Of course I was right in that. But I have to admit that I had no idea how badly they would fail and how well the stoats would do. There are now a lot of them and they are all over the place. They present a huge threat to Orkney's traditional wildlife assemblages, particularly to ground-nesting birds such as curlew, redshank and other waders. In the case of the island's very important hen harrier population, the stoats pose a serious threat, both directly through chick predation and indirectly by competing for the supply of Orkney voles, which make up an important part of the harriers' diet.

All this has produced a particularly difficult problem, especially for the RSPB. According to my reading of their bag data, nowhere in mainland Britain does the RSPB report killing stoats on their reserves. Nowhere do they accept that killing stoats is necessary to protect ground-nesting birds and they appear to have persuaded other organisations to follow their line.

Now, if something isn't done and done quickly, Orkney will go from being a paradise for ground-nesting birds, including being a major source of hen harriers, to being yet another wader sink. Another place where the perfect habitat lures the birds into nesting, but where, instead of fledging healthy offspring, they simply produce bite-size snacks for an efficient mammalian predator.

The problem is, if you have to kill stoats to protect ground-nesting birds on Orkney, how can you then maintain that you don't need to kill them to protect the same birds on the mainland? The first answer is that the stoats are not native to Orkney. However, whilst that is a good reason for getting rid of the stoats, it doesn't answer the question. A curlew is a curlew, whether it nests in Derbyshire or Orkney. These species are all exactly the same as those found on the mainland; they are not some flightless curiosity on a remote antipodean island. There must be another special reason, or the RSPB and others might have to rethink their approach to mainland stoat control.

This gets us back to our vole. The unique reason why the stoats have to be killed on Orkney and not in Derbyshire or Suffolk is that they are preying on the Orkney vole. Thank God for the dear old vole, a rare native mammal about to be eaten by an invasive alien. So, it is different after all – the slaughter of the chicks of ground-nesting birds is not the main reason for exterminating stoats, but it's the voles, which were brought to Orkney by humans, albeit a long time ago.

But here we encounter another anomaly. The third problem the RSPB shared with me in 2010 was their plan to eradicate black rats from the Shiant Islands where they lived in the presence of some of the largest and most successful seabird colonies in the country. The black rat is far more delicate and agile than its ubiquitous brown cousin and has been exterminated throughout mainland Britain, partly by humans but mostly by the brown rat. It is, like the Orkney vole, a species that hitched an illicit lift. It arrived a long time ago, albeit after the vole. The last-known survivors of this now incredibly rare species in the whole of the British Isles were on the Shiants, where I was told that they didn't seem to be having any significant impact on the huge seabird colonies but might be stopping other species nesting there. I have to admit I said that, personally, I would not want to have a hand in exterminating the last sad remnant of a species that had shared these islands with us for centuries.

We are therefore faced with one animal that arrived by human agency, but which is so important that it must at all costs be protected, and another that also arrived by human agency, a bit later but still long ago, that must be exterminated and has been. It seems extraordinary, but the fact is that the first long-established mammal species to be entirely exterminated in these islands since the wolf was at the hands of the RSPB.

So, whilst I am not entirely convinced about the uniqueness of the situation, it is a free country and you can believe whatever you like. However, forget the justification; think of the cost. When I heard some time ago that over £60,000 was being spent as a consequence of the stoat problem on Orkney, I have to say that I thought it sounded relatively cheap, but that was before I discovered that the £60,000 was only to draw up the plan! The real figure to kill some stoats on an island was around £6 million and, in the way of these things, will almost certainly rise again. For instance, the project is spending £90,000 to buy and train six dogs and to teach their handlers what to do – you could run a village school for less. But that is only the start-up cost, the estimate for the handlers and their six dogs for the planned five years is £300,000. Interestingly, running seven packs of beagles for five years would cost less than six dogs, so it seems a bit pricey to me, but I'm used to spending my own money and this sort of profligacy can only ever take place with other people's.

I have no problem whatsoever with killing stoats and I certainly support the idea of eradicating them from Orkney – after all, a decade ago, when there was a small localised population, I suggested how it could done quickly and economically. What I object to is the appalling waste of time, allowing the problem to get entirely out of hand, and the consequent outrageous cost. If the people and organisations involved had done the right thing a decade earlier, the problem would not now exist or, if it did, it would be at a level far more amenable to cost-effective control or eradication. The people and organisations who made the catastrophic decisions then, are the same ones handling these vast sums of money now.

One reason may be that, if anyone else other than the RSPB were doing this, all hell would break loose. Their celebrity vice-president would be all over Twitter, raising his troops, accusing poor old SNH staff, yet again, of having blood on their hands, with all the consequences of death threats and protests.

In these circumstances it is not unreasonable to ask if this pattern of behaviour has been noticed by the key players. Have SNH noticed that, if the RSPB gets the money, there is little or no adverse comment from their vice-president and his fellow-travellers, but if someone else gets involved or receives funding or even permission to cull predators, the sky falls in. You don't have to be bad to take the path of least resistance. Anyone who was moderately risk-averse and averagely aware of social media, could hardly be blamed for doing so. I might myself in their position, especially when you look back at the personal consequences of the alternative. But, as the RSPB is involved, happily none of this has happened. The fact that in the fifty years leading up to their involvement they have apparently killed just one stoat and have done little more than watch as the situation deteriorated for nearly a decade, clearly makes them uniquely well suited to the task in hand.

But whatever the reason for the decision, the eradication programme has begun and the first results were released at the beginning of 2021. They make interesting reading. The total bag for the first tranche of stoat trapping was:

750	Stoats	48	Mice	9	Frogs and toads
2,068	Brown rats	18	Hedgehogs	4	Cats
242	Rabbits	12	Birds	2	Blackbirds
111	Starlings	10	Voles	2	Water rails

It is unclear how this extraordinary mixture of wildlife managed to get into the specially designed stoat traps, assuming they were properly set. The trap is enclosed in a robust wooden box and can only be reached by the stoat insinuating itself around mesh baffles designed to stop non-target animals and birds such as hedgehogs or cats reaching the trap itself.

It is not unreasonable to make two assumptions. First, that if a professional gamekeeper, who knew exactly how traps should be set, had been employed a decade ago, the mayhem would have been hugely reduced. Second, that if that gamekeeper had caught a fraction of the bye catch the project has already achieved, there might have been a tiny bit of a fuss. As it is the RSPB's vice-president remains strangely silent. There are apparently plenty more starlings, hedgehogs and water rails where they came from, so there is no need to dwell.

As has already been said, the RSPB regularly publishes its bag data and the numbers for 2018 and 2019 make interesting reading. The stoat return for 2018 shows that on the whole of their substantial Orkney estate they caught one stoat. A small enough beginning, but better that the nil returns that preceded it. In 2019 this leapt to an impressive 121 (they are silent on the issue of non-target species). The only reasonable assumption that can be drawn from this is they decided not to kill stoats on their Orkney reserves until the EU agreed to pay the bill. It is fair to ask why not? The EU funds were provided on the basis that exterminating the stoats was essential and that every legal means must be urgently applied to eradicate them from the islands. That is the case that the RSPB itself put.

Yet, for a decade they appear to have done nothing to deal with the problem. What possible reason can there be for an organisation that generates annual financial surpluses running into tens of millions of pounds, to do nothing to deal with an ecological problem of this seriousness on their own land? There are small grouse syndicates who spend more on stoat control in a year than the RSPB appears to have spent in a decade on its own holdings on Orkney, faced with, what it says is, the worst stoat problem in Britain. It is almost as though they decided to watch the situation deteriorate until it became bad enough to justify the huge grant from the EU.

We seem to have reached a point that is both ridiculous and tragic. Huge sums of public money are being spent on conservation, often without any apparent concern for value for money or the delivery of real sustainable outcomes, and this money is being channelled into a small number of already rich and powerful organisations. No one seems interested in asking why they do not use their own funds to achieve their aims, especially when a glance at their accounts reveals that they have the funds to do so, at no greater cost than a marginal adjustment to their balance sheet. All too often these organisations show greater skill in acquiring and spending huge sums of money, than they do in achieving sustainable outcomes.

In summary

- *The Orkney stoat problem has been managed in such a way that the people largely responsible for the looming catastrophe, and who own large parts of the area affected, are, as a consequence of their incompetence, now the recipients of huge sums of public money.*

- *To date the project has trapped three non-target birds and mammals for every stoat, including species such as cats and hedgehogs that should find it impossible to get to the trap were it properly set.*

13. The tale of two vegetarians

My biggest worry is that truth doesn't matter anymore. I understand that people will see things differently but when you see what is going on now it's frightening. It's not just some animal rights nutter from a city, who never leaves his keyboard – although there are plenty of them – it's what used to be respected organisations, like the RSPB. I'm prepared to believe that mountain hares have declined by 99% somewhere, but on all the grouse moors I know, they haven't. There are as many as there ever were. No one will tell me where this place is, and to hear them talk it's everywhere. It's not, it's just a lie. I keep saying 'Come and have a look. I'll take you out and you can see for yourself', but they won't come. Then they're on TV again saying there is a 99% decline. It is disgraceful.

Then deer are the opposite. They cause everything from car accidents to global warming. I'm not joking. The RSPB were on TV saying that the methane they produce was affecting the climate. They hate them and most of these conservationists and rewilders want them shot on sight. Of course you can have too many deer, and of course you have to cull them, but it is a question of balance. They're not interested in balance. For them the only good deer is a dead one. Now they want wolves and bears let loose to kill them, with the added advantage that these eco-tourists will pay to watch. If I was an old stag I'd rather have an HV bullet than have my guts pulled out by a pack of wolves but apparently it's going to attract tourists, so it's great.

A.F., Perthshire

THERE ARE SEVERAL species of herbivorous mammal that are commonly found on grouse moors, but two attract all the interest and controversy. These are red deer and mountain hares. The one is large and magnificent, the other is small and looks cuddly. Despite the fact that both create similar problems for moorland managers, they elicit very different reactions in the hearts and minds of the conservation industry. The one must be shot on sight, the other protected at all costs.

The approach of grouse moor managers is more practical and pragmatic. They see both species as having a legitimate place in the open landscapes of the heather moors. They believe that both can be harvested for food without compromising their conservation status and that both may, from time to time, reach population densities that require periodic, or sometimes regular, control.

The mountain hare

As has already been mentioned, the shooting of mountain hares is controversial. It is suggested that grouse shooting has been a major factor in an alleged 99% decline in mountain hare numbers in Scotland and that the survival of this extraordinary animal is endangered by grouse moor management. The grouse shooter's position is diametrically opposite. They say that mountain hares do better on grouse moors than almost anywhere else, that the population on grouse moors is healthy and that the species is thriving under their stewardship.

The mountain hare is our only native hare. The brown hare survived the last Ice Age in an enclave around where the Black Sea now is, and slowly spread westward. Its progress was, in fact, so slow that by the time it got to Calais it would have needed a boat to get to Britain, as the land bridge had already gone. This problem did not affect the mountain hare, able to digest much rougher food than the brown hare, and adapted to harsher climatic conditions. It had followed the retreating ice much faster and arrived at the French coast when it could still hop across. It therefore had the run of the place, all to itself, for thousands of years. As the climate continued to improve it seems likely that the population in the lowlands would have lost its trait of turning white in the winter, as this is what happened to the Irish subspecies, and turning white in a green landscape is not the best way of staying hidden or alive.

The brown hare was a very important animal to Gaulish tribes, who eventually dominated much of Britain. They used hares in divination, but the hare they saw back home in Gaul was a brown hare, which by then had replaced the mountain hare in much of Continental Europe, restricting them to the higher mountain regions. For whatever reason, the brown hare was brought across the English Channel and released. Eventually it replaced the indigenous mountain hare from everywhere except the uplands.

So, the situation we find today is that, all across Europe, the mountain hare is only to be found in areas in which the brown hare cannot thrive. The mountains, where the weather is too severe and the vegetation too coarse for brown hares, is all that is left for the mountain hares. In Britain this means that they are restricted (with the single exception of a reintroduced population in the Peak District), to the hills and mountains of Scotland. Even there it seems likely that climate change will do the species no favours. Less winter snow will make them more vulnerable to predation. Milder, wetter summers, don't help either species, as the leverets, born above ground, can die from exposure in heavy rain. In the mountains, if the rain falls as snow, the problem is intensified.

What mountain hares need for their survival is food, shelter, freedom from predation and, apparently, the absence of competition from brown hares. These are precisely the conditions they are likely to encounter on a driven grouse moor in Scotland. The short heather from a burn a few years ago is their favourite food, the longer old heather provides ideal cover, and the keepers reducing predation pressure by controlling the foxes, stoats and crows reduces mortality. If you or I were mountain hares we would live there ourselves. So why are they so scarce?

They aren't. On well-managed grouse moors there are lots and lots of them. The greatest concentrations of mountain hares anywhere in Europe are on grouse moors in Scotland. This may not be immediately apparent if you go for a walk on a grouse moor; it will seem that there are no hares because you will see none. This is because they are nocturnal and spend the day hidden. If you went back at night with a powerful lamp or night vision equipment, or joined the beating line on a driven grouse day, you would see them all over the place, and in large numbers.

There exists a peer-reviewed paper claiming that the number of mountain hares has declined by 99%, apparently as a result of mass shooting by gamekeepers. A moment's reflection might lead anyone to question how you can have mass shootings of something that apparently isn't there and what the world would have looked like if, for every hare you can find now, you would have seen a hundred? The reality, based on peer-reviewed research, is that mountain hares do best on driven grouse moors, quite well on walked-up moors, and worst on moorland that is not managed for shooting at all.[1]

It is, of course, true that hares are shot on grouse moors, sometimes in large numbers: they always have been, and it has had no long-term effect on their range or abundance. It is also true that hare numbers fluctuate: they are known to be subject to natural population cycles throughout their range and their breeding success is very weather-dependent. Nonetheless, these facts do not alter the directly observable fact that mountain hares do better on well-keepered moors than anywhere else.

This is not the biased opinion of someone who approves of grouse shooting. It is an inevitable conclusion of any unbiased person who examines the observable facts. The Mammal Society said that:

> Mountain hare numbers have declined locally where favourable habitat such as former grouse moors have been afforested or heather has been removed by excessive grazing. Young forestry plantations can support high densities of hares which sometimes cause significant damage to trees, but these high densities decline once the forest canopy closes, and the ground vegetation is diminished.
>
> ***The Moorland Balance*, 2017**

To suggest that grouse moor management is bad for mountain hares is to fly so directly in the face of easily observable reality, that it is difficult to see it as anything other than intentional deceit. What might also be worth considering is what it feels like to be a gamekeeper on a moor that has hundreds, if not thousands, of mountain hares living on it, and have to listen to the representatives of what is supposed to be a respectable conservation body repeatedly claiming that the animal has declined by 99%.

The enormous effort made to get full protection for mountain hares before there was an agreed system for counting them was successful in June 2020, when sixty members of the Scottish Parliament voted to give the animal full legal protection. The most likely explanation for this particular example of putting the cart before the horse, is that those involved knew that once a robust system of population assessment came into operation it would demonstrate what they really knew all along – that there are far more mountain hares on grouse moors than you can find on most nature reserves and they, the conservation industry, entirely understandably wanted to get their way before they were found out.

The rushed piece of parliamentary business that saw the animal protected was followed by further rushing about to establish a licensing system to enable them to be killed when the need arose. The urgency and pressure for such a step comes, not from the moors, but from the forestry interests that the Scottish Government needs to deliver its tree-planting targets to achieve its aim of vastly increasing the amount of tree cover.

Thus there are, indeed, parts of the mountain hares' Scottish range where they are or may be more or less exterminated, but these are not grouse moors, or at least they are no longer grouse moors. The most dangerous place to be a mountain hare is in newly planted woodland, since licences are issued routinely to exterminate mountain hares out of season in newly planted forestry. If, as has often been the case, the planting takes place on what were heather moorlands, those responsible will not only succeed in destroying one of the world's rarest and most valuable landscapes, replacing it with one of its most abundant and least valued, they will have to kill huge numbers of mountain hares in the process. Even worse, the new habitat they create is one in which the mountain hare does not thrive. The people who have just 'protected' the hare are planning to do permanent and irrevocable damage to the mountain hare population.

There are greater ramifications to this forestry venture than its potential impacts on the mountain hare. To grow trees on a large scale by planting on open ground, you need to exclude species that will eat the trees – essentially, all deer species, rabbits and hares and, eventually, presumably beavers. This is done by mass culls, or fencing, or usually both. In the case of deer and rabbits, the problem may only last for a decade or two, as once the trees have grown they will do little harm to them and both these species live happily in forestry, but the mountain hares do not. As far as they are concerned, a forest is no more amenable than a housing estate. They are gone forever, along, of course, with all the other open country species that lived on the moor before it was turned into a forest. The curlew, redshank, ring ouzel, short-eared owl, hen harrier, merlin, red and black grouse, snipe, skylarks, meadow pipits, wheatears, whinchats, stonechats and golden eagles are no more at home in or, in most cases even near, a forest, than the mountain hares. But what is the destruction of one of the earth's rarest eco-systems when compared with the temporary benefits of an ill-informed gesture?

There are few things in the world more important at the start of the third decade of the twenty-first century than tackling climate change, but that must not mean that every half-baked scheme dreamt up by people who may find themselves enriched as a consequence, and which gets an approving headline or television sound-bite, should be allowed to destroy that which is rare and precious.

A former Head of the UN World Conservation Monitoring Centre, Jon Hutton, said in 2019:

> There is a real danger that radical climate action might, in reality, involve a rush to solutions that are anything but biodiversity friendly. A renewed drive to biofuels perhaps, or more indiscriminate hydro-power, or an escalation of forest restoration based on fast growing non-native species.

Obviously, that won't apply on the heather moors of Scotland because planting there will involve only sensitively selected native species, which grow slowly and have little commercial value. However, when you tell the people who will do it that this is what you have been told, they smile and walk quickly away. There will be bits and pieces of such species planted as showcases, but the rest will be, as it always has been, great swathes of alien conifer, because that is what makes the money.

In any event, from a loss of wildlife point of view, it doesn't really matter; as far as a curlew or a mountain hare are concerned, a wood is a wood and, whether it is aspen and ash, or larch and lodgepole, they don't live there. When you plant the trees, you do so in the full and certain knowledge that the existing eco-system is being destroyed. So the Scottish Parliament has protected a species essentially to spite the people who look after them best, and is now looking for ways to kill them to facilitate the permanent destruction of the habitat they need to survive. What's not to dislike?

In England the only sustainable population of mountain hares south of the Scottish border is in the Derbyshire Peak District. These few thousand animals are descended from animals reintroduced from Scotland in

Victorian times by grouse moor owners. For many years conservationists were distinctly sniffy about them. They were 'introduced' and therefore a second-rate species. As the reintroduction was carried out by grouse shooters they were relegated still further and, on occasions, even referred to as 'feral'. That has now changed.

The nature of this change is telling. They were reintroduced by grouse shooters, they mostly live on the managed moors, they live at a higher density on the grouse ground than elsewhere and they are not killed by the grouse shooters. The reason why they do well on the Derbyshire grouse moors and badly elsewhere is fairly obvious. It is the same reason that pertains on well-managed Scottish grouse moors. The moorland management creates an ideal habitat with mixed aged stands of heather providing food and shelter, and protection from excessive predation by foxes, stoats and corvids allows the leverets to survive to adulthood.

The campaigners want to follow the Scottish model and protect the mountain hare from the evil grouse shooters. The NT, the RSPB and the Derbyshire Wildlife Trust obviously don't burn heather or kill stoats; their friends in the Moorland Monitors are facilitating the destruction of countless legal traps and snares, and are campaigning to stop the control of foxes, stoats and corvids. Thus we are in a fantasy land where the people who make it possible for the mountain hare to thrive in the Peak District are being attacked by people who are doing everything they can to stop the use of the techniques that make it possible for the mountain hare to thrive in the Peak District.

The red deer

Perhaps surprisingly to those unused to the *Through the Looking Glass* world of the debates about moorland management, while there was an endless torrent of outrage directed at any moor owner who allowed mountain hare populations to be controlled by culling, killing deer elicits an equal and opposite reaction. Deer, especially red deer, are the only animal that the conservation industry considers nearly as distasteful as red grouse or pheasants.

In Scotland red deer are totemic creatures, tragically caught up in a battle about land ownership and rewilding. Frankly for many, including those in the conservation industry, the only good red deer is a dead one. It seems surprising, but many people who have difficulty in controlling their emotions at the mere thought of a dead stoat, are deeply relaxed about killing Bambi's mother. A famous vegan and rewilding guru George Monbiot went so far as to learn to shoot with a rifle so that he could kill a red deer himself. It was, of course, so that he could be filmed shooting it, as part of a television programme promoting himself, veganism and rewilding, and he obviously made sure that the cameras caught him being suitably emotional after the shot, but he made a point. From his point of view, killing any wild red deer is a public service.

Interestingly, the RSPB kills a lot of deer. In fact, they kill far more deer than they kill predators. It might seem odd that it is more important to kill a deer so a tree can grow under which a capercaillie might nest in forty years time, rather than killing a stoat or a fox that will kill the one that is nesting under one now, but it is their land and they can do as they wish. Just to make clear that this is the case, the RSPB bag returns for 2019 showed total for foxes of 509, whilst the deer bag was 1265. Other elements within the 'conservation' industry are even more draconian than this, with some going so far as to follow the deer into places where the carcases can't be removed for human consumption, so they are left to rot on the hill.

In many parts of Scotland a good deal of estate income, which is essential if these rare habitats are to be successfully managed, derives from deer stalking. This means that these estates try to maintain a balance in deer numbers, which allows a steady income stream without excessive impact on important habitats. The existence of these deer in open habitats means that one of the most memorable wildlife experiences of many people's holidays in the Highlands is seeing wild red deer. For the hardened eco-tourist this obviously is pretty naff: 'deer sneer'. They would far rather spend a week *not seeing* a rewilded lynx. But for ordinary mortals, who have escaped into these wonderful wild landscapes for a few days, seeing a herd of stags grazing on the river flats in the evening sunlight will be something they never forget, even if it is out of the window of a parked car.

It is surely odd that people who are making such huge claims about the economic potential of eco-tourism are the keenest on more or less wiping out the only large mammal that most tourists are ever likely to see.

It is also odd that deer stalking is being attacked as a form of the dreaded trophy hunting by the same people who are intent on killing huge numbers of red deer to encourage trees to grow. This leads to the even odder idea that if we just let lynx, bears and wolves out, the deer 'problem' would be solved and no one would have to be beastly to a deer ever again. This is based on the claim that the reintroduction of wolves into Yellowstone National Park in the USA resulted in deer changing their feeding behaviour and trees returning to what had previously been seen as natural open meadow land. This then allowed beavers to exploit these areas, which were now dominated by short rotation willow that the beaver activity favours.

There are several lessons that can be drawn from this. The first and most obvious, although the least mentioned by the proponents of reintroducing bears and lynx, is that these species have zero impact on deer populations. These predators had been living at or above natural densities in Yellowstone for a hundred years without any impact on the deer population. It was the wolves that did the trick.

I don't think there is any doubt that wolves would kill a lot of deer if you let them out in the Highlands. I don't imagine that any rewilder would be impressed by farmers moaning that they will also kill their sheep. Sheep are non-native and even worse than deer in the world of rewilding and land reform. But what mystifies me is that people who become incoherent with rage at the idea of someone paying to shoot a deer with a rifle are enthusiastically promoting the idea that eco-tourists, presumably including themselves, will pay large sums to see packs of wolves pulling down deer.

When the campaign was taking place to get the three packs of staghounds that operated in the West Country banned, enormous efforts were made to get film or photographs of a hound biting a deer. Fifty years of herculean effort resulted in a couple of blurred pictures and a shaky video or two. These were said to be evidence of the most outrageous cruelty. What is proposed as a tourist attraction to replace grouse shooting and deer stalking is way beyond this. The wolves will not have a man with a gun following them around to shoot the deer before they can touch it. They have to do it themselves. Can I be the only person who finds it odd that someone who is outraged by the idea of shooting a stag, can enthusiastically promote watching the same animal being pulled down and disembowelled alive by a pack of wolves as a tourist attraction?

The Scottish Highlands are managed by the people, who have made a sometimes precarious living from the land for generations, running sustainable multifunctional farming and sporting estates. They are regularly under fire. Land campaigners, rewilders and eco-warriors of various sorts claim that the 'natives' have ruined the landscape and its biodiversity by sheep farming, deer stalking and grouse shooting. It was therefore with some trepidation that I examined the 2020 National Biodiversity Network Atlas. You may imagine my surprise and relief when I discovered that of all the United Kingdom's regions, the one with the greatest biodiversity was the Scottish Highlands, with a staggering total of 16,273 different species. The next on the list was over 2,000 behind. How could this be? There must be some mistake. Surely, all the self-proclaimed experts and campaigners couldn't be wrong – again?

In summary

- *Mountain hares are abundant on driven grouse moors because the landscape management provides food and shelter and the predation control by gamekeepers allows their leverets to survive in greater numbers.*

- *Mountain hares have not, as claimed, declined by 99% on grouse moors – the suggestion is ridiculous. They can be up to thirty-five times more abundant on a well-managed driven grouse moor than on similar unmanaged moorland.*

- *The spread of forestry into the uplands, replacing heather moorland with trees, risks completely eradicating mountain hare populations and destroying one of the world's rarest eco-systems by replacing it with one of the commonest and least valued.*

- *Sporting estates have integrated red deer, grouse, mountain hares, farming and forestry successfully for generations. It is not necessary to exterminate deer or hares to improve biodiversity. There is no evidence that the State or NGOs can produce better outcomes than are already achieved by private landowners.*

14. Ticks

I hate ticks. They are pointless and ugly and dangerous. If a loving God made everything, why on earth did he make ticks?

When I first came here years ago you hardly ever saw a tick. There were more sheep and they had to be dipped and the winters were colder and the summers were sunnier. Now they seem to be everywhere all the time. I have to take all my clothes off and do a body search every time I come off the hill. Doing my job, I'm not likely to be squeamish, but even I find they make my skin creep. Especially when they in a mass. The worst is when you find a chick blinded by them. It would be bad enough if they just attached themselves anywhere but they go for the eyelids and you'll see chicks blundering about and when you pick them up, their eye lids will be encrusted with dozens of ticks. It's one of the worst sights in all of nature and I've seen some bad ones. The other is when you pick up a dead hare and the ticks have begun to abandon ship, there can be hundreds of them crawling through its fur, looking for anything with a pulse.

We are starting to improve things with the sheep being dressed regularly to go out as tick mops but we have got Lyme disease and I don't think the tourist board makes enough fuss about it. You still see walkers with no protection at all, and you can't blame people if they've never been told. I suppose they don't want to frighten people but it's better to be slightly worried than slightly dead.

Round here, it's really only the shooting estates that try to keep the ticks down, and to be fair, we wouldn't do it if it wasn't for the grouse. It is labour intensive and labour is always the most expensive part of a job. The estate gets no income from the walkers or the bird-watchers, although they get the benefit. It's the income from the shooting and the bosses' own money that pays for it. Without the grouse you wouldn't do it. I always tell people if you're going to walk on a moor, go to one that has tick mops. If I ran the Tourist Board I'd mark them on a map. Better still they could always pay to get everybody else to join in. But I'm not holding my breath.

T.R., Aberdeenshire

TICKS ARE AN increasing problem. As the world warms, and winters become milder and summers wetter, they spread and multiply. They now occur in places where they were unknown a few years ago and they can build up to huge populations when conditions are right, a situation made worse by the removal of the legal requirement for graziers to dip their sheep. To make matters more serious, the UK has for centuries been fortunate in having none of the more dangerous tick-borne diseases found in warmer countries. That has already changed with the appearance of Lyme disease and is very likely to change again as the warmer climate enables the causal organisms to complete their lifecycles. What used to be an unwanted nuisance can already kill you and the risk is only going to get worse.

For the avoidance of doubt, this is what one of the nation's experts, Professor Roy Brown, said recently:

> The number of tick-borne diseases is increasing dramatically (seven diseases currently pose serious health risks to birds, mammals and people in the UK). The rate of infection in ticks and multiple pathogen loads are also increasing. New pathogen strains (e.g. the Flavivirus causing Tick Borne Encephalitis [TBE]) have become 'native' in the UK in the recent past.
>
> It was estimated by the NIHR (National Institute for Health Research) that there could be as many as 18,000 cases of Lyme Disease in the UK in 2020, against 4,000 in 2015. Lyme Disease is a 'head line' problem but there are several other chronic (as well as acute) tick transmitted infections affecting a much larger number of people, as well as companion animals, stock and wild mammals and birds.

These unfortunate circumstances are relevant to ground-nesting birds in general and red grouse in particular. The sheer number of ticks can debilitate the tiny chicks of lapwing, curlew and red grouse, simply because they take so much blood or, going for the eyes as they often do, they blind them and prevent them from feeding. With the red grouse, in some parts of the uplands, the problem is even more serious. In places where the sheep flocks are infected with a disease called louping ill (which can also affect humans), red grouse will have difficulty in surviving at all, let alone reaching levels that permit sustainable shooting. The virus, which is transmitted by the bite of a tick, causes very high levels of mortality in the chicks, up to 90% and rarely below 70%. The reasons why this is the case are unclear, as the chicks of the closely related black grouse are hardly even inconvenienced by the infection and can thrive in areas where red grouse can hardly survive.

For both these reasons grouse moor managers would like to see a lot fewer ticks and have cast about for means of bringing the situation under more control. Two systems seemed to offer some hope of reducing the tick problem. One was to reduce the capacity of the landscape to carry large numbers of ticks by reducing the availability of host species such as hares and deer, the other was to reinstate an amended form of the old dipping regime, designed to go beyond keeping the sheep clear of ticks to a point where the treatment actually reduces the number of ticks.

The first system involves large-scale culling of deer and mountain hares and has proved both controversial and not as effective as was hoped. The practical problem is that ticks can still survive happily on small mammals and birds, so you cannot achieve your aim by simply reducing the number of large host species. Expert advice now is that large culls for this purpose are to be discouraged, although it is obviously sensible to maintain the populations of both hares and deer at levels where they do not adversely affect the environment.

The tactic of regularly treating sheep with acaricide and turning them onto the moor to function as so-called tick mops does work, at least to an extent, and is currently the only practical way of reducing the numbers of ticks in the landscape. It is time-consuming and requires care and skill. But if it keeps a grouse moor functioning successfully, it will be worth the trouble and expense. It also has a collateral public health benefit in reducing the number of ticks that could transmit Lyme disease to people who work and walk on the moor. It does not remove the need to inspect yourself immediately you get home for these unlovely parasites, but it does reduce the likelihood that you will find one.

As Professor Brown made clear, it is entirely predictable that the problem of tick-borne infection will get worse. These new diseases will make a walk in the countryside a lot more challenging for the medical profession than is currently the case. At the moment the problem is in the 'too difficult' box. Tick mops are unpopular in some quarters because they are not free, and risk giving some credit to grouse shooting. They are, however, a practical option which might have an application in the wider countryside.

The other factor in this worrying saga is the remorseless spread of bracken. Ticks love bracken. If you want to pick up ticks, take a walk in the bracken. If you want to try it, it shouldn't be too difficult as the plant is more common than it has ever been. The area of the UK covered by dense stands of bracken is estimated to be nearly a million hectares and increasing by 1–2% every year. A further 700,000 hectares has bracken present and increasing, so finding a patch should be easy.

If you do, ticks will not be your only concern. The fronds, spores, rhizomes and roots are all toxic and the same goes from the water flowing over and out of it. Apart from the ticks, toxins and carcinogens, there is nothing to worry about. It is a native plant so some within the conservation sector don't like it harmed, but moorland managers and water companies take a different view and are amongst the very few who spend substantial resources to combat the threat posed by the plant to birds, mammals and people.

In summary

- *Climate change is favouring the spread of ticks and increasing the range of diseases they carry.*

- *Operating 'tick mops' and eradicating invading bracken, as some grouse moor managers are doing, are currently the only practical means of reducing tick populations and the risk to wildlife and human*

15. The search for a level playing field

Indigenous knowledge of how to live with nature has been routinely dismissed or downplayed. Scientists and indigenous people come with very different world views. Science is more utilitarian and sees the world in pieces, indigenous knowledge is more about the interconnectedness of things.

Eli Inns, Canadian Indigenous Circle of Experts, Vienna, 2019

One of those morning television programmes spent a week talking about the Peak District. Every morning the presenter sat on a settee in a field with a chap from RSPB and guests from various NGOs and talked about how wonderful they had made everything and how marvellous the view was and its wildlife. What they failed to tell the viewers was that the wonderful view and its wonderful wildlife had absolutely nothing to do with them. Leaving aside the appalling incongruity of sitting on a sofa in a field, nothing in that view, absolutely nothing, belonged to any them or was managed by them or funded by them. Absolutely nothing.

Some of it belonged to me, the rest to my hard-working neighbours. They were right. It is a very lovely view. They were right, it is rich in wildlife. But they completely excluded everyone who was responsible for making it like that. They sat there, Mr Smug

and Mr Know All and talked as though they were responsible for everything when they were responsible for nothing. The farmers and gamekeepers did not exist, it was all thanks to some strangers pontificating on a sofa in a field.

G.E., Derbyshire

THE CONFLICT IN Britain's uplands is as much about community and culture as it is about conservation. There are essentially two tribes. On the one hand is what might be seen as the indigenous people, those who have owned, managed, lived and worked on these landscapes for generations, and who want to maintain their management, traditions and culture. Their knowledge is largely experiential, they have high levels of acquired skill and understanding, but they may lack scientific qualifications, the experience of operating in a bureaucratic environment and networks within the regulators and the NGOs who dominate the increasingly authoritarian conservation industry. They have formed strong communities of place and interest, which are vitally important to and within the locality, but they are not used to engaging with the media and the population at large.

On the other hand, are what might be seen as the colonists – they are, after all, intent on taking over control of the land from those who currently manage it, which is what colonists do. They are likely to be lacking in practical experience or skill, and generally have no interest in the traditions and history of the place and its community. They are, however, adept at the selective use of science and procedure, and they have excellent networks within the NGOs, the regulators and the media. They have access to vast resources and are more likely to be dismissive of the interests and values of the 'indigenous' community than they are to share them.

This is not to say that there are no scientists owning or involved in managing grouse moors – of course there are, and some very good ones. The community also has the assistance of the ecological research charity, the GWCT, which has been conducting first-rate research into moorland matters for decades. Without the GWCT demonstrating the ecological and biodiversity value of grouse moor management through peer-reviewed science, the current struggle would be even more one-sided than it already is. Sadly, it is the GWCT's habit of saying, 'Excuse me but I think you might have got that wrong', that has made it an object of loathing with elements within the conservation industry who, when they say 'jump', believe that the only acceptable response is to ask: 'How high?'

The balance of power has moved to the colonists and is continuing to do so. In part, this is because the key players, the RSPB, NT, NE and so on, appear to be a range of disconnected, altruistic organisations, who happen to agree with and thus validate each other's positions. This appearance is misleading. The regulator, say NE, the campaigner, say Friends of the Earth (FoE), and the local conservation body, say the County Nature Wildlife Trusts, are all different, aren't they? Yes, except that a previous campaigns director of FoE runs the regulator, a former chief executive officer of FoE now runs the Wildlife Trusts, and a former chairman of the Wildlife Trusts now chairs the HLF. These are just examples of a wider reality. There are relatively few large employers in this field and, if you look at the employment histories of the people meeting to discuss the future of any moorland, you will often find that, whilst they represent a variety of NGOs and regulators, the personnel are largely interchangeable.

This also crosses over into accessing resources. Grant-giving bodies looking for someone to sit on their board wearing an environmental hat will go to the best-known organisations, and whoever they recruit is likely to have had fingers in all the usual pies. To stack the cards even further, government agencies pay the NGOs, who will eventually access grant funding, to advise on the policies that generate the grant funding, and even give them grants to enable them to access grants.

When some unfortunate moorland manager meets the regulator, they are likely to be talking to a past or future employee of the RSPB, or the NT, or FoE, or all three. When they apply for a grant, in the unlikely event that they even know that the opportunity exists, the people making the decision will be advised by someone from a local Nature Trust who previously worked for the RSPB and has applied for a job in the NT, or someone from the RSPB, who previously worked for the local Wildlife Trust and has applied for a job in the NT.

To this can be added the ability of the colonists to call down wrath on anyone who steps out of line. When the Scottish regulator SNH, following an extensive, detailed and exhaustive process, which involved everyone they could think of, including the RSPB, decided to issue a licence to cull a small number of ravens as part of a project to discover if such a cull made it possible to conserve curlew, lapwing, redshank and other ground-nesting birds, all hell broke loose. RSPB Vice-President Chris Packham went on to social media to accuse the person responsible at SNH of having blood on their hands, and all rational discussion ended. After death threats, petitions, abuse and all the other horrors of an orchestrated campaign of outrage, SNH caved in and what was a perfectly legal licence, for a perfectly legal purpose, carefully negotiated and supported by the local community, went into the bin.

In all the furore several things went unnoticed. First, the campaign was actually designed to prevent the acquisition of knowledge – of a sort that might not have suited the prejudged position of Chris Packham or, for that matter, the RSPB itself. How can it be right to use such tactics to prevent a better understanding of what needs to be done to protect species, simply because the answer may not suit your personal view?

Second, SNH already regularly issues licences for the lethal control of ravens, to enable farmers to protect their sheep and lambs. They do this, apparently without a sign of a complaint from anyone, including the vice-president of the RSPB. Chris Packham is a vegan, and therefore presumably does not even approve of sheep farming; indeed, he is on record saying that livestock farmers 'could be going into organic vegetable production, and we should support them with training schemes'. Yet he remained silent on the granting of licences to kill ravens to protect sheep, which he would like to see replaced by organic vegetables, whilst reacting violently to the idea that ravens might be culled to protect the rare birds he is supposed to care about.

Finally, when the RSPB were part of the Langholm Project, there was much discussion about the impact the ravens, which bred on the estate, might be having on ground-nesting birds. It was agreed that, if the farmer applied for a licence to cull them to protect his sheep, it would provide an excellent opportunity to assess the impact they were having on the birds. The licences were indeed granted, but never used. The granting of the licences obviously did not bother the RSPB (they were party to it), nor its celebrity vice-president, nor any of the other keyboard warriors who made the life of the unfortunate officer at SNH utter hell.

What is the only lesson that can be learnt from this saga of hypocrisy and double standards? 'Do what we tell you or else take the consequences!'

It is often claimed that the moor owners, gamekeepers and farmers are wholly resistant to change or compromise. This is simply not true. Moorland management in the third decade of the twenty-first century is different from that which went before. It is designed to optimise, not maximise, the production of grouse. What it does seek to maximise is the contribution it is making to the conservation of endangered habitats and species, and the eco-system services it provides to the wider community. It does this for a very simple reason. The research by Professor Denny into the impacts of moorland management[1] states that every one of the moor owners and leaseholders who responded to his survey saw themselves as custodians of the land and believed that 'it was very important that they leave a positive legacy, and an environment better than the one they inherited'.

Those involved also see that their best chance of being able to continue to run their estates as they should be run, lies in doing what they understand those in power want them to do, up to, but not including, destroying what they love. If you consider that grouse moors have re-wet their land, improved their heather management techniques, accommodated open access and more, you would have to be very biased to say that there is no evidence of change or that there is no willingness to change further. Unfortunately, bias is the one thing of which there is a superfluity.

A mistake that the grouse moor managers make is that they assume people know what they are doing and that they will be seen in a good light as a result. They are wrong – very few outside their community have a clue. As a result, any crazy claim is likely to be believed. What needs to happen –and quickly – is that every moor should conduct an audit of its natural capital and the contribution it is making to achieving the nation's ambitions in terms of clean air and water, flood reduction, carbon storage, biodiversity and landscape-scale conservation. Every moor should have an up-to-date species inventory and a plan to enhance its performance. The fact that these moors form an integral and essential element of the complex web of community and culture of these remote and precious places must be made clear to policymakers. If it is not understood and valued by those in power, the people seeking to destroy this way of life will win.

There are, of course, risks. Whenever the 'indigenous people' make a compromise, it is simply pocketed and the next bid is higher, sometimes ridiculously so. The Langholm Moor project[2, 3], which was designed to see how hen harriers could fit into a successful grouse moor, involved the RSPB from the outset. When it was winding up, they held a meeting with the regulator (SNH) and other partners. At that meeting it was made clear that the owner of the moor (a SPA by virtue of the large number of hen harriers nesting there) had decided enough was enough, and there would be no further attempts to recover grouse shooting. The five gamekeepers had left and would not be replaced. The RSPB, represented at a very high level, informed the regulator that the estate must not be allowed to operate without gamekeepers, and that replacements must be recruited, as their predator control was essential if the moor was to retain its SPA status for hen harriers. They made it clear that they expected a private individual to spend over £250,000 every year in perpetuity, doing something that generated no income and which created no discernible advantage for his family or the estate, simply because he had been generous enough to allow his land to be used for their failed experiment.

Of course, like any other group, the preparedness to compromise varies amongst grouse moor managers, but at least it exists. Those resistant to positive science and outcome-based change are rare and subject to steady peer pressure to understand the need for workable solutions. The same is obviously true of significant elements on the other side. The difference is that the peer pressure is almost all against any compromise. When NE employees were seeking to make sense of the European Court's decision to ban even cool burning on peat shallower than you can find in a bag of garden compost, they were taken back to the European Commission by the RSPB and humiliatingly presented with not just defeat but the threat of a huge daily penalty if they didn't do as they were told.

The aggressive Lawfare, pioneered by the animal rights organisation Wild Justice, has been aimed at the regulators with such effect that they are now tying themselves, and those who wish to obtain licences for conservation purposes, into knots. They are desperate to avoid being dragged into yet another judicial review at enormous cost, both personal and financial. The licensing and consenting processes are now no longer fit for purpose. Judged by direct observation, the people who manage privately owned land are treated in an entirely different manner from the NGOs. It is clear that, as far as many within the regulator are concerned, issuing a licence or a consent to someone managing a grouse moor is tantamount to failure.

One example out of many that can illustrate the utterly different way in which regulators deal with the supposedly altruistic NGOs (of which they may, of course, be members) and the rest of us, let alone estate owners, is provided by the RSPB flagship Titchwell reserve on the North Norfolk coast. It is a designated site, just like many grouse moors. If you want to build a new grouse butt or even refurbish an old one, you may well need consent and it is very likely to take a long time and result in rejection, despite the fact that it is designed to blend into the moor, is very small and is an intrinsic part of a cultural landscape. The RSPB wanted to build a new bird hide, a concept not dissimilar to a grouse butt, only on this occasion what was intended was not the discreet heather-covered hole in the ground that caused such outrage on a grouse moor, but a huge, sprawling concrete structure said to cost over £1 million, stuck in a SSSI beside one of Norfolk's most beautiful beaches. Obviously, no problem there. The planners and the regulator were perfectly happy and the rent-an-outrage crowd, who rush to social media at the sight of some tyre marks on a Google map of a grouse moor, remain utterly silent.

It could be said that this is largely the fault of the indigenous inhabitants for not making friends with the regulators, not understanding the paperwork as the NGOs do, and not attending the meetings. For not sitting on the boards of grant-giving and decision-making bodies, and not putting their views across in a sufficiently persuasive way to convince the open minded. There is some truth in that, but not much. It assumes that you know there is a meeting, that you are allowed to attend, that you will be allowed to speak and will be listened to and that there are open minds. If any one of these elements is missing (and it usually is) you are wasting your time and may find later that your mere ineffectual presence has been used to add a tick to the consultation box.

It is difficult to believe that there is not a strategy to keep local landowners, farmers and their representatives off the decision-making and grant-giving bodies that matter to their lives. If one examines the relevant board memberships, the level of under-representation of this obviously vital stakeholder group is extraordinary and stark. If this occurred in an urban setting in relation to any minority, those responsible would be at great risk. Even to survive, they would have to be able to demonstrate very clearly the measures they had put in place to ensure adequate representation. When it comes to conserving the countryside, it doesn't matter at all that the people who own and manage the land are somewhere else when the strategies are agreed and the funds are allocated. In fact, that seems to be the plan.

There is no doubt that members of the indigenous community now consider themselves effectively voiceless, and with good cause. They belong to a recognisable cultural minority, who are entitled to their way of life and to respect. They have, by their actions, to their own cost, and at their own expense, preserved an ancient landscape of great rarity and worth. They have strong views on what needs to be done to preserve it and its wildlife, in perpetuity. Their views are based on generations of experience and a not inconsiderable amount of sound science. Why has it been almost impossible to get anyone in authority to listen?

Whatever the strategy actually is – or if, indeed, there is a strategy – the people we have been calling indigenous, the people who own and manage these landscapes and the people who live and work in them, are entitled to draw their own conclusions from their own direct observations. What they conclude is that the NGOs and the regulators who, from their perspective, are virtually the same thing, see them as a temporary, boring inconvenience, and the sooner they give up and get out of the way the better. They are entitled to this view. They may be wrong. The National Parks Authorities, AONB boards, the RSPB, the WildlifeTrusts, HLF and the other grant-giving bodies, NE etc., may be able to point out the enormous efforts they are making to engage with the local community, to recruit respected individuals from those communities onto their boards and, perhaps, the number of these people that their boards and advisory committees already contain. They might – but they can't.

On the basis of the available evidence, the conservation industry believes that it can run what is left of the best of the uplands better than the people who currently do so. They appear unconcerned that they are alienating and ignoring the people who own, manage, work and live in the landscapes they want to control. Anyone who compares the outcomes of management by an NGO with those of a competent grouse shooting estate, will understand why the people who are to be so casually pushed aside consider this to be outrageous.

Why does it have to be like this? Why can't the sensible people in either party just work together and leave the extremes of both sides to wither? What needs to happen, and as rapidly and as comprehensively as possible, is that the regulators, and many within the conservation industry, need to stop treating the locals, who own and manage most of the landscape, as the enemy. Sadly, this applies to the lowlands as well as our heather moors. They are not the enemy. They are the surest route to salvation – in fact they are probably the only route. The idea that you can solve the conservation problems of a small country with 67 million inhabitants by more nature reserves and more regulation, whilst at best ignoring and at worst alienating and demonising the people who currently manage it, is simply mad.

Remember the RSPB's electric fences to protect lapwing and curlew, a grand total of 874 hectares protected by the largest and richest conservation body in Europe, if not the world? There are millions of hectares of potential lapwing and curlew country, most of it privately owned, the best of it grouse moor or adjacent to grouse moors, and the plan is to ignore the views of the people who own these vast spaces and just tell them what to do. What idiot thought that was the way to improve things?

The majority of people who own, farm and manage the rural landscape want it to be beautiful and rich in wildlife. The main reason it isn't is that external forces, imposed by our own governments, historically by the EU, by supermarkets and the preferences and prejudices of the people who buy what they produce, operate very powerfully to drive them to increase cost-effective production at the expense of beauty and richness. Of course farmers and landowners make mistakes and do things they wish they hadn't – so do we all – but more often than not they are doing what the market or the ministry wants. To that can be added the impact on the landscape and its wildlife of nearly 70 million people, a significant minority of whom are happy to cover the countryside in litter, to fly-tip and, when they feel like a barbecue or a cigarette, set fire to it.

It is, of course, true that the conservation industry does much that is good. It has achieved a great deal and continues to do so. Without its achievements we would be in a far worse place. The problems faced by our wildlife are so great that it is essential that the conservation industry is well resourced and delivers the necessary outcomes in a cost-effective and sustainable way. It is also beyond question that the vast majority of the people who support these organisations are entirely and laudably committed to conservation and are happy to work with the people who own and manage the landscape in genuine partnership in order to improve things, in the same way that upland communities are happy to work with them. The problem lies elsewhere further up the hierarchy. It is the result of a fatal combination of the need to acquire vast resources at almost any price and the hubris that accompanies wealth and power.

The fastest-growing idea in rural conservation is one almost no one has heard of: farmer clusters. The GWCT, one of the very few genuinely farmer and landowner facing organisations in UK conservation, came up with the idea as a means of overcoming the twin problems of scale and exclusion. The challenge for much wildlife is that, whilst this farmer might want lapwings, and that landowner might want partridges, each, alone, has neither the space nor the resource to make it sustainable. The idea was to get groups of farmers whose land and resources, taken together, would overcome the problem of scale, to cooperate in the achievement of agreed wildlife outcomes.

The key to all this was that the farmers decided for themselves what outcomes they wanted. Thus, one group might be keen on harvest mice, another on snakes, a third on lapwings and so on. What horrified the usual suspects was that the farmers and landowners had not been told what to do and what species to focus on. To make matters worse, the small amount of money that was available from government – and it was small compared to the millions swallowed up annually by the conservation industry – was given to them to hire an adviser of their choice. There are now over 150 of such clusters: just one series of them spans the vast swathe of land stretching from the Jurassic Coast to Swindon, and they are achieving wonderful sustainable improvements. Allowing farmers to band together for the greater good of wildlife, allowing them to select for themselves what outcomes they want, and giving them money to hire advisers of their own choosing, all without being told what processes to use and what to do by the regulator and the conservation market leaders – and it works! No wonder hardly anyone has heard of it.

If we, as a nation, are to make the best of our landscapes and maximise the wildlife they can support, the only rational way is to work with the people who own, manage and work on the land. To work successfully with any group you need to respect them and their views, even if you don't entirely agree about everything. You need to find common goals toward which everyone can work. You must be prepared to do your share of the heavy lifting and accept, from the outset, that there are going to be mistakes and setbacks and disagreements along the way. You must be meticulous in giving credit where credit is due. You must look for reasons to praise, and avoid blame like the plague it is. When there is success you must make sure everybody shares in the credit. These are the simple and well tried and tested means of achieving successful outcomes in any complex environment and they are about as far away from what is currently occurring in our uplands as it is possible to get.

In summary

- *It cannot be right that the people who own and manage the moors are effectively excluded from participating in the strategic decisions which impact on the landscapes they have created, protected and maintained.*

- *The idea that the best way to improve conservation performance is to ignore, traduce and demonise the people who own, manage and work in these moorland landscapes is utterly absurd and counterproductive.*

- *A strategy of preserving a few key sites and using regulation to obtain control over the rest of the rural landscape is doomed to fail.*

- *Most landowners and farmers want to live in beautiful and biodiverse places. Doing things with them is far more likely to succeed than doing things to them.*

- *The grouse moor community is prepared to do whatever it takes to continue to exist and, in spite of the way it has been treated by regulators and elements of the conservation industry, it will continue to offer to work in partnership with anyone of goodwill.*

16. Grouse shooting and its community

Individuals who participate in grouse shooting in all roles, not just firing a gun, but also those acting as beaters, pickers-up, loaders, drivers, caterers, etc. often do so for reasons of tangible cultural heritage (as defined by UNESCO). Individuals participating in grouse shooting feel a strong link to their individual and local heritage.

Prof. Simon Denny BA, MA, PhD.,
University of Northampton

I SAID THAT this book is not about grouse shooting and it isn't, but I can't avoid the subject entirely. If I did, I might be accused of ducking the issue and so I'll explain something about how it works.

First, an explanation of the different systems. There are essentially three. Walking-up, shooting over dogs (setters or pointers) and driven. Walking-up consists of usually four to eight people walking in line abreast about twenty yards apart, typically accompanied by one or more gamekeepers and dog handlers. The dogs are not encouraged to roam but kept at heel except when they are needed to pick up shot grouse.

Shooting over dogs is similar, but instead of walking at heel, the dogs, who have a special ability to react to the scent of a bird carried on the wind, range widely trying to find the grouse. When they scent grouse they freeze in the classic pointing or setting pose that can be seen in sporting prints.

The two nearest shooters then walk quietly to the dogs who flush the birds.

In driven shooting the eight or nine shooters are each placed in a separate butt, the butts being in a line or arc, twenty or thirty yards apart. A larger number of people, anything from twenty to eighty, walk towards the butts attempting to drive any flushed grouse over them. There will be flankers, who wave flags to try to stop flushed birds drifting right or left and avoiding the butts, and pickers-up (dog handlers) sitting watching, well behind the shooters, whose job it is to pick up the shot grouse.

There will be several such 'drives' in a day, usually with a break for lunch. Because this is a more efficient way of covering a given area, more ground can be covered in a day and consequently more grouse flushed than by walking-up. As a result, in spite of the individual grouse flying faster and tending to change direction at the last moment, making them the most challenging game bird in the world to shoot consistently, the bag tends to be larger on a driven day.

It is important to understand that grouse are entirely wild. They live where they want to live and they take flight when they want to take flight. Walking-up only works because their instinct is often to trust in concealment. If the grouse decide to fly before the shooter is reasonably close, these systems stop working because, by the time the shooter can react, the grouse is already out of range. In August and September most grouse can be approached close enough by a dog and a shooter to make walking-up work most of the time, but as the season progresses the percentage that sit tight declines and before long everything except driven shooting becomes labour in vain.

With driven shooting, later in the season the grouse become easier to get into the air but more inclined to go in the wrong direction. Despite this, it is at least still possible to shoot successfully. So, while the legal season is the same, the practical season for driven shooting is longer than for walking-up. The cost is also different. Because of the large number of people who need to be paid to make the day work, a driven day is far more expensive to put on. That is balanced by the fact that a driven grouse is such a difficult and exciting game bird to shoot consistently, and consequently the most valuable, whereas walked-up grouse are not usually as challenging and do not command as high a price.

I have not had a lifetime shooting grouse. I celebrated my sixty-third birthday by driving almost the length of England to Otterburn Towers Hotel, with the plan of shooting my first-ever grouse the following day. I arrived in the midst of a tempest, with rain falling in lumps and a wedding in full flow. It was immediately apparent that a large section of the wedding party was reaching the excitable stage, so I went straight to bed and fell asleep with the rain hammering on the windows and people running up and down the corridor screaming. I'm a good sleeper, especially after a horrendous drive in the rain, and I awoke eight hours later, and wondered what the noise was. The screaming had gone, but the rain still lashed the window panes. When I opened the curtains I could just see through the murk that the little River Rede was half a mile wide. Not the sight I was hoping for.

I had never met my host, Martin Edgar, a friend of my cousin Sinclair, or any of his friends who were also shooting, and I was fairly certain that the day would be cancelled as shooting anything in a howling gale and torrents of rain would be impossible. So I packed my stuff, loaded the car and waited for the inevitable, 'Sorry, when you have come so far but I'm sure you understand.'

I had gravely underestimated Martin: 'Don't be ridiculous. Of course we will shoot. It could be worse.' I left my car in the hotel car park and got into a vehicle with better road clearance, wondering exactly how it could be worse. But even the 4x4 couldn't get us through a normally tiny tributary of the Rede that had decided that it was more fun flowing over, instead of under, a bridge we had to cross. A second attempt using the main road got us there, by which time it was clear that the only two people still keen to get out into the maelstrom were me and Martin. Even the dogs wanted to stay in the car.

I had assumed that any grouse would be crouched, waterlogged in the lee of a stone wall and said as much, suggesting that we could just creep up on one, shoot it and then we could all go home. Martin explained that the opposite was true. The worse the weather, the wilder the grouse. Grouse are as tough as any wild goose and will sit out even the worst wind and rain in short heather. They don't like pushing into long heather in the wet; it forces water through their feathers and wets and chills their bodies. In the open they just shake themselves every now and again and their bodies stay dry and insulated. Because they are in short heather, they don't try to hide when they are approached, but simply fly. As the wind is so strong they fly down it and reach very high speeds. As it is pouring with rain, and bitterly cold, shooting accuracy suffers. So I had been dealt just about the worst hand possible and I had an audience whom I had never met before, and who were being dragged around in conditions that would kill a horse, just for me. Apart from that, there was no pressure.

Just to prove the wildness point, as we got out of the cars, a covey sprang from the heather some two hundred yards away and went sweeping down the wind at enormous speed, disappearing in the direction of Newcastle. The moor was magnificent: a picture of wild desolation. Few places have as many moods as a moor. I love the drowsy, bee-heavy days of summer, when your boots are dusted with pollen, and the spring mornings, with the wonderful soundscape of curlew, golden plover and, if you are very lucky, the bubble and squeak of black grouse. But there is something uniquely exciting about moorland when it is obviously trying to kill you or, at the very least, drive you back where you belong. This was one of those days, when the wind was so strong you had to turn your head to inhale and the rain drove in one side and out the other.

We formed a line and began to trudge into the wind, hardly able to see. After half an hour we had put up several grouse, but all were out of range. Then a single bird rose out of the heather and went tearing across my rear at about the limit of my range. I fired two pointless barrels at it and missed by a fast bowler's run up. I opened the gun to reload and a covey rose a hundred yards in front and came straight over me. If I'd had a tennis racket instead of an empty gun, I would have got my first grouse. We trudged on. Everything went wrong. I missed again. Then I couldn't get the safety catch off because my hands were not functioning. I fell over just as a covey rose in easy range. The list of 'God help me, who is this idiot' incidents grew in length and severity. Martin took it all in good part and the others kindly pretended to.

At last, after three hours of purgatory, when all seemed lost and we were walking across the wind in the general direction of the cars, someone to my left flushed a small covey, they came racing across my front and I sent my first grouse crashing into the heather. That was that, we got back to the cars and then to the hotel. I changed in the gents, put my entire ensemble into two bin liners and went to express my extreme gratitude by buying everyone a drink. The recipients of my largesse were the first fragment of the grouse shooting community that I had encountered at first hand. They were not rich, nor were they aristocratic. You could have put a stranger amongst them and they might have taken them for golfers, or rugby fans, or fishermen. In that, the stranger would have been right: all those interests were represented in that little group, but it was their love of the grouse and its pursuit and the places it frequents that bound them together and it was a community I was happy to join.

I had, of course, known some grouse shooters before I shot my first grouse and, once word got out that I was interested, a very old friend invited me to shoot driven grouse on his moor in Cheshire. I instantly accepted, not only because I had never shot driven grouse before, but because I was keen to see his grouse moor, which he had created from scratch or, more correctly, from a large expanse of upland pasture. As he said himself, when he had the idea of creating a grouse moor, the nearest heather was in a garden centre in Macclesfield. You would not have known by the look of it. When we walked out to the first set of butts, it looked as though it had been a driven moor since time out of mind. In reality, that day was the first time it would ever be shot over. The grouse that had colonised it had been left for several years to develop a population that would allow a sustainable harvest and today was to be a first for me and the moor.

I had read the books, seen the videos and talked it through with everybody I knew who could tell me what to do. As a result I was completely confused. I settled into my butt, which was like a large, upended pallet, painted green, and awaited events. The sun was shining, larks and pipits pottered about and in the far distance I could make out a tiny flag or two as the beaters descended into dead ground. A few little black dots materialised in the periphery of my vision. I turned to see what sort of insects they might be and was confronted by a covey of grouse hurling themselves through the landscape in the general direction of my head.

It was too late to shoot them in front so I turned to shoot them behind, only to see them dip below the horizon before I could get the gun to my shoulder. Brilliant, what a farce. I could only hope no one had noticed, but even that was ridiculous – everyone was watching. The next covey struck the line of butts at a shallow angle and a couple of shots from my neighbour told me they were coming and I shot at the nearest as they swept passed and, by some miracle, my first driven grouse was in the bag. We finished the day with a total bag of eight brace, of which I shot three, but we had a great time and I went home to eat my first driven grouse, which happily tasted as good as the walked-up one – as they always do.

Is there an identifiable grouse shooting community? Yes, of course. How big is it? That depends on how you define the community. If it is limited to those who actually own and manage grouse moors, it is measured in hundreds, and as that number would include the RSPB, it is probably not the most useful way to look at it.

What about the people who shoot grouse? Well, that's measured in tens of thousands, but it still excludes the much larger number who otherwise participate in the sport: the keepers, beaters, flankers, drivers, caterers, dog handlers, and camp followers – they would take it to hundreds of thousands. However, the number associated with grouse shooting is still bigger because you have the publicans, hoteliers, shopkeepers and to that you can add the spouses and offspring of all the above and the number gets bigger again. You have the even larger number of people who shoot other things, pheasants, pigeons or partridge, but who are grouse shooters in their hearts and who read about it and dream of one day having a chance to do it.

If you define it by place, you get a different answer. There are village schools that would close without grouse shooting, and hotels that depend on the months of August to October to put the icing on the cake, and many places where the loss of grouse shooting would cause real problems for small rural communities. But the moors are generally the most inhospitable parts of the landscape. They may be beautiful but they are not going to grow corn and make beasts or men fat. The populations in many of these places are inevitably small by city standards and, whilst there may be a significant number who work full- or part-time thanks to the grouse, it will still be a smaller number than the average viewing figures for *East Enders* or *Big Brother*.

Whichever way you look at it, the grouse shooting community is, as those who wish to destroy their way of life constantly tell anyone who will listen, a minority. Why wouldn't they be, and what's wrong with being in a minority anyway? If our interests relate, as they do, to a rare landscape and the harvesting of the sustainable surplus produced annually by a wild bird only found in that landscape, how could we be anything else? Fortunately we live in one of the most sophisticated democracies in the world. One of the fundamental tenets of our democracy is that the majority protects the rights and interests of minorities. Our system recognises that being different, believing differently, and being in a cultural minority, does not allow the majority to force that minority to conform to their opinions and views.

That the grouse shooting community is a cultural minority is beyond doubt. Even its detractors agree. Their endless work at isolating and demonising the community only makes sense if they see us as a discrete minority with a recognised and recognisable culture.

So what are the beliefs that are held by this community?

- ❖ They believe that participating in grouse shooting, either directly or vicariously, is an essential and entirely beneficial part of their chosen way of life.

- ❖ They believe that the management of heather moorland for grouse, in a way that facilitates their chosen way of life, is the principal reason that these beautiful places still exist.

- ❖ They believe that grouse shooting compares favourably with any other system of producing meat, in terms of the quality of life of the animal concerned and the benefits it generates to biodiversity and the environment.

- ❖ They believe that without grouse shooting there would be far fewer ground-nesting birds, and that rare species and eco-systems would be lost.

- ❖ They believe that grouse shooting and grouse moor management are an essential part of both the culture and the economy of the areas in which they take place.

- ❖ They believe that we cannot just 'let nature take care of itself' but, rather, we have a duty to do what is needed to maintain a healthy balance of species, and maintain rare habitats, without which action many would simply disappear.

- ❖ They believe that they have as much right to enjoy their chosen way of life as anyone else. They understand that some people may not approve of what they do, that the list of what people disapprove of is a long one, that they are free to do so, and they are not forced to participate in grouse shooting or grouse moor management.

- ❖ They believe that they are as law-abiding as any other community, that their behaviour is ethically sound and that their way of life is in no way morally inferior to that of the many millions of citizens who pay others to kill livestock and fish for their culinary pleasure.

- ❖ They believe that members of their community should be allowed, as other cultural minorities are, to continue to live the life of their choosing, within the law, without being attacked, demonised, stigmatised, harassed or discriminated against.

It might seem ridiculous to suggest that grouse shooting is a belief system, but all of the beliefs listed are held by the individuals who identify themselves as a recognisable community. What else is it? After all, the courts recently recognised veganism, which is a set of particular dietary choices, as a belief. The court also ruled that, as such, those believing in veganism should not be harassed or discriminated against on the basis of their belief. Why is the grouse shooting community different?

In fact, the grouse shooting community is not even seeking what has been afforded the vegan believers. That group got separate fridges for vegan food in the workplace, and the right to absent themselves from the workplace if there is a risk that they might encounter meat. We, on the other hand, don't want employees to have grouse shooting breaks or employers being forced to have a grouse option in the canteen.

The grouse shooting community should be treated like any other cultural minority. It should be protected from generalised and gratuitous abuse and demonisation. We are tired of being called barbarians, scumbags, psychopaths and criminals. No other identifiable minority can be treated like this with impunity. Remember the blog asking its followers to send in collective nouns for gamekeepers? We are tired of the lazy and casual language that damns a community on the basis of unsubstantiated allegations, or wild extrapolation from an individual to thousands of people who have never heard of them and do not agree with their actions. Remember the steady and skilfully orchestrated dissemination of generalised half-truths and assertions by even the apparently respectable elements in the conservation industry and ask yourself, 'How long would this be tolerated with any other minority?'

One of the difficulties that has to be faced by grouse shooting is that it can be very expensive and most big, productive grouse moors are owned by rich people. This should surprise no one. It is the universal experience of mankind that rich people own things that are expensive to buy and costly to maintain, whilst the rest of us don't. Curiously, almost uniquely, the direct consequence of this universal truth is, in the case of grouse shooting, a cause of celebration. This is not a private Cornish beach, a walled luxury home or even a hyper-exclusive golf course. It is heather moorland, one of the world's rarest and most precious habitats; it is somewhere that we are all allowed to visit for lawful recreation and it produces a range of public goods. All of this is provided and maintained at the expense of the owner. Exactly, why is that a bad thing?

The most obvious equivalent one can find in ordinary life is a football club. No one is surprised, alarmed or finds it reprehensible that a football club is owned by someone rich. Manchester City FC is hardly likely to be owned by a syndicate from the local supermarket. Who cares? Nobody. Why should they? The fact that a rich person is pouring his own money into the team you support is a cause for celebration, not complaint. The only difference from a grouse moor, is that, unlike football, you don't have to pay anything at all when you turn up to enjoy yourself on a Saturday afternoon. What is the problem?

That said, not all grouse shooters are rich. The cost of a day's grouse shooting is very variable. Walked-up days with no beaters, pickers-up and other staff, with a small bag, often let on the poorer, less productive edges of the moors, can be had for the price of family meal at a good restaurant. There are quite a lot of small moors which are run by do-it-yourself cooperatives at a reasonable cost. Of course, the big, driven days are expensive – they have to be; there are beaters, pickers-up, loaders and flankers to be paid, not to mention the catering, and people driving the cross-country vehicles to get everyone into position. If you add to that the cost of actually running the moor for the bulk of the year, when it is not being shot, there is a lot of money being spent one way or another. Money that could come from no other source than grouse shooting, and money that almost entirely stays within a few miles of where it is spent, in some of the most economically challenged parts of rural Britain.

If a farmer's son or a young woman from the village goes out for a day's beating, not only have they had a great day out with friends, they've met people who they would never have encountered otherwise. They have been to places to which they wouldn't normally go. They will have seen lots of wildlife. They've vicariously enjoyed the sport and they've been paid for their efforts. There is no other activity that could take place on that land that can match this. The chances of getting any other recreational user of that moor to pay a penny to anyone is zero. The chances of any other recreational activity even trying to involve the local community, let alone paying them, is even less.

Where grouse shooting takes place, it is part of a complex web of community. It is not the only thing. There will be farming, shepherding, other sorts of game shooting, maybe forestry or fishing, cricket, football, market, pubs, the parish church, the school and all the things that make up the life of remote but interconnected and robust rural communities. There will be sheep and pheasants, cattle and grouse, and countless birds and mammals, some extremely rare, and some very common. There will be moors, and woods and wildflower meadows and bogs and burns and rivers. All of this, and the people who live there and the different shades of interest they take in everything that makes up that place, matters, and they have a right to be there.

It is in the interests of those who attack grouse shooting to isolate and stereotype the community. They intentionally create two-dimensional caricatures that can be progressively ridiculed and demonised. In their view, grouse moor owners are rich, uncaring despoilers of the landscape, gamekeepers are, to quote the RSPB, armed gangs of criminals, turning our moorlands into industrial landscapes. None of this is true. These people are as reasonable and complex as any other community. There is, of course, no interest from within the conservation industry in doing anything that might risk diluting these stereotypes, but there is ample evidence that shows they are unjustified. The GWCT publication *Moorland Conservationists, The Untold Story*[1], provides case studies that show that the owners and gamekeepers, so casually and persistently traduced, are frequently the exact opposite of their cartoon image. GWCT's recently published *Community Spirit*[2], which deals with attitudes and opinions of the shooting community in Wales, shows a complex, caring, environmentally engaged cross-section of the whole of Welsh society a long way from these caricatures.

The study led by Professor Denny of the impacts that integrated moorland management, including grouse shooting, have on moorland communities had some interesting things to say about these communities:

> Compared to national data, respondents that live in moorland communities we surveyed have a stronger sense of belonging, strong social networks, lower levels of loneliness, greater sense of job security and a strong sense of identity based on a shared heritage and culture, with those involved in grouse shooting in any role having statistically significant higher levels of wellbeing. All these factors are associated with more positive health and wellbeing outcomes. We think this is extraordinarily interesting.[3]

Any reasonable person must find extraordinary the idea that people from outside this community, who have no knowledge of, or interest in, its complexity or its values, feel that it is acceptable to turn up, and say, 'We will tolerate most of what you lot do, at least for the moment, but not you grouse shooters, we find you morally repugnant, you've got to go', which is essentially what is happening.

Incredibly, if grouse moor management and grouse shooting took place in France or Italy or Spain, we would have more chance of protection for our community and its culture. This is because these countries signed the United Nations Educational, Social and Cultural Organisation (UNESCO) 2003 treaty that recognised Intangible Cultural Heritage (ICH). For some strange reason the UK did not. The treaty defines ICH as:

> ... the practices, representations, expressions, knowledge, skills – as well as the instruments, objects, artefacts and cultural spaces, associated therewith – that communities, groups and, in some cases, individuals recognise as part of their cultural heritage. This intangible cultural heritage, transmitted from generation to generation, is constantly re-created by communities and groups in response to their environment, their interaction with nature and their history, and provides them with a sense of identity and continuity, thus promoting respect cultural diversity and human creativity.

In summary

❖ *There is an identifiable grouse moor community. It is made up of respectable people from all walks of life and they are no more or less law-abiding and moral than every other identifiable minority.*

- ❖ *This community gets a great deal from its engagement with grouse shooting and its wider effects. Its members' sense of well-being and community is enhanced by their involvement.*

- ❖ *The community is one of the few that are routinely demonised by otherwise respectable charitable organisations, in a manner that would hardly be tolerated with any other group.*

17. Economics

If we look at the economics of my moorland, each ewe will have an average of 1.5 lambs worth £40 each in the market. So each ewe can produce £60 income. You can have one sheep on four acres of moor without doing damage to the land. You can have a pair of grouse on four acres and they average 6 or 7 young. Their value is £80–100 per bird each. For a thousand acres of moorland you can earn £15,000 from sheep, or £120,000 from grouse. On a well farmed moor grouse provide a much better return. In addition, whereas for 1000 ewes you need one full-time worker, you need a full-time worker for every 500 brace of grouse. Because grouse produce such a good return, you employ more staff, and they have families and live locally. Cattle are less profitable than sheep due to the overheads such as silage, sheds, machinery, etc. However, cattle improve the land for ground-nesting birds including curlew, lapwing, woodcock. Cattle work brilliantly as part of an integrated system.

Farmer and landowner, North Yorkshire

Grouse shooting occurs on some of the poorest land in Britain, so the question becomes whether driven grouse shooting is the best use of this land in economic terms. This is a hard question to answer because, whilst grouse shooting survives only because of private investment, farming and forestry survive only because of public investment. The wider environmental damage (in terms of erosion, downstream flooding and acidification) caused by these three activities is much less from grouse shooting than from hill farming or forestry, but clearly varies between areas.

... much of the private income that goes into grouse shooting enters the local economy, supporting people in some remote areas where alternative employment is scarce. This includes not only people involved in grouse management, but those working in hotels and other local businesses. Grouse shooting and other game shooting undoubtedly attracts some people to the uplands when other visitors are scarce, and further adds to the cash flow from the city to the countryside.

Ian Newton OBE, FRS, FRSE and former chairman of the RSPB in *Uplands and Birds* (2020)

ANOTHER CONTENTIOUS ISSUE is the economic impact of grouse shooting and grouse moor management. The opponents dismiss the idea that grouse shooting has any economic significance by pointing to the self-evident fact, that, whatever contribution it makes, it can only ever be trivial on a national scale because of the vast size of Britain's economy. While this is true, it is also pointless, as the same could be said for a myriad small and medium-sized businesses. Individually each is of only local significance, but together they make up one of the key drivers of a successful economy. None, including grouse shooting, should be destroyed on a prejudiced whim. The economic impact of grouse moor management is essentially local, but that arguably makes it more important rather than less. More than almost any other business, the money from grouse shooting comes into the immediate locality and stays there.

Let us compute a typical day. Nine people shooting and a bag of 100 brace. This will cost them £180 plus VAT per brace, so the estate will receive £18,000 and the tax man £3,600. In addition, the shooters, known as 'guns', will pay for loaders who will get £90–110 each. They will also tip the keepers around £100. Thus the total funds going directly into the estate and its full- and part-time employees is around £20,000. The guns would normally stay in a local hotel on the nights before and after shooting, so if we take a conservative estimate of £200 a night for dinner and accommodation and then add in the drinks bill you are probably near to £5,000. Thus, just one day's driven grouse shooting has injected £25,000 into the local economy.

The high cost of driven grouse shooting is not simply a result of demand exceeding supply. There are a lot of people to pay. There are the beaters who walk miles across the moors trying to get the grouse to fly over the butts, the pickers-up who bring their dogs to collect the shot birds, and many others, who all have to be paid for their day's work. Most importantly there is also the endless day-to-day management, which obviously includes the full-time keeping staff, but also a wide range of local businesses and craftsmen. So the money goes round and round a largely closed loop within the community. This, it must be remembered, is just one day. In a good year, when the grouse have bred well and there is a good harvestable surplus, on a large moor there may be many days, each one contributing similar amounts to the local economy. If there are a hundred days like this, spread over all the moors in a dale – and there may well be more in a good year – that is £2.5 million flowing into the local community.

But this is only the direct economic benefit and the easiest to compute. The income from the shooting and the direct costs of the keepers and contractors and rents and fees are only the tip of a financial iceberg whose scale is almost impossible to calculate. To the obvious elements must be added other important layers of value and worth. How much are hundreds of curlew, lapwing and redshank worth? What is the value of the landscape, the privately maintained public access, the enhanced quality of the retail and hospitality sector in remote locations that, without the grouse, would have difficulty keeping a shop open? How can a value be put on the human health benefits of eradicating toxic bracken and reducing the risks of a lethal tick bite? Is anyone ever going to put a value on the eco-system services the moors provide? The clean water, the carbon safely stored, the river flow modulation, even the well-being these magnificent places engender – all are literally priceless, but currently have no value. All are provided free by the people who manage the grouse moors at their own expense.

There is simply nothing that can replace this level of economic activity if it disappears. Most of the things that are suggested as alternatives already exist alongside grouse shooting. Grazing sheep and cattle and tourism would not increase in the absence of grouse moor management and might decline if traditional management were stopped. Forestry and wind turbines would generate income but all the regular money would go to the landowner. There would be a short period using peripatetic, specialist contractors, focused around construction and planting. There might be a burst of spending in the local hotels for a few months and then nothing.

It is, of course, true that grouse shooting will not single-handedly save the nation's economy but it does make a significant contribution to the local economy where it occurs. That is essentially all we can ask of any business. What is more, the money that flows into these communities is private money, freely given and taxed. It is not the public funds that keep the conservation industry's efforts at moorland management afloat. Remember the scale of the alternative. A figure of €7 million to kill Orkney stoats, £6 million not to rid the Uists of hedgehogs, over £3 million lottery money not to stop curlew, hen harriers, merlin and red grouse disappearing from Lake Vyrnwy. Millions to re-wet and re-vegetate moors that are now burnt and blackened.

Perhaps the last words on the impact of grouse shooting and grouse moor management should go to Professor Denny:

> Communities in areas where integrated moorland management, including grouse shooting, is practised have a more diverse economy, and are less reliant on tourism than comparable upland areas where land management practices do not include grouse shooting.
>
> The study concludes that integrated moorland management, including grouse shooting, results in a complex web of economic, social and intangible benefits that can have direct and indirect financial benefits.

In summary

❖ *It is beyond doubt that grouse shooting, especially driven grouse shooting, is an important source of income in the areas where it occurs.*

❖ *The money that flows into grouse shooting is largely private and stays in the immediate locality.*

❖ *Some activities, such as forestry, and conservation in various forms, rely to a large degree on public finance. Others, such as energy generation, will generate income but very little will enter the local community.*

18. Ethics and politics

The council met monthly, and halfway through they used to break for what was called tea. It is actually a very fine three-course buffet dinner with a range of cooked main courses, and, if you wanted it, wine. Senior officers were expected to attend. Some dived into the food with as much enthusiasm as the elected members, but I always limited myself to a cup of tea. I can't say I ever really enjoyed it, not because the people weren't pleasant and engaging – a lot of them were – but because I always felt I was at someone else's party.

I was sipping my tea, and chatting to some Labour councillors, when a colleague turned up and, seeing a chance to cause me some grief, asked if I wasn't eating because there was no pheasant on the menu. This set off a somewhat disjointed discussion about the moral destitution of game shooting, which I did my best to keep out of. Telling someone who may decide your future career that they are talking hypocritical nonsense has always been an option I've sought to avoid.

Luckily the little weasel who started all this was joining the fray between mouthfuls of chicken curry, so I could deal with him and not the councillors. When he finally stuffed another piece of chicken in his mouth, I explained to the councillors that I rarely ate chicken and never at the council house. But I did eat game I had shot myself whenever I could. The reason was that I rather thought killing a 32-day-old animal just so I could enjoy eating its tender young body, seemed a little harsh. Furthermore, as some time before they were elected, their colleagues had, in their wisdom, voted in favour of a motion to serve only halal chicken and lamb at tea, whilst I had no view on others eating it, my personal choice, based on having inspected a variety of slaughterhouses in my younger days, was not to do so. On the other hand the pheasants I enjoyed pursuing and eating were full grown, in their natural environment and died in a manner far better than the most fortunate chicken.

He was going on about the absolute necessity of eating tender young animals, when a senior member of the Labour group, who I knew was a vegetarian, walked past. I pulled him into our little group and asked him to settle our argument: 'Chairman, do we, as David is suggesting, eat chicken from necessity?' He said, 'Of course you bloody don't. What a stupid idea.' My tormentor was still trying, and said, 'Yes, Chairman, but would you rather be a chicken or a pheasant.?' What he got back was not what either of us expected: 'God, David, what are you on tonight? A pheasant, every time.' You never know where you are going to find a friend.

S.C., West Midlands

WHEN GROUSE SHOOTING, or any form of shooting for that matter, is attacked it seeks, not unreasonably, to defend itself by pointing out the consequences of stopping it: the lost employment, the reduced biodiversity, and the environmental damage. In the particular case of grouse shooting, those seeking its curtailment or abolition have lately sought to say, albeit erroneously, that these losses do not matter, as grouse shooting is itself inimical to conservation. But now, when faced with a perfect grouse moor, sequestering carbon, producing pure water from a restored water table, groaning under the weight of breeding curlew, black grouse and redshank, and loved by the community who live by it and take recreation upon it, replete with every designation, it doesn't matter. The thing that matters is 'we think it's immoral and unethical'. It doesn't matter that the consequence of indulging an ill-informed prejudice is an ecological, economic and cultural disaster. *We*, whoever 'we' are, don't like what you do, and we have the power to force you to stop it and we will.

Thus, the biggest question may not be about biodiversity, or culture, or carbon or the economy. It may be about morality and ethics. We have had some warnings that this will be the case. The Welsh Assembly spent a lot of taxpayers' money on a review of shooting on their land. The state regulator (NRW) took a mass of evidence, and produced a comprehensive report, which showed that shooting on state land had many benefits and virtually no disadvantages, and recommended a continuation of the *status quo*. The relevant Minister completely ignored it and banned shooting anyway, on the grounds that it was immoral and unethical. So it happens. It is not a hypothetical position and it deserves careful consideration.

Morals have certain characteristics: they have to be both absolute and universal. If it applies to me, it has to apply to you. If it is wrong for me to fiddle my expenses, it is wrong for anyone, even politicians. Theft is theft, whoever does it and whatever form it takes.

If you apply these tests to killing mammals, birds and fish, it is undoubtedly true that people in the grouse shooting community derive pleasure and enjoyment from an activity that involves the killing of sentient creatures. But then so do a lot of other people. Whilst a few thousand grouse end up on the plate each year, they are a tiny fragment of what is killed for the pleasure and enjoyment of human beings. In the UK we kill 2.2 million chickens every day, the majority of which, far from enjoying the freedom of the heather moors, live all their seven or eight weeks of life indoors. No one – not even a Welsh Minister – has yet been found who eats the bodies of these birds from necessity. The existence of healthy vegetarians and vegans demonstrates, beyond all doubt and argument, that we eat chicken because it gives us pleasure.

Of course we also derive nutritional benefits, but we could get them without killing something that has been alive for a few weeks of an intended lifespan of around eight years. Of course, in the vast majority of cases, people who eat chicken didn't kill the chickens themselves, whereas I kill my own dinner – but attempting to use that as an escape route from moral responsibility is obviously shameful. As a position of pretended ethical superiority, it would not even stand comparison with Al Capone believing he had nothing to do with the St. Valentine's Day Massacre, because he only told the boys what to do, but avoided pulling the trigger himself. At least I can be sure that my dinner has lived a natural life, that its existence contributed to sustainable management of the landscape and that it was killed where it lived, in as humane a way as practicable. Anyone who thinks any of those things apply to their Chicken Kiev needs to strengthen their grip on reality.

Support for this view comes, ironically, from those most desperate to see the end of all shooting, let alone grouse shooting – the animal rights activists, in organisations like the Moorland Monitors. They are very clear, at least in private and amongst themselves, that killing any mammal, bird, fish or invertebrate, for any reason, is the moral equivalent of murder. The declaration of animal rights to which they subscribe could not be clearer. It states that 'All sentient creatures have the right to life, liberty and the pursuit of natural enjoyments.' I don't agree with a word of it but it is unquestionably clear, and it puts me in one rational position and them in another. Unfortunately it leaves the Welsh minister swinging in the wind. Both sides think she is an awful hypocrite. The only difference is that the other side are prepared to keep quiet about her hypocrisy as long as she is prepared to help them to take another little step on the way to their ultimate goal, ending the use of any sentient creature for the benefit of humanity, whereas the honest, law-abiding and entirely moral citizens she has casually abused, may not be.

There are, of course, people, vegans and fruitarians, who have abandoned all use of animal products and their position has to be respected. It is an ethical choice, and it demonstrates beyond any doubt that eating and using the bodies and products of animals, birds and fish is indulged in by the overwhelming majority of adult human beings from choice. But does the abstinence by such people from using animal products justify them trying to stop what I and my community do? Of course not. Does the fact that I choose not to eat bivalve shellfish make those who do immoral? Does someone being teetotal mean that drinking wine is unethical? Of course not. It is a free country and they are free to abstain from what I choose to do and I would not dream of trying to force them to do otherwise. Conversely, the fact that they choose to live differently from my own community neither gives them a position of moral superiority nor the right to force me to change my way of life to conform to a morality and ethical code that I do not share.

Shooting game is not evil or immoral; it stands on the same moral basis as enjoying eating meat and fish. People who object to either activity are not entitled to assert moral superiority on that basis. Furthermore, they are no more likely to be generally 'good', in a moral sense, or in their behaviour towards other human beings, than those of us who enjoy hunting.

The Mayor of Liverpool, Mr Anderson, led a campaign of unrestrained invective against game shooting in 2019, calling people who enjoyed shooting, amongst other things, barbarians, and made it clear that they were not welcome in that city. He was also one of the politicians who had supported the campaign to get the public research university of that great city named 'Liverpool John Moore's University', in honour of a great philanthropist and benefactor to innumerable good causes over many years. Mr Anderson fully recognised Sir John Moore's humanity, kindness and generosity. What he appears to have been unaware of was that Sir John was a very keen game shooter, and so, according to Mr Anderson, would, if he were alive today, be both a barbarian and unwelcome in the city to which he gave so much.

In this context it is of course hardly worth mentioning the well-known antipathy to hunting of famous humanitarians such as Hitler and Pol Pot. But what is less well known on the other side of the coin is that Nelson Mandela enjoyed hunting. A love of hunting, or a profound antipathy to it, are life choices, with no more moral relevance than keeping a cat, and are no more an indication of someone's character or moral status than playing golf or eating seafood.

Why does any of this matter? Who cares if people who shoot grouse are accused, rightly or wrongly of being immoral or unethical, simply because we kill our own dinners? What's the problem? The problem is that this mixture of half-baked morality, casual abuse and hypocrisy, when combined with clever and aggressive campaigning, can lead to decisions being made that could destroy a way of life and the support system for one of the world's rarest habitats and the rare species it supports.

The Welsh Minister's decision is a case in point. She was encouraged to indulge her personal prejudice by the usual online petition. This pretended to show that there was overwhelming support in Wales for stopping shooting. The abolitionists are adept at these tactics and the Minister's position was bolstered by a 12,000-signature petition showing that the people of Wales were strongly in favour of stopping shooting. There was another petition on a government website that called for more rigorous personal checks to prevent multiple voting, and this only reached a less striking total of 119. But 12,000 is a lot. However, later analysis showed that 88% of them did not live in Wales and 8% did not even live in the UK. Of the huge total, just over a thousand had Welsh postcodes. Thus, what seemed like overwhelming support from the people of Wales turned out to be little more than a convenient fiddle. But it enabled the Minister to calm any of her colleagues who thought there might be problems in marginal rural seats as a result of her indulging her personal view, that people who shoot are her, and her party's, moral and ethical inferiors.

How this played out in the subsequent election is a matter for speculation, although it is a fact that her party did badly in rural marginals. What needs to be considered is that there are far, far more people who shoot in Wales than are campaigning to ban it. Noise and numbers are very different things. In England and Wales there are about three-quarters of a million shotgun and firearm certificate holders. The numbers for Wales are not separated, but in a rural country, it can be assumed that they have their fair share. Indeed, Dyfed and Powys have the second highest shotgun certificate holder level in the whole of England and Wales, at 2637 per 100,000 population. This means that a typical Welsh parliamentary constituency of around 56,000 electors is likely to have more shooting people voting in it than were mustered from the whole of Wales to support the petition. Why would any sensible politician go out of their way to casually offend over a thousand of their electorate? The problem is that most politicians, even open-minded ones, have little first- hand knowledge of most things, and can be persuaded by skilful lobbyists, especially, when what is proposed fits in with their personal prejudices.

There is no evidence that being against game or grouse shooting wins elections for politicians – indeed on the current evidence it appears, unsurprisingly, to be the reverse. Unsurprising, because taking such a position implies moral superiority. This is always a dangerous thing for a fallible human being to do and it is something that many electors will find hard to stomach, from any politician, let alone one who has no interest in their lives beyond the caricatures promoted by the people who hate them. While the grouse shooting community is a minority, it has many friends, far more than many urban politicians realise, and is, in any event, far bigger, certainly in many key marginals, than the tiny number of dedicated keyboard warriors who cleverly create the impression of an abolitionist army where none exists.

Politicians need to be aware that, perhaps uniquely, the people who shoot grouse and manage the nation's rare and beautiful heather uplands want absolutely nothing from them. All the community wants is to be allowed to carry on enjoying their culture, as they have done for so long. They want to continue to help each other through good times and bad, as they have always done. They want to spend their own money on the things they love. Just left alone, they will maintain rare and beautiful landscapes. They will keep populations of rare birds safe. They will continue to put out wildfires. Their moors will produce pure water, provide recreation and put millions of pounds into delicate rural economies. What is wrong, immoral or unethical about that?

I freely admit that the reason I go grouse shooting is that I enjoy it. I do not consider that makes me wicked or evil, nor do I believe that I am too stupid to understand that there is an ethical dimension to my chosen way of life. No one is forced to shoot grouse, any more than they are forced to eat chicken.

If the grouse shooting community's actions hurt other people, then there might be a case for interfering in their lives, but they do not. On the contrary, on balance, what they do enhances the lives of millions unaware of the benefits that accrue from the actions of the moorland communities. Of course, not every single person in the community behaves as they should. Of course, some let the side down. But laws exist to deal with them, as they do throughout society, and the existence of an occasional wrongdoer cannot justify the condemnation of a whole way of life.

People who hunt and fish are almost the only people who are asked why they do what they do. I do lots of things unconnected with shooting, and I discuss lots of things with lots of people. Apart from shooting, and sometimes fishing, whilst people may ask how or where, they never ask why. The only answer I ever give to the question 'Why do you shoot grouse?' is that I absolutely love it. It is one of the best things I ever do. I love the company of the people I do it with, and the places I do it in. The reasons why people should not interfere with my freedom to do it and put at risk the manifest advantages that come from people doing it, are a different matter. I do it for the love of it and that is the truth.

In summary

❖ *Morals are absolute and universal. If they are not, they are simply prejudice in disguise. For someone who pays others to kill 30-day-old chickens so that they can enjoy eating their tender young bodies to complain about others enjoying shooting their own dinner is the essence of hypocrisy.*

- *If every interaction between humans and animals currently occurring in the UK were examined in detail, taking account of the whole life experience of the creature concerned, grouse shooting would be one of the least open to criticism.*

- *Politicians are misled by noise, especially when what is asserted is in line with their personal prejudices. It is wiser to take a more balanced view.*

- *In a liberal democracy our elected representatives are traditionally expected to avoid inflicting their prejudices on minority groups whose lifestyle choices do no harm to others.*

- *It is entirely reasonable for someone to dislike shooting game, and therefore decide not to take part. It is neither reasonable nor right for such people to seek to force others to conform to their pretended moral position.*

19. What should happen

The following are opinions of residents of Llanwddyn at Lake Vyrnwy who took part in a community consultation in 2010 on the possible change of ownership of the estate:

- *'I strongly believe that the RSPB partnership will have a huge detrimental impact on the community and the estate.'*
- *'The rumour that the RSPB may acquire the estate is a recipe for continuing disaster. Just look at the mess they have created.'*
- *'The RSPB have done little for the community in thirty years.'*
- *'I hope whoever buys the estate will manage it better than Severn Trent and RSPB have done in the past.'*
- *'Please keep the RSPB out – they are a self-centred organisation and care little for the community.'*
- *'What benefits have RSPB brought to the local community?'*
- *'The RSPB is useless to all but a few.'*
- *'I strongly feel that an independent buyer would benefit the local people of Llanwddyn, with a good estate manager, something that has not happened when in the hands of RSPB.'*
- *'I think RSPB have upset far too many locals and made too many mistakes.'*
- *'RSPB first made their appearance thirty years ago and personally I have seen no positive impact towards the people of Llanwddyn.'*
- *'It would be the final nail in the coffin if RSPB take over.'*
- *'I would like to see Llanwddyn run by brand new management, a*

new start for Llanwddyn and the people. Not RSPB.'

- *'It would be a blessing if RSPB were not involved in the future, so we can have a future.'*
- *'If RSPB buy the lease will they have the money to invest?'*
- *'Not interested in RSPB.'*
- *'RSPB is the worst thing that came to the area.'*
- *'Whoever ends up purchasing the estate will need to have a good rapport with the local community and this is one of the worries I have with RSPB.'*
- *'I would not like the RSPB to run Lake Vyrnwy.'*
- *'No to RSPB; got to be a new owner.'*
- *'The RSPB are not farmers and bring no jobs.'*
- *'The RSPB have done nothing for the estate, only looked after themselves.'*
- *'Hopefully the RSPB is not successful in the bid.'*
- *'Great if RSPB take over half the estate.'*
- *'The RSPB had the chance to get it right for the locals ... Lake Vyrnwy, beauty has always been here, before RSPB set foot on the place don't change the beauty just change the management.'*
- *'How are RSPB going to run the estate for 125 years? All volunteer labour, it could be a big mess.'*
- *'With RSPB Cymru, maybe the organisation is not as unpopular as the staff they have running the place.'*

ONE OF THE aims of this book is to give a voice to the communities who live and work in the uplands and who have to watch as the conservation industry takes away their heritage and culture, and puts what they love, the landscape and its wildlife, in jeopardy. Only rarely is a community ever asked what they think. Even more rarely do we discover what they said. The only example I can find is provided by the community consultation which took place in the Welsh village of Llanwddyn beside Lake Vyrnwy. The small community was asked their opinion about a possible change of ownership and management of the Lake Vyrnwy reserve, which had by then been run by RSPB for over thirty years. A total of 92 people filled in the survey form, 44 went beyond the ticking of boxes and filled in the free text section to express their views. Of those, 29 specifically mentioned the RSPB.

You have read their views. Who knew? Who cared? What difference did it make to the decision? The RSPB still run the place.

The uplands have become a battle ground. On the one side are the people who have managed these places for generations and whose stewardship has resulted in the safe storage of billions of tonnes of carbon, and the survival, against the odds of one of the world's rarest landscapes and the rare wildlife it supports. On the other side are people who believe that everything that has gone before is anathema and needs to cease immediately. Ideally, they will replace the present owners and, if not, at least tell them how to manage their land. The conservation industry in general, and the RSPB in particular, are intent on winning the battle at whatever cost. Something as trivial to them as the attitude of the people who live there is not going to stand in their way.

Not long ago the RSPB, judging by its actions as well as its words, was of the view that, apart from the vexed matter of raptor persecution, grouse moor management was generally a good thing. If that were not the case, there would have been absolutely no point in them engaging in the Langholm projects. These were intended to discover if it was possible to run a commercially viable driving moor whilst sustaining an extraordinary number of breeding hen harriers. If, at that time, they had thought that everything about grouse moor management was bad, evil and immoral, as they now do, what would have been the point of taking part?

Furthermore, whilst they were involved in Langholm, they were content to see rotational burning taking place, the trapping, snaring and shooting of foxes, stoats and crows, and the farmer applying for a licence to cull ravens. They even occasionally suggested that predator control needed to be stepped up. All that has gone and, along with it, any wish to listen to anything that the people who have created and maintained these wonderful places have to say. Judging by the actions and words of the people who run the RSPB, they consider that the only acceptable outcomes are the end of driven grouse shooting and the end of traditional moorland management. The latter is to be replaced by its own brand of moorland conservation, which specifically excludes the management techniques that have created and maintained the landscape and its unique wildlife.

If they are successful, they can see that the capital value on moorland estates will fall. That will enable the conservation industry to acquire vast swathes of the uplands at prices that any good funding appeal should cover.

If government has been persuaded that people who own moorland that can sequester peat should be paid to do no management and simply watch the carbon accumulate, they can enter a financial golden age.

When the people who have kept these places safe for centuries are proved right, and the huge build-up of fuel results in one catastrophic wildfire after another, this will be just another excuse for an appeal. They won't even get the blame. There will be no awkward grouse moor managers to point out their incompetence, and NE won't say anything because it will be complicit. When the birds disappear, it's another reason to have an appeal for more money.

While the upland communities continue to resist extinction, there is still money to be made – huge amounts of it – and the RSPB is perfectly deployed to take its share. To that can be added mastering the art of getting money on the back of self-confessed failure, and, all the while, appearing so altruistic that there is no need to consider other providers or even to test for value for money.

The sums are vast. The RSPB's 2020 accounts show over £11 million from the UK's governments and quangos, £3 million plus from the EU, and an incredible £4 million from apparently cash-strapped local councils. The RSPB's total grant income was just short of £30 million.

But these figures could be dwarfed by the money that will flow into carbon sequestration. Almost the only things that stand between the RSPB and a gift that will keep on giving, are the grouse moors and their communities. The moor owners and their communities keep pointing out that the prospectus that the RSPB and others are peddling is fatally flawed. What, they ask, is the point of increasing peat depth by, say, a few extra centimetres every thousand years if, as a consequence, in twenty or thirty years' time, you lose far more than can be accumulated in a thousand years to a single wildfire? Where is the evidence that the RSPB can produce more ground- nesting birds? Show us where re-wetting, sensible though it may be, has actually stopped a flood or a wildfire? Excuse me, but didn't Crowden / Winter Hill / Marsden just go up in smoke? If you are so good at curlew conservation, why are there none on Vyrnwy? If you want to see lots of breeding curlew, why not go to a grouse moor?

There are several possible explanations as to why the RSPB has become obsessed with grouse shooting, as distinct from lots of other widespread and more damaging human interactions with the natural world, from forestry, through open-cage salmon farming, to domestic cats that kill millions of small mammals and protected birds every year. It may simply be a combination of personal prejudice in some key individuals and that targeting a minority group with links to rich aristocrats is less risky than going for your own members' pets. The frequently stated cause, the continued persecution of raptors, provides the perfect excuse to belabour anyone and anything associated with grouse, irrespective of all the good that is done, but with raptor populations reaching levels not seen for generations and raptor persecution lower than it has ever been, the virtual eradication of such persecution is a practical goal if all sides worked together.

But, whatever the cause of their outrage, it cannot be denied that if grouse shooting disappears the conservation industry, including the RSPB, can be predicted to benefit hugely as a result. The RSPB has made its position clear, and if it doesn't get grouse moor licensing it will campaign to ban all driven grouse shooting, irrespective of the consequences to upland communities and the retention of rare heather habitat and the special wildlife it supports. In the meantime it campaigns remorselessly against virtually everything that grouse moor managers do and takes common cause with some of the darker exponents of direct action. It is in institutional denial about all the good that grouse moor management achieves and it makes it almost impossible for those who want to do the right thing to be seen as anything but fools.

This is made worse by the RSPB's exponential growth. The RSPB's 1975/76 accounts show a total income of approximately a million pounds. By the time the 2020 accounts were published the annual income had grown to £146 million. The organisation is now 146 times richer than it was in 1975/76. This is the sort of growth you see in a balloon and, like a balloon, as it expands its skin gets thinner and thinner. Even twenty years ago the RSPB still understood, and accepted, the need to work in partnership to win the argument and to persuade. Now it expects obedience.

Grouse moor management has made itself a target partly by answering back. When it has been admonished, it has had the audacity to ask, in effect, 'Who are you to tell us what to do? Show us where you have managed things better than we have?' All that has done is make the opposition angry, and they will have their way, even if every grouse moor has to turn into a Lake Vyrnwy, or a Forsinard, and we have to wave goodbye to rare habitat and wildlife.

As the organisation has grown, so has its appetite for resources and power. The people who have the closest view of what it is like to have the RSPB move into their world, like the good citizens of Llanwddyn, have long since been disenchanted, but what was bad has become worse. The RSPB does not appear to have any time for doubt or self-reflection. Have they ever asked whether they are 146 times 'better' than they were in 1976? Do they have a governance system capable of making a judgement of the magnitude of the one we are discussing?

How do the trustees, who appear to have little practical knowledge or experience of grouse moor management, assisted by a CEO who (as she would probably admit herself) is no better equipped, come to a balanced and considered judgement that their strategic aim should be the destruction of long-established communities and their way of life? By what process did they decide that they would destroy a system of land management that has, for generations, protected one of the earth's rarest habitats and its vast carbon stores, and, perhaps most damning of all, a system that outperforms them in their own core business, the production of rare ground-nesting birds? Well, whatever the system by which they came to their decisions, it did not involve listening to the other side of the argument. I can find no one (and I have searched) who understands grouse moor management from the other side of the fence that the RSPB has built around its trustees, who has been invited or even allowed to discuss these issues with them. When I was Chairman of GWCT, the trustees instructed the CEO to invite the RSPB to visit our research farm at Loddington to discuss its work and anything else they wanted. They didn't even reply.

Remember that the RSPB is not some fringe conservation group. It is the conservation equivalent of the NHS. Huge, loved and trusted. That gives it power beyond even that which its vast resources can buy. But this power should bring with it a greater sense of responsibility. Sadly, where some moorland communities are concerned, it does not.

It is understandable that the RSPB strategists are upset when the organisation is criticised or subjected to slighting comparisons with other land managers. They need to raise around £150 million every year, around a billion pounds every six or seven years, just to feed the monster they have created. These are eye-watering sums. Nothing can be allowed to stand in the way of acquiring money. To be fair, they are very good at raising cash. They should be – they spend a lot on it – over £30 million a year. That is thirty times more than it took, in 1976, to run the entire, respected and effective organisation as it was then. This is a vast sum even by the standards of the conservation industry. To put it into context, in 2020/21the total cost of running the BTO was £6.3 million, around a fifth of the RSPB's fundraising budget, to run one of the most effective and respected ornithological research charities in the world.

We can sympathise with people who are faced with the challenge of raising a million pounds every two or three days, forever, but it cannot justify the crude treatment of the people who currently manage the uplands. In any rational world the best way to improve things is to sit down and discuss what the problems might be, and how everyone can work together to achieve mutual goals. The RSPB has decided to take a different course, and appears to have given up any pretence at engaging with the grouse moor community. They may from time to time claim to be interested in dialogue, but they are no more genuine than the school bully. If you have abused and blackguarded people at every opportunity, can you really expect to be taken seriously when you say you want dialogue? Of course not. On the basis of their actions it is reasonable to assume that the RSPB has lost interest in working with landowners and managers in the uplands.

It appears they have formed the view that a baleful combination of the conservation industry (preferably, but not exclusively, themselves) and their fellow travellers in the statutory agencies will, one way or another, take control of the heather moorlands. The NGOs will acquire as much land as possible and use their friends in the regulators to control the parts they do not yet own or manage. Their strategic aim is that driven grouse shooting will become impossible. That will be achieved by preventing the people who currently manage the land from using the techniques that have made these places what they are in the first place. The people who own and manage these moors, the people whose livelihoods and communities depend on them and who love them, as they have known them for generations, are just so much collateral damage.

This would be bad enough if the people who were planning to take over had a record of excellence in moorland management. But their record, severally and collectively, mostly varies between poor and appalling. The idea that the organisation responsible for Lake Vyrnwy has the nerve to think that they are entitled to take the management of Swaledale or the Angus Glens, or any one of a hundred well-run grouse moors, away from its community and its owners, is simply outrageous.

But couldn't we solve these problems by talking to one another? Is it not possible to reach a consensus about a rational, science-based way forward that allows the grouse moor community to live their lives, and manage their land, more or less as they wish, whilst having clean water, safe carbon storage, beautiful landscapes, masses of ground-nesting birds and raptors? Yes, of course you could and can.

If we take the vexed issue of raptor persecution as an example, there can surely be no doubt that the best and swiftest route to solving the problem is through dialogue. If we turn again to Ian Newton, an ex-chairman of RSPB and no apologist for raptor persecution, he says, in Uplands and Birds, 'Progress requires continued dialogue between the main stake holders and more understanding of the costs, acceptability, legality and feasibility of these different approaches, as well as their environmental, economic and social consequences', and later, 'Only dialogue and compromise on both sides can lessen this conflict.' Amen to that.

Are the organisations, who one way or another can be seen as on the side of the moorland community, prepared for dialogue and compromise? Yes. Does the same apply to the RSPB? Not on the current evidence. They long ago engineered the situation whereby any mention of raptor persecution destroys rational discussion. They will do nothing that risks compromising their most potent weapon. It is the gift that keeps on giving and they will countenance no discussion and no compromise.

Consider hen harriers. The implementation of a long-negotiated plan for the recovery of the species in England, which included the brood-management trial and the southern reintroduction, resulted in the RSPB not just walking out, but launching a judicial review against the trial, hoping to have it destroyed at birth. Having lost that, they went to the Appeal Court to try again. At the same time, according to NE, they used their soft power in France and Spain to starve the hen harrier southern reintroduction trial to death by preventing access to eggs or chicks.

Both the projects they set out to destroy were designed to result in more hen harriers, and both are techniques which have been used by the RSPB with other species. The most plausible explanation for the RSPB's opposition to them is that, having turned the lack of hen harriers into a perfect weapon with which to undermine the legitimacy of grouse moor ownership, it had no intention of seeing it blunted by having more hen harriers about the place. There is little evidence that the RSPB is interested in negotiation and compromise. Such evidence as exists indicates that it is far more interested in control.

Is the RSPB likely to change its stance? Hardly: they have invested a huge amount of resources and reputation into the demonisation of almost everything to do with grouse shooting and grouse moor management, so the current regime would lose too much credibility if they took a single step towards a more balanced view.

In the absence of any realistic prospect of the RSPB engaging in meaningful negotiation or even reappraisal, what can the grouse moor community do to prevent the places they love being taken over by them and the other exponents of their version of bureaucratic and authoritarian conservation?

Manoeuvre is pointless before a fixed position, and the RSPBs position is as fixed as they get. Grouse moor managers should therefore simply do what they can to run their land to the greatest community and national benefit, make their achievements known as widely as possible and work in partnership with the widest range of organisations who share their ambitions for issues relating to water, carbon, wildlife and landscape.

Obviously, it is essential that everyone involved stops shooting themselves in the foot. Everything about grouse moor management must be legal and operate to the highest ethical standards. But even when people do the right thing and obey the letter and spirit of the mass of legislation that moor managers need to comply with, they will be given no credit, and will continue to be attacked by generalisations and innuendo. So what? The world is not fair. The mere fact that the people who hate the grouse moor community refuse to recognise the good that is done is no reason to not do it.

Those involved in grouse moor management can be proud of what they have achieved and of their preparedness to continually improve. But they must come out of the shadows and tell the world. They should follow the pioneers in their community who already record everything. Every grouse moor should maintain a robust and constantly updated species inventory. They should all have management plans, which set out how they intend to maximise biodiversity, sustainability and wider environmental benefits, without compromising the fundamental purpose of the estate. Without these things, those who wish to destroy them and take away their ability to manage as they believe is right, will simply dismiss everything they say as anecdote.

The process of constructing these records and plans should involve as broad a church of individuals and groups as possible. There will be fungi or bat or amphibian enthusiasts in the locality, who may welcome the chance to get involved. This can facilitate the spread of understanding and tolerance along new channels. The RSPB is not the be all and end all of conservation. There are lots of small and dedicated groups who need support and access. Building relationships and understanding with them, and making these partnerships work and celebrating that success, is time well spent. To be successful, partnerships do not have to include everyone. They simply need to be a coalition of the willing.

Perhaps, the moor owners' most valuable assets are their gamekeepers. If they look at what their keepers achieve, it is arguable that they should, these days, be more accurately called conservation managers. Consider the litter, fly-tipping, wildfires, off-road vehicles, abandoned dogs, damaged gates, walls and fences, and lost and injured walkers they have to deal with. Think about the lapwing and curlew, the sphagnum moss and juniper, the adders and newts, and the brown and mountain hares, and so much more, that thrives under their care. These gamekeepers / conservation managers are too often a light hidden under a bushel. When it comes to communicating the good that grouse moors do they are almost always the best people to do it. They have a depth of knowledge and an authenticity which open-minded people recognise and relate to. Not all are natural communicators, but those who are should be able to play their part in explaining the vital nature of our moorland, and be celebrated and rewarded as a consequence.

Moor owners, the wider moorland community, and the organisations that recognise and celebrate the vital nature of grouse moor management must make every effort to communicate directly with national and local government, local politicians, statutory agencies and the civil service, to do all in their power to make clear that the narrative promoted by the RSPB is flawed and doesn't accurately represent the current position, or the ambition of those who own the moors to contribute fully to the achievement of the government and the nation's goals for the environment.

Finally, moor owners are well placed to deliver on a landscape scale. Individual moors are extensive; taken together they can encompass huge areas, entire dales or straths, or river catchments. They should all do as some are already have, and operate their own bespoke variants of GWCT's farmer clusters (see Chapter 15). They should negotiate with the regulators collectively when it suits their purposes, and from a position of strength generated by their detailed knowledge and track record of success.

Governments have a choice. They must decide if they want to retain what is left of Britain's heather moorland, and facilitate the operations of those who currently own and manage much of the best of it. By so doing they will maintain the steady flow of private finance and investment into upland communities and ensure that, where grouse moor management takes place, there is a sustainable mixed economy that is not entirely dependent on seasonal tourism.

Alternatively, governments may decide to bow to the increasingly shrill demands of the conservation industry for ever-more restrictive legislation. They will also be under pressure to allow the regulatory authorities such as NE or NRW to interpret legislation in the most authoritarian way possible with the aim of constraining moorland management to a point where it becomes impossible to operate any grouse moor successfully. This would allow the conservation sector to take over the ownership and management of the heather moorlands, but it would also require public funds of various sorts, in vast quantities, and in perpetuity. It can also be predicted that, on the basis of currently available evidence, there would be a number of serious negative consequences including, for example, the collapse and disappearance of entire eco-systems, the local extinction of rare ground-nesting birds (in what are now their main strongholds), and an increase in the risk and severity of wildfires.

It cannot be stressed too strongly that these choices are not based on theory or speculation. They are already available for inspection. One of the most baffling elements of this conflict is the extraordinary difficulty in getting even the major proponents of dramatic change to actually go and look at what already exists. It is not a theory that the Cheviot Forests displaced merlin and redshank, or that the curlew have all but gone from the Berwyn's. You don't need to speculate that the moors and fields of Upper Teesdale pulse with life on a May morning, or that the first successful inland sea eagle nesting site was on a grouse shooting estate. The thousands of hectares of NGO-managed, no-burn moorland that are now blackened ash can be visited at any time by anyone. The most obvious reason why those who are in denial of these things (and much else) will not go and see for themselves, is that they do not want to jeopardise their prejudices.

Whatever anyone's personal view of Brexit, it is difficult to imagine that anyone interested in conservation can be sorry that we have escaped the Common Agricultural Policy (CAP). The idea that you can have a system that fits everywhere from the Cairngorms to Alicante was always mad and the CAP's disastrous consequences were predicted and predictable. Governments should take the opportunity presented by leaving the EU to take a pragmatic and practical approach to improving environmental performance.

In England the Environmental Land Management Scheme (ELMS) appears to be a huge step towards what is needed: a system with which farmers and landowners and managers will want to engage, and which will allow them to do what they want and what is needed, without layers of useless bureaucracy and meddling third parties. As it focuses on outcomes rather than process and as it deals directly with the people on the land, it is not surprising that it is not popular with the conservation industry.

There must also be a move away from pretending that giving huge sums of money to the conservation industry is not, in itself, conservation. The recipients of the money are happy to go along with the deceit – but they would, wouldn't they? There is a finite sum available for even the most worthy purpose, and government must ensure value for money and break the cosy links between those who get the money and those who give it out.

It would be an excellent first step if government could put a stop to the extraordinary system whereby the first many people know about something happening on their land is when an NGO, which has obtained several million pounds to do whatever it is, turns up at their door. There will be enormous resistance. The conservation sector will be very angry and vindictive but, in the long run, they will benefit from being weaned away from their dependence.

A major challenge for any government has been created by the expectation that the statutory agencies, such as NE, will be the means by which some of their ambitions are delivered. This has proved to be problematic and needs sorting out urgently. The repeated fiascos around licensing, which shows little sign of abating, are just one example; there are many more. Government needs to create a regulator that is capable of delivering the outcomes it knows are needed, and does not make everything ever-more complicated and obsessed with process. It is to be hoped that NE has seen the light and is pleading with government to take advantage of the new world to make things simpler, more outcome-focused and less vulnerable to vexatious challenge in the courts.

There are some indications that there are people within NE, and the other nation's regulators, at fairly senior levels, who would agree with this ambition, but they face enormous challenges from within and from the conservation sector, as Andrew Sells and his CEO found when they attempted to do what is needed during his chairmanship. Is it not time that government helped NE to reform itself into an organisation that is admired for its achievements, rather than pilloried for its failings?

The current process-driven model suits the authoritarian and bureaucratic form of conservation that is almost universally espoused by the NGOs and the statutory agencies. When yet another State of Nature report is launched by the conservation industry and everything is getting worse – again – do they never think that it might be wise to look in the mirror? Do they never reflect that the systems they use and their own actions are not working? Is it not time to try something else before it's too late? Can they not see that telling people what to do is not as effective as asking for their help. No one has ever used a directive to save a single curlew chick. You can't put out a wildfire sitting in a desk in Smith's Square or The Lodge, but you can create one.

The authoritarian model of conservation has not worked. This should surprise no one, as we know that authoritarian regimes rarely do. They fail for many reasons, but in the world of conservation probably their greatest flaws are that they alienate rather than engage and they fatally prevent the innovation and adaptation that are essential to obtaining successful outcomes in a complex and dynamic world.

In summary

- *Judged by their actions and statements, it is the intention of the RSPB and some other elements within the conservation industry to bring about the end of driven grouse shooting.*

- *That this will destroy the way of life of the communities who currently live on and manage these moors, is obvious, and well understood by those whose ambition it is.*

- *Such an outcome is predicted to reduce the capital value of what is left of the UK's heather moorland and make its acquisition more easily affordable by the conservation sector, commercial forestry, wind farmers, and others.*

- *There is no evidence that such acquisition would benefit the landscape, its wildlife, the provision of eco-system services, its culture or its economy. Indeed, the current evidence indicates that they may all be adversely affected by such a change of ownership.*

- *The RSPB, in particular, has invested so much into its attacks on every aspect of grouse moorland management that, whatever the consequences, the current regime cannot, and will not, change their stance.*

- *It is in the hands of governments to create a system that facilitates the delivery of its environmental ambitions, by those who manage and own most of the nation's land, or alternatively continue with the failed system of authoritarian and bureaucratic conservation.*

- *Britain's exit from the EU creates an opportunity for governments to establish sound, simple legislation and assist the statutory agencies who are to help in delivering their ambitions to reform themselves into outcome- and user-focused exemplars of best practice.*

Epilogue

I SET OUT to explain two things. That our heather moorlands matter and that the people who have looked after them for generations have a valid point of view. When they disagree with, say, NE and the conservation industry on how they may best be looked after, they deserve to be listened to, and not, as is currently too often the case, excluded and marginalised.

These moors are rare, beautiful and rich beyond price. They are not barren, industrial landscapes. They support communities and cultures that are as valid as any others in the land. They are of course minority ones – how could they be anything else – but that does nothing to diminish their right to exist.

The people who own and manage them and who got them into a state worthy of all the designations they have, are frequently shocked and disgusted by the behaviour of both the regulators and the conservation industry. But they can do little or nothing about it, as they have been systematically excluded from the policy and funding decisions that will determine the future of these wonderful places.

They are victims, as are the farmers and landowners elsewhere in Britain, of an arrogant conceit. The idea is that, if the regulators are given enough power and the conservation industry enough money, the views of the people who manage and live on the land can be ignored and they can simply be told what to do, and all will be well.

The capacities of the regulatory bodies to acquire more powers and the industry to take more money are almost certainly limitless. But there is scant evidence that they have the least idea how to use either the power or the money appropriately.

If what remains of these precious places is not to be lost forever, something must change. What is needed is simple, and only in the least bit radical because the current appalling status quo has persisted for so long that it is taken for normality. The views of the people who own and manage the land, and whose skill and knowledge have made these places what they are, must be an intrinsic part of the decision-making process, in relation to both policy and funding.

I am an outsider. I have spent my working life in a great city. I don't own a moor. I have only rarely shot grouse. However, I have become so appalled by the way these communities and these beautiful places have been treated that I have made this issue my study for many years. In the course of that study, I have learnt much from many great people. But what no one has ever been able to begin to explain is why it is a good idea, or even acceptable, to intentionally exclude these people from any involvement in the decisions that affect their land, their community and their culture. I have said elsewhere, but it bears repeating, that such conduct would rightly be viewed as utterly intolerable in any imaginable urban context.

Thank you for persisting to the end. I am sorry if I have appeared, at times, too strident. My only excuse is that I care too much and time is short.

References and further reading

THIS BOOK IS my personal opinion based on my own experiences, the multitude of discussions I have had with the people who live and work on the heather moors and on my understanding of the science and the practice of moorland management. I am no more or less unbiased than anyone else and it would be entirely reasonable if readers want to decide for themselves what the science says.

I have kept references to a minimum; if this were a scientific paper there would have been hundreds, but each reference will lead to dozens or even hundreds more.

If you do want to decide for yourself on what the science says about the key issue of heather management, I would recommend reading Glaves, followed by Ashby, also known in the trade as 'post-Glaves', but most importantly the GWCT Peatland Report 2020, which pulls together the widest possible range of existing knowledge. Don't blame me for it being complicated, it just is. I would also recommend the Royal Society paper by Davies et al. It provides a very unusual insight into how febrile the issue of heather management has become.

More generally, for a concise but well-referenced look at the issues, *The Moorland Balance*, again produced by GWCT, is hard to beat. To go beyond the two-dimensional stereotype of grouse moor owners and people who shoot and get an insight into the minds and actions of the multi-faceted people who make up these communities, you could read *Moorland Conservationists*, and *Community Spirit, what game shooting means to the Welsh people*, both published by GWCT.

Chapter 1

1. United Nations Environment Programme. Rio Declaration on Environment and Development. United Nations Conf. Environ.Dev. (1992) http//www.unep.org/documents.multilingual/default.asp?documentid=788carticleid=1163.

2. Tallis J., Meade R., Hulme P., 'Blanket Mire Degradation' in: Tallis J., Meade R., Hulme P. (eds), British Ecological Society, Manchester, 1998, pp. 1–2.

Chapter 2

1. Evans et al., (2007) 'Implementation of an emissions inventory for UK Peatlands', report to the Department for Business, Energy and Industrial Strategy. Centre for Ecology and Hydrology, Bangor, 88 pp.

2. Glaves D., Morecroft M., Fitzgibbon C., Owen M., Phillips S., Leppit P., 'Natural England Review of Upland Evidence 2012 – the effects of managed burning on upland peatland biodiversity, carbon and water', *Natural England Evidence Review*, Number 004, 2013.

3. Ashby M.A., 'A review of the post-Glaves et al. (2013) evidence investigating: "The effects of managed burning on upland peatland biodiversity, carbon and water"', 2020.

4. GWCT Peatland Report 2020, 'A review of the environmental impacts including carbon sequestration, greenhouse gas emissions and on peatland in England associated with grouse moor management'.

5. Davies G.M., Ketteridge N., Stoof C. R., Gray A., Ascoli D., Fernandes P.M., et al., 'The role of fire in UK peatland management: the need for informed unbiased debate', *Philosophical Transactions of the Royal Society London B Biological Sciences*, 2016: 371.

Chapter 3

1. Glaves D., Morecroft M., Fitzgibbon C., Owen M., Phillips S., Leppit P., 'Natural England Review of Upland Evidence 2012 – the effects of managed burning on upland peatland biodiversity, carbon and water', *Natural England Evidence Review*, Number 004, 2013.

2. *Fieldsports* Volume III Issue IV August/September 2020.

3. Lee H., Alday J. G., Rose R. J., O'Reilly J., Marrs R. H., 'Long-term effects of rotational prescribed burning and low-intensity sheep grazing on blanket-bog plant communities', *Journal of Applied Ecology* 2013; 50: 625–35.

Chapter 4

1. Ratcliffe D.A., *Bird Life of Mountain and Upland*, Cambridge University Press, Cambridge (1990).

2. Ratcliffe D.A., *Galloway and the Borders. New Naturalist 101*, HarperCollins, London (2007).

3. Hammond N., RSPB *Nature Reserves* (1983) ISBN 0-903138-12-3.

4. Warren P., Baines D., 'Changes in abundance and distribution of upland birds in the Berwyn Special Protection Area North Wales 1983–2002' *Birds in Wales* 2014; 11: 32–42.

Chapter 5

1. Fletcher K., Aebischer N. J., Baines D., Foster R., Hoodless A. N., 'Changes in breeding success and abundance of ground-nesting moorland birds in relation to the experimental deployment of legal predator control', *Journal of Applied Ecology* 2010; 47: 263–72.

2. Aebischer N., Baines D., Ewald J., Jones C., Fletcher K., Foster R., et al., *Waders on the Fringe*, Game and Wildlife Conservation Trust, 2010.

3. *Fieldsports* Volume III Issue IV August/September 2020.

Chapter 6

1. Smallwood K.S. and Thelander C.G. (2008), 'Bird mortality in the Altamont Pass Wind Resource Area, California', *Journal of Wildlife Management* 72: 215–25.

2. Perrow M.R., *Wildlife and Wind farms, Conflicts and Solutions*, Vol 1, Pelagic Publishing (2017) ISBN 978-1-78427-119-0.

3. May R., et al., 'Collision risk in white-tailed eagles', NINA Report 639. Trondheim: Norwegian Institute for Nature Research (2010).

4. Voight et al. (2015), 'The catchment area of wind farms for European bats: a plea for international regulations', *European Journal of Wildlife Research* 61: 213–9.

5. Lehnert L.S., Kramer-Schadt S., Schonborn S., Lindecke O., Niermann I. and Voight C.C., (2014) 'Wind farm facilities in Germany kill noctule bats from near and far', PloSONE9(8):e103106.doi:10.137/journal.pone.0103106.

Chapter 8

1. Aebischer N., Baines D., Ewald J., Jones C., Fletcher K., Foster R., et al., *Waders on the Fringe*, Game and Wildlife Conservation Trust, 2010.

2. Fletcher K., Aebischer N.J., Baines D., Foster R., Hoodless A.N., 'Changes in breeding

success and abundance of ground-nesting moorland birds in relation to the experimental deployment of legal predator control', *Journal of Applied Ecology* 2010; 47: 263–72.

3. Merricks P. (2010), Lapwings, farming and environmental stewardship. *British Wildlife*, October 2010, 10–13.

Chapter 11

1. Baines D., Redpath S., Thirgood S., 'The direct and indirect effects of predation by hen harriers *Circus cyaneus* on trends in breeding birds on a Scottish grouse moor' Ibis (*London 1859*) 2008; 150: 27–36.

2. Baines D., Richardson M., 'Hen Harriers on a Scottish grouse moor: multiple factors predict breeding density and productivity', *Journal of Applied Ecology*, 2013; 50: 1397–1405.

3. Ludwig S., Roos S., Bubb D., Baines D., 'Long term trends in abundance and breeding success of red grouse and hen harriers in relation to changing management of a Scottish grouse moor', *Wildlife Biology* (2016).

4. Newton I, *Uplands and Birds*, The New Naturalist Library, London (2020).

Chapter 13

1. Hesford N., Fletcher K., Howarth D., Smith A., Aebischer N., and Baines D., 'Spatial and temporal variation in mountain hare (Lepidus timidus) abundance in relation to red grouse (Lagopus lagopus scoticus) management in Scotland', *European Journal of Wildlife Research* (2019).

Chapter 15

1. Denny S. and Latham-Green T., 'What impacts does integrated moorland management including grouse shooting have on moorland communities, a comparative study', Northampton University 2020.

2. Ludwig S., Roos S., Bubb D., Baines D., 'Long term trends in abundance and breeding success of red grouse and hen harriers in relation to changing management of a Scottish grouse moor', *Wildlife Biology* (2016).

3. Baines D., Richardson M., 'Hen Harriers on a Scottish grouse moor: multiple factors

predict breeding density and productivity', *Journal of Applied Ecology*, 2013; 50: 1397–1405.

Chapter 16

1. *Moorland Conservationists. The Untold Story*, Game and Wildlife Conservation Trust, March 2020.

2. 'Community Spirit. What game shooting means to the Welsh people and countryside', Game and Wildlife Conservation Trust (2021).

3. Denny S. and Latham-Green T., 'What impacts does integrated moorland management including grouse shooting have on moorland communities, a comparative study', Northampton University 2020.